THE UPANAYANA

THE UPANAYANA

The Hindu Ceremonies of the Sacred Thread

Translated by

DR. R.C. PRASAD

MOTILAL BANARSIDASS PUBLISHERS
PRIVATE LIMITED • DELHI

*3rd Reprint: Delhi, **2014***
First Edition: Delhi, 1997

ISBN: 978-81-208-1240-6

MOTILAL BANARSIDASS
41 U.A. Bungalow Road, Jawahar Nagar, Delhi 110 007
8 Mahalaxmi Chamber, 22 Bhulabhai Desai Road, Mumbai 400 026
203 Royapettah High Road, Mylapore, Chennai 600 004
236, 9th Main III Block, Jayanagar, Bangalore 560 011
Sanas Plaza, 1302 Baji Rao Road, Pune 411 002
8 Camac Street, Kolkata 700 017
Ashok Rajpath, Patna 800 004
Chowk, Varanasi 221 001

Printed in India
by RP Jain at NAB Printing Unit,
A-44, Naraina Industrial Area, Phase I, New Delhi–110028
and published by JP Jain for Motilal Banarsidass Publishers (P) Ltd,
41 U.A. Bungalow Road, Jawahar Nagar, Delhi-110007

DEDICATED

With Profound Respect
To the Memory of

The Late Svāmī Sahajānanda Sarasvatī

'tvadīyaṁ vastu he deva tubhyameva samarpaye'

Contents

PREFACE
ix

CHAPTER I: INTRODUCTION
1

CHAPTER II: THE PŪJĀS
31

CHAPTER III: THE TONSURE
99

CHAPTER IV: UPANAYANA
113

CONCLUSION
157

APPENDICES

APPENDIX I
165

APPENDIX II
171

APPENDIX III
175

SANSKRIT GLOSSARY
181

INDEX
187

Preface

In days gone by every Hindu was socially and religiously required to have a family priest, a brāhmaṇa, who was revered and admired for his scholarship, especially for his vast knowledge of the Vedas and the Hindu saṁskāras. He functioned as a family preceptor and spiritual guide, not as a casual brāhmaṇa visitor whose services are solicited only on certain festive occasions by the needy when no other priest is available. The work of such roving vendors of ceremonial decrees is more business-oriented than in keeping with the sacred laws. It is surely difficult today to come across a *guru* who models his living on that of the *ṛṣis* dedicated to the performance of self-purifying penance and sacrifice. The seers in days of yore were mostly enlightened men who had realized during their studentship that were they to guide the laity and be called 'Ācāryas' or 'Paṇḍitas' the sobriquets which are often attached to their names, they must renounce all sensual pleasures. Manu, their great lawgiver, had ordained with his inimitable clarity that

यश्चैतान् प्राप्नुयात् सर्वान् यश्चैतान् केवलांस्त्यजेत् ।
प्रापणात् सर्वकामानां परित्यागो विशिष्यते ।।
yaścaitān prāpnuyāt sarvān yaścaitān kevalāṁstyajet ।
prāpaṇāt sarvakāmānāṁ parityāgo viśiṣyate ॥

"If one man," Manu declares, "should obtain all those sensual enjoyments and another should renounce them all, the renunciation of all pleasure is far better than the attainment of them." A student was expected to practice renunciation, detachment, and self-restraint. Here again Manu's instruction was respectfully acquiesced in and the forest celibates remembered both in theory and in practice that

> न तथैतानि शक्यन्ते संनियन्तुमसेवया ।
> विषयेषु प्रजुष्टानि यथा ज्ञानेन नित्यशः ।।
> *na tathaitāni śakyante saṁniyantumasevayā* ।
> *viṣayeṣu prajuṣṭāni yathā jñānena nityaśaḥ* ॥

"Those organs which are strongly attached to sensual pleasures, cannot so effectually be restrained by abstinence from enjoyments as by a constant pursuit of true knowledge."

It appears from Manu's institutes that they are meant as much for the householder in the second order of life—gārhasthya—as for the student. The laws for the brāhmaṇas are severer and they are expected to subject themselves to harder physical and mental disciplines, forsaking all attachment of their organs to sensual pleasures. A brāhmaṇa student must keep them under complete control and bear in mind that desire is never extinguished by the enjoyment of desired objects; it only grows stronger like a fire fed with clarified butter.

> न जातु कामः कामानामुपभोगेन शाम्यति ।
> हविषा कृष्णवर्त्मेव भूय एवाभिवर्धते ।।
> *na jātu kāmaḥ kāmānāmupabhogena śāmyati* ।
> *haviṣā kṛṣṇavartmeva bhūya evābhivardhate* ॥

Even those people who did not belong to the trivargas conceded with reluctant admiration that the majority of the purohitas were adepts at their priestly duties and had acquired considerable merit by subduing their organs. They were taught by their enlightened teachers during their gurukula days that one gains all one's aims if one keeps all the ten organs as well as the mind in subjection. The teacher along with his students stood during the morning twilight muttering the Sāvitrī until the sun appeared; he recited it, seated, in the evening until the constellations were seen distinctly. They all knew how meritorious it was to stand during the early morning hours muttering the sacred mantras, how they removed the guilt contracted during previous night and how those who recited them seated in the evening were able to destroy the sin committed during the day.

But all this appears to have vanished. It is unfortunate that many brāhmaṇas, starkly ignorant of the Vedic ṛcās and scriptural teachings, are often called upon to perform the ceremonies. There is substance in their contention that since the times have changed, the ceremonial laws too must be thoroughly revised and modified to bring them in conformity with the present-day ethos. They also argue that, as the mantras are in Sanskrit, very few people are able to chant them with complete understanding of their inherent meaning and importance. Their bewilderment is understandably genuine in the face of the difficulties involved in following the instructions given by the institutors. It is to meet their demand for a simple text with explanatory instructions that this book has been written. Its readers can be scholarly priests or non-scholarly householders or both. To some this may sound a profanation of the ceremonial laws, but the intention is pious and therefore this attempt to democratize and expound the esoteric is forgivable.

I am considerably indebted to Mr. Digvijay Narayan Singh of the Department of English, Patna University, who came to my rescue when my eyesight was failing due to a sudden eye haemorrhage. With exemplary patience and devotion, he worked day and night preparing the rough and final drafts of the manuscript, checking the typescript and giving it the last Midas touch.

CHAPTER I

Introduction

I

The Law Books, no less than the Gṛhyasūtras, provide ample materials on the sixteen saṁskāras or ceremonial rites performed in Hindu homes under the guidance of a family priest. Sometimes the manner of performing the ceremonies is given at length, while at other times the details are scanty. There is, however, unanimity among the law-givers and institutors of the rules with regard to the qualifications of the priest. He should be a brāhmaṇa, they maintain, to whom the most resplendent Lord assigned teaching and studying the Veda, sacrificing for his own benefit and for others, giving and accepting of alms. In one of his well-known verses Manu says:

भूतानां प्राणिनः श्रेष्ठाः प्राणिनां बुद्धिजीविनः ।
बुद्धिमत्सु नराः श्रेष्ठा नरेषु ब्राह्मणाः स्मृताः ।।९६।।
bhūtānāṁ prāṇinaḥ śreṣṭhāḥ prāṇināṁ buddhijīvinaḥ ।
buddhimatsu narāḥ śreṣṭhā nareṣu brāhmaṇāḥ smṛtāḥ ॥

But all brāhmaṇas are not suited for the job of family priest. Manu rejects even those brāhmaṇas who are learned in the Vedas. Of the learned, only those should be preferred who recognize the necessity and the manner of performing the prescribed duties. Of those who possess this knowledge, those should be preferred who perform them, and of the performers, those who know the Brahman. Manu based his preference on his simple conviction expressed in the following verse:

उत्पत्तिरेव विप्रस्य मूर्तिर्धर्मस्य शाश्वती ।
स हि धर्मार्थमुत्पन्नो ब्रह्मभूयाय कल्पते ।।
utpattireva viprasya mūrtirdharmasya śāśvatī ।
sa hi dharmārthamutpanno brahmabhūyāya kalpate ॥

"The very birth of a brāhmaṇa," he maintains, "is an eternal incarnation of the sacred law; for he is born to fulfil the sacred law, and becomes one with Brahman."

The test laid down for the choice of the officiating priest—the purohita—is rigorous. He must be learned in the Vedas; he must recognize both the necessity and the manner of following the prescribed rules or performing the prescribed duties; he must not only possess this knowledge but also know the Brahman. He comes into existence for the protection of the treasury of the law and eats but his own food, wears but his own apparel, bestows but his own in alms; other mortals, adds Manu, subsist through the benevolence of the brāhmaṇa. The latter was expected to carefully study the institutes of the sacred law and to duly instruct his pupils in them, 'but nobody else shall do it'. This was deemed imperative because it was held that a brāhmaṇa, who studied the institutes and faithfully fulfilled the duties prescribed in them, was never tainted by sins, arising from thoughts, words, or deeds.

The brāhmaṇa's services were sought to conduct the ceremonies and guide the householder for the assurance contained in Manu's Institutes:

पुनाति पङ्क्तिं वंश्यांश्च सप्त सप्त परावरान् ।
पृथिवीमपि चैवेमां कृत्स्नामेकोऽपि सोऽर्हति ।।
punāti paṅktiṁ vaṁśyāṁśca sapta sapta parāvarān।
pṛthivīmapi caivemāṁ kṛtsnāmeko'pi so'rhati ॥

The very presence of the brāhmaṇa as instructor and guide sanctifies any company with which he may enter, seven ancestors and seven descendents, and he alone deserves to possess this whole earth. The brāhmaṇa priest learned in the

Vedas studied the smṛtis (and the Gṛhyasūtras) because they were (and still are) the best means of securing welfare; they increased understanding, procured fame and long life, and led to supreme bliss.

Among the qualifications of an eligible family priest is not only great learning but also a knowledge of the rule of conduct and of the sacred law. The rule of conduct has been described by Manu as transcendental law—

> **आचारः परमो धर्मः श्रुत्युक्तः स्मार्त एव च ।**
> **तस्मादस्मिन् सदा युक्तो नित्यं स्यादात्मवान् द्विजः ।।**
> *ācāraḥ paramo dharmaḥ śrutyuktaḥ smārta eva ca* ।
> *tasmādasmin sadā yukto nityaṁ syādātmavān dvijaḥ* ॥

—whether it be taught in the revealed texts or in the sacred tradition (śrutyuktaḥ smārta eva ca). All the four castes were therefore expected to follow the immemorial rule of conduct and a brāhmaṇa, who transgressed this rule, was cautioned that he would not reap the fruit of the Vedas. Manu added that he who duly followed it could obtain the full reward. "The sages who saw that the sacred law is thus grounded on the rule of conduct, have taken good conduct to be the excellent root of all austerity."

What is lamentable is the dearth of efficient and learned purohitas who are also masters of the rules of the sacraments, the ordinances of studentship, and the most excellent rules of bathing and offering oblations. Instead of eating their own food and wearing their own apparel, they act solely from a desire for rewards, though they know that such a desire must not be nursed. According to Manu, "The desire for rewards, indeed, has its root in the conception that an act can yield them, and in consequence of that conception sacrifices are performed; vows and the laws prescribing restraints are all stated to be kept through the idea that they will bear fruit."

The officiating priest, ācārya or guru used to be a snātaka whose duties were as hard as those of a celibate. One of his duties was to avoid cutting, breaking, scratching and crushing anything. According to Gautama, he was expected to be a stay-at-home, nor was he to go to perform a sacrifice without being chosen to officiate as priest. He could go to see it only at his pleasure. Some of the most unavoidable rules of conduct, according to Gautama, were:

> He shall always speak the truth.
> He shall conduct himself as becomes an Aryan.
> He shall instruct virtuous men only.
> He shall follow the rules of purification taught in the śāstras.
> He shall take pleasure in the study of the Vedas.
> He shall never hurt any being, he shall be gentle, yet firm, ever restrain his senses, and be liberal.
> A snātaka who conducts himself in this manner will liberate his parents, his ancestors, and decendents from evil, and never fall from Brahman's heaven.

The rules of internal and external purification were no less rigorous. No ceremony can be performed unless the host and the priest have duly performed the rite of purification for which the rules were clearly defined. According to Baudhāyana, the sacrificial thread has to be made of kuśa grass, or cotton, and consist of thrice three strings. It shall hang down to the navel. In putting it on one is expected to raise the right arm, lower the left, and lower the head. The contrary is done at sacrifices to the manes. If the thread is suspended round the neck, it is called nivīta; if it is suspended below the navel, it is called adhopavīta. Both the priestly brāhmaṇa and his host were expected to perform the rite of purification, facing the east or the north, and seated in a pure place. They had to place their right arms between their knees and wash both hands up to the wrist and both feet up to the ankles. None was advised to use for sipping the remainder of the water with which he had washed his feet. But if one used that for sipping, he was allowed to do so after pouring a portion of it on the ground. Here again the rules enjoined that he should sip out of the tīrtha sacred to Brahman. The part of the hand at the root of the thumb is called the tīrtha sacred to Brahman and that above the thumb is called the tīrtha sacred to the manes, the part at the tips of the fingers that sacred to the Gods, the part at the root of the fingers that sacred to the ṛṣis. Going still further, Baudhāyana ordains not to use for sipping water that has trickled from the fingers, nor that covered with bubble or foam nor water that is hot, alkaline, or salty, or muddy, or discoloured, or that which has a bad smell or taste. Foreseeing that future generations may be lax in the performance of some of these ceremonial duties, Baudhāyana ruled that water must not be sipped laughing, nor talking, nor standing, nor looking about, nor bending one's head or one's body forward, nor while the lock on one's crown is united, nor while one's throat is wrapped up, nor while one's head is covered, nor when one is in a hurry, nor without wearing the sacrificial thread, nor stretching one's feet out, nor while one's loins are girt with a cloth, nor without holding one's right arm between one's knees, nor making a sound.

The sacred laws of the Āryas lay considerable emphasis on purity and account for it by saying that the gods enjoy only that which is pure; they are, Baudhāyana says, desirous of purity and themselves pure. He quotes the following in support:

> To you, O Maruts, the pure ones, pure viands; to you, the pure ones, I offer a pure sacrifice. They who love the pious rites, who are of pure origin, themselves pure and purifiers of others, came duly to the truthful worshipper.

In the *Vāyu Purāṇa* a separate chapter is devoted to this subject and due emphasis is laid on the relationship between purity of conduct, righteousness, and the observance of vows:

> Seeking of water for purity is the excellent state of sages.

> He who is not negligent in regard to these comes to no trouble. Insult and honour, they say, constitute what is called poison and nectar. Insult is poison; honour is nectar. The sage who does not err in regard to these comes to no trouble. He should remain with the preceptor for a year engaged in what is pleasing and beneficial to him. He should not be negligent in the observance of vows, major (*yamas*) or minor (*niyamas*). After attaining supreme knowledge, he should seek permission from his preceptor and move about the earth consistently with dharma. This is the holy dictate of *dharma,* viz. one should go along the path purified by (i.e. observed carefully by) the eyes; one should drink water filtered with a cloth; and one should utter words purified by truth, i.e. state the truth only. It is the considered opinion that the knower of Yoga should never accept hospitality in *śrāddhas* and *yajñas* and that it is only thus that a yogin becomes non-violent. An intelligent yogin should go out for alms when the fires in the kitchen have become smokeless and have been extinguished and the people have practically taken their meals. He should not constantly beg in the same houses lest he should get insulted or people offended. It is thus without violating the code of conduct of the good, that he should carefully go out for alms.

The *Agni Purāṇa* mentions no less than forty-eight purificatory rites:

> One would reach the world of Brahmā by doing the forty-eight purificatory rites. They are the impregnation, causing the birth of a male child, the parting of the hair, rites done at the birth of a child, naming the child, the first rice-feeding of the child, the tonsure, investiture of the sacred thread, the collection of four Vedic observances—the completion of one's studies, marriage, the collection of five devotional acts—towards

> the gods, manes, mortals, beings and sages, seven simple domestic sacrifices—the *aṣṭakā* and *pārvaṇaśrāddha, śrāvaṇī, āgrahāyaṇī, caitrī,* and *āśvayujī*, then the *haviryajñas* (such as) the *agnyādheya, agnihotra, darśapaurṇamāsa, cāturmāsya, āgrahāyaṇeṣṭi, nirūḍhapaśubandhaka,* and the *sautrāmaṇī*, the seven *somasaṁsthās*—commencing with *agniṣṭoma—atyagniṣṭoma, uktha, ṣoḍaśī, vājapeyaka, atirātra*, etc. and the eight basic human qualities—compassion, forbearance, freedom from malice, absence of exertion, propitiation, charity and absence of desire. Whoever possesses these attains the supreme. One should observe silence in the six acts—evacuation of bowels, copulation, passing urine, cleaning the teeth, bathing and eating. One should avoid making a gift again of an article received as a gift, drinking separately the ghee and milk in the night, removal of teeth and hotness in the seven kinds of flours. One should not gather flowers without bathing. It is said to be unfit for the worship of gods.

The rules of conduct demand that the sacrificer and his wife as well as the officiating priest shall put on clothes which have been cleaned and dried by the wind, and which are not deformed and ungainly. One looks elegant and imposing if one's clothes are spotless and suited to the occasion. That is why both the sacrificer and the officiating priest are required to perform every little ritual connected with the sacrifice dressed immaculately and to see to it that while importance is attached to physical purity, what really conduces to the purity of the soul is not neglected. According to the *Agni Purāṇa* one should "pursue righteousness entertaining purity of thought in whichever order of life he may be interested. He should treat all beings equally. The cause of righteousness does not lie in the symbol associated with the different orders of life." It is unfortunate that these rule of conduct are fast vanishing and the officiating priest is as much to be blamed for this as the householder. Very few of us care for the sacred rules laid down in the law books dealing with the saṁskāras. Those who should have observed them with punctilious and meticulous care are either negligent or ignorant and in their craze for being modish and non-conformist belittle them or discard them altogether. Most of the officiating priests, finding the Vedic texts, the ṛcās and the mantras too recondite, have not only remained ignorant themselves but have kept their hosts no less ignorant. The sacrificial rites conducted by them are seldom in conformity with the modes and rules prescribed by the sacred books.

The forbiddingly difficult language and meaning of the sacrificial formulas have, in addition to scaring away the reader, largely contributed to this widespread ignorance of the karmakāṇḍas. The brāhmaṇas, moreover, by forbidding a sizeable chunk of the Hindu population to read Sanskrit, deprived it of a right the ancients had given them. As a matter of fact, even the śūdras were in some distant past permitted to study the Vedas and the Niṣāda chieftains and mechanics to perform the Vedic sacrifice called aveṣṭi (see, for instance, the sixth chapter of the Pūrva Mīmāṁsā, I.xii-xiii, sūtras 44-52). The rathakāras who belong to the class of the śūdras, had, and still have the right to study the useful Vedic mantras. It is important in this connection to remember that one of the principal motives underlying the writing of the *Mahābhārata* and the Purāṇas was to educate the śūdras. The kṣatriyas and the vaiśyas were no less entitled to study the Vedas than the brāhmaṇas. In their overweening selfishness the priestly class stopped teaching Sanskrit to the śūdras and then to the vaiśyas and kṣatriyas. Then came a time when only those brāhmaṇas came to learn Sanskrit who desired to adopt their ancestral profession—paurohitya or teaching. To teach Sanskrit to a non-brāhmaṇa was, to the brāhmaṇas, like serving a snake with milk. Dwelling on the reason "why the karmakāṇḍas remained the soie monopoly of the brāhmaṇas?" Sahajānand Sarasvati remarks:

> I say this on the ground of their own repeated assertion. They not only say this but also act on it and try first not to admit non-brāhmaṇa boys into their schools. If at all the latter succeed in securing admission, they are so ill-treated by the teachers and students that they are forced to give up their studies. There are hundreds of such instances. When, therefore, will it be possible to teach the Vedas, Sanskrit, or Karmakāṇḍas to the non-brāhmaṇas? In ancient times when the sacrificer and the officiating priest were well read in Sanskrit and the saṁskāras every ceremony was performed according to the prescribed rules. Whenever an officiating priest committed an error, the host and others stalled him at once . . .

That is why, says the learned Svāmī, the officiating priest was intellectually always alert and fully prepared. Ordinarily the kṣatriyas and the vaiśyas performed homas with their own hands, for all the three varṇas alike possessed the right to make offerings to the sacrificial fire. Only when services of the ācāryas were unavoidable on such festive occasions as marriage, the brāhmaṇa scholar was invited and the officiating priest conducted the sacrificial rites according to the prescribed code. The reason was that kṣatriyas and vaiśyas are debarred from receiving dakṣiṇā, fee or gift.

The glory with which the purohita was vested gradually vanished. Most of his tribe ceased to be real spiritual guides, purifiers, and preceptors. The gap which separates the ideal guru from the mercenary purohitas of today is much too wide if not unbridgeable. Describing the former the *Śiva Purāṇa* says:

> He who is the preceptor is Śiva and he who is Śiva is the preceptor. Whether the preceptor or Śiva the same person is stationed in the form of knowledge. As is Śiva so the knowledge. As is knowledge so is the preceptor.

> The benefit is similar in the worship of Śiva, knowledge or the preceptor. The preceptor is in the form of gods and the mantras. Hence every endeavour shall be made to accept his behest with bent head.

Not many of the purohitas of today will stand the rigorous test implied in these lines. But one must also bear in mind that no purohita, however learned in and faithful to the ancient codes he may be, can afford in the present-day circumstances and living conditions, especially prevailing in the cities, to follow them or make others—his hosts—to abide by the rules governing the performance of each and every saṁskāra. He finds the codes too irksome and impracticable.

If the purohita had to live a life of extreme abstemiousness and austerity, the teacher was no less bound to all kinds of rigorous observances.

> Let him who teaches, says Āpastamba, avoid connubial intercourse during the rainy season and in autumn. And if he has had connection with his wife, he shall not lie with her during the whole night. He shall not teach whilst he is lying on a bed. Nor shall he teach sitting on that couch on which he lies at night with his wife. He shall not show himself adorned with a garland, or anointed with ointments. At night he shall always adorn himself for his wife. Let him not submerge his head together with his body in bathing, and let him avoid to bathe after sunset. Let him avoid to use a seat, clogs, sticks for cleaning the teeth, and other utensils made of palāśa-wood. Let him avoid to praise himself before his teacher, saying, 'I have properly bathed or the like'. Let him be awake from midnight. Let him not study or teach in the middle of the night; but he may point out their duties to his pupils. Or he may by himself mentally repeat the sacred texts. After midnight he may teach. When he has risen at midnight and taught during the third watch of the night, let him not lie down again

> saying, 'Studying is forbidden'. At his pleasure he may sleep leaning against a post or the like. Or he may mentally repeat the sacred texts. Let him not visit inferior men such as Niṣādas, nor countries which are inhabited by them, nor assemblies and crowds. If he has entered a crowd, he shall leave it, turning his right hand towards the crowd. Nor shall he enter towns frequently. Let him not answer directly a question that is difficult to decide.

The technicalities involved in the performance of the saṁskāras make them somewhat incomprehensible to the common reader. It is to simplify these technicalities and make the ceremonies more practicable that the following section of the Introduction has been appended. Unless the essentials of the manner in which a Hindu performs the purificatory rites, offers oblations of several kinds, uses kuśa blades as a ladle for sacrificial purposes, worships the elements, especially Agni and the quarters, invokes the deities celebrated in the Vedas, etc. are grasped, the ceremonies will all sound a chaotic jumble of mystic formulas and no less elusive instructions beyond the comprehension of an ordinary householder. The following definitions must therefore be borne in mind.

II

All ceremonies, whatever their goal, begin with what is called śānti-pāṭha, an Invocation, which we find at the beginning of the *Īśa Upaniṣad:*

ॐ पूर्णमदः पूर्णमिदं पूर्णात् पूर्णमुदच्यते ।
पूर्णस्य पूर्णमादाय पूर्णमेवावशिष्यते ।।
ॐ शान्तिः शान्तिः शान्तिः ।।

om pūrṇamadaḥ pūrṇamidaṁ pūrṇāt pūrṇamudacyate ।
pūrṇasya pūrṇamādāya pūrṇamevāvaśiṣyate ॥

oṁ śāntiḥ śāntiḥ śāntiḥ ॥

Om. That is full; this is full. This fullness has been projected from that fullness. When this fullness merges in that fullness, all that remains is fullness.

Om. Peace! Peace! Peace!

The mantra purports to liberate the Self from the grief, delusion, and other evil traits of saṁskāra in which it has been entangled on account of ignorance. To be attached to matter amounts to killing the Self.

Not only is the invocatory mantra identical in almost all ceremonial worship and on all festive occasions; certain other imperatives are common to all saṁskāras. The performer is required to be physically clean and fresh and the place where the pūjā is to be offered spick-and-span. Before the function starts, he must have a bath and his clothes must be properly washed, without any trace of impurity on them. The officiating priest should let him know that in most of the Hindu saṁskāras such pūjās as svastivācana, puṇyāhavācana, grahapūjā, etc. are the same and are performed with due humility and devotion. Having performed his daily ablutions and routine duties he should be fresh and carefree, all set for performing the pūjā. Here the treatises on the saṁskāras do not forget to remind the performer that bathing in a sacred river or at a sacred place is preferable to bathing in a stagnant pond or at the countryside well. They tender a piece of salutary advice and ask the bather to mutter the following mantra, entertaining the feeling that he is bathing at a holy place or in a holy river:

पुष्कराद्यानि तीर्थानि गंगाद्याः सरितस्तथा ।
आगच्छन्तु पवित्राणि स्नानकाले सदा मम ।।
विष्णुपादाब्जसम्भूते गंगे त्रिपथगामिनि ।
धर्मद्रवीति विख्याते पापं मे हर जाह्नवि ।।
यन्मया दूषितं तोयं मलैः शरीरसम्भवैः ।
तस्य पापस्य शुद्ध्यर्थं यक्ष्यमाणं तर्पयाम्यहम् ।।

puṣkarādyāni tīrthāni gaṁgādyāḥ saritastathā ।
āgacchantu pavitrāṇi snānakāle sadā mama ॥
viṣṇupādābjasambhūte gaṁge tripathagāmini ।
dharmadravīti vikhyāte pāpaṁ me hara jāhnavi ॥
yanmayā dūṣitaṁ toyaṁ malaiḥ śarīrasambhavaiḥ ।
tasya pāpasya śuddhyarthaṁ yakṣyamāṇaṁ tarpayām-yaham ॥

The six primary duties of the performer after this are, in addition to putting a sandal mark on his forehead and with his face towards the east occupying a seat made of kuśa blades, pavitrīkaraṇa, ācamana, śikhābandhana, prāṇāyāma, nyāsa, and pṛthvīpūjana. These are to be accomplished in the following manner:

The ritual of sanctification involves taking a little water in the left-hand palm and covering it with the right hand and then uttering the following formula:

ॐ अपवित्रः पवित्रो वा सर्वावस्थां गतोऽपि वा ।
यः स्मरेत् पुण्डरीकाक्षं स बाह्याभ्यन्तरं शुचिः ॥
om apavitraḥ pavitro vā sarvāvasthāṁ gato'pi vā ।
yaḥ smaret puṇḍarīkākṣaṁ sa bāhyābhyantaraṁ śuciḥ ॥

The citation of the mantra is followed by sprinkling the water with the right-hand fingers on the body. But for the purity of mind, speech and action one needs to perform what is called ācamana. What is required for it is an *ācamanī*—a spoon—with which one sips water three times one after another. If no such spoon is available, perform the ācamana with the help of the right-hand palm and with the intonation of such an appropriate mantra as the following:

ॐ अमृतोपस्तरणमसि स्वाहा ॥ १ ॥
ॐ अमृतापिधानमसि स्वाहा ॥ २ ॥
ॐ सत्यं यशः श्रीर्मयि श्रीः श्रयतां स्वाहा ॥ ३ ॥
om amṛtopastaraṇamasi svāhā ॥ 1 ॥
om amṛtāpidhānamasi svāhā ॥ 2 ॥

om satyaṁ yaśaḥ śrīrmayi śrīḥ śrayatāṁ svāhā ॥ 3 ॥

Having done the ācamana, wash those hands which were used for sipping water. Then begins the ceremony of tying the tuft on the crown of the head (śikhā-bandhana); it is one of the most essential ceremonies of the Hindus. It is for this that the tuft is well combed, deftly arrayed and disentangled. Those not having the crown tuft should just touch the crown with their hand and while doing so or tying the knot should rehearse the following sacred verse:

चिद्रूपिणि महामाये दिव्यतेजःसमन्विते ।
तिष्ठ देवि शिखामध्ये तेजोवृद्धिं कुरुष्व मे ॥
cidrūpiṇi mahāmāye divyatejaḥsamanvite ।
tiṣṭha devi śikhāmadhye tejovṛddhiṁ kuruṣva me ॥

The breath-control is practised for the purification of the pañcavāyus and upavāyus, namely, prāṇa, apāna, samāna, udāna, and vyāna, etc. It consists of three parts called in yoga pūraka, kumbhaka, and recaka. The first involves inhalation, the second retention and the third exhalation. While performing the prāṇāyāma the following mantras need be chanted:

ॐ भूः ॐ भुवः ॐ स्वः ॐ महः ॐ जनः ॐ तपः ॐ सत्यम् । तत्सवितुर्वरेण्यं भर्गो देवस्य धीमहि धियो यो नः प्रचोदयात् । ॐ आपोज्योती रसोऽमृतं ब्रह्म भूर्भुवः स्वरोम् ।
om bhūḥ om bhuvaḥ om svaḥ om mahaḥ om janaḥ om tapaḥ om satyam । *tatsaviturvareṇyaṁ bhargo devasya dhīmahi dhiyo yo naḥ pracodayāt* । *om āpo jyotī raso'mṛtaṁ brahma bhūrbhuvaḥ svarom* ।

The nyāsa aims at energizing, refining and purifying the sensory organs as well as the organs of action. For this one needs to take a little water in one's left-hand palm and touch all the organs with the right-hand fingers as one mutters the following mantras:

ॐ वाङ्म आस्येऽस्तु ।। १ ।।
ॐ नसोर्मे प्राणोऽस्तु ।। २ ।।
ॐ अक्ष्णोर्मे चक्षुरस्तु ।। ३ ।।
ॐ कर्णयोर्मे श्रोत्रमस्तु ।। ४ ।।
ॐ बाह्वोर्मे बलमस्तु ।। ५ ।।
ॐ ऊर्वोर्मे ओजोऽस्तु ।। ६ ।।
ॐ अरिष्टानि मेऽङ्गानि तनूस्तन्वा मे सह सन्तु ।। ७ ।।

om vāṅma āsye'stu ‖ 1 ‖
om nasorme prāṇo'stu ‖ 2 ‖
om akṣṇorme cakṣurastu ‖ 3 ‖
om karṇayorme śrotramastu ‖ 4 ‖
om bāhvorme balamastu ‖ 5 ‖
om ūrvorme ojo'stu ‖ 6 ‖
om ariṣṭāni me'ṅgāni tanūstanvā me saha santu ‖ 7 ‖

With the repetition of the first mantra touch the mouth, with that of the second the nostrils, with that of the third the eyes, with that of the fourth the ears, with that of the fifth the arms, with that of the sixth the thighs, and with that of the seventh sprinkle a little water on your body.

Of earth is born man and by it he is reared and sustained, which is the reason why paying obeisance to Mother Earth is common in all important ceremonies. The following mantra should be chanted while making offering of raw rice, flowers, incense, unguents, water, festal lamp, etc.:

ॐ पृथ्वि त्वया धृता लोका देवि त्वं विष्णुना धृता ।
त्वं च धारय मां देवि पवित्रं कुरु चासनम् ।।

om pṛthvi tvayā dhṛtā lokā devi tvaṁ viṣṇunā dhṛtā ।
tvaṁ ca dhāraya māṁ devi pavitraṁ kuru cāsanam ‖

At the start of the proper ceremony the officiating priest should see to it that the host has performed the six acts to his satisfaction and will participate in the saṁskāra with due dedication and commitment; beginning with the installation of the ceremonial jar, called kalaśa, an indispensable constituent in all important ceremonies. The kalaśa has been deemed so integral to every saṃskāra, whether it is for laying a foundation stone or for an investiture ceremony, because of its symbolical role it represents all that is conducive to one's well-being and all that augurs well for the believer. A Hindu is duty-bound, therefore, to revere the kalaśa as the very abode of all sacred tīrthas, celestials and heavenly splendour. An earthen pot is preferable to all other jars, say the purohitas. But many among them advise, as an alternative measure, the use of non-earthen vessels as well, such as those made of gold, silver, copper, brass, etc. Before establishing it draw a benedictory mark (svastika) on its outward wall and on its mouth keep pañcapallava, flowers and a coconut. On certain ceremonial occasions a wooden seat should be earmarked for the purpose; spread a beautiful bed-sheet on it and carve on it with either raw rice or with rolī (a mixture of lime powder and turmeric) a picture of an eight-petalled lotus. Due homage should be paid to the kalaśa with sandal, rolī, raw rice, incense, festal lamp, naivedya (an offering of eatables presented to a deity or an idol) and flowers and the following mantra should be entoned:

ॐ कलशस्य मुखे विष्णुः कण्ठे रुद्रः समाश्रितः ।
मूले तस्य स्थितो ब्रह्मा मध्ये मातृगणाः स्मृताः ।। १ ।।
कुक्षौ तु सागराः सप्त सप्तद्वीपा वसुन्धरा ।
ऋग्वेदो'थ यजुर्वेदः सामवेदो ह्यथर्वणः ।। २ ।।
अङ्गैश्च सहिताः सर्वे कलशन्तु समाश्रिताः ।
अत्र गायत्री सावित्री शान्तिः पुष्टिकरी सदा ।। ३ ।।
त्वयि तिष्ठन्ति भूतानि त्वयि प्राणाः प्रतिष्ठिताः ।
शिवः स्वयं त्वमेवासि विष्णुस्त्वं च प्रजापतिः ।। ४ ।।
आदित्या वसवो रुद्राः विश्वेदेवाः सपैतृकाः ।
त्वयि तिष्ठन्ति सर्वेऽपि यतः कामफलप्रदाः ।। ५ ।।

om kalaśasya mukhe viṣṇuḥ kaṇṭhe rudraḥ samāśritaḥ ।
mūle tasya sthito brahmā madhye mātṛgaṇāḥ smṛtāḥ ॥ 1 ॥
kukṣau tu sāgarāḥ sapta saptadvīpā vasundharā ।

ṛgvedo'tha yajurvedaḥ sāmavedo hyatharvaṇaḥ ॥ 2 ॥
aṅgaiśca sahitāḥ sarve kalaśantu samāśritāḥ ।
atra gāyatrī sāvitrī śāntiḥpuṣṭikarī sadā ॥ 3 ॥
tvayi tiṣṭhanti bhūtāni tvayi prāṇāḥ pratiṣṭhitāḥ ।
śivaḥ svayaṁ tvamevāsi viṣṇustvaṁ ca prajāpatiḥ ॥ 4 ॥
ādityā vasavo rudrāḥ viśvedevāḥ sapaitṛkāḥ ।
tvayi tiṣṭhanti sarve'pi yataḥ kāmaphalapradāḥ ॥ 5 ॥

The worship of the kalaśa should be followed by the worship of the gods, the centrality of which on all festive occasions cannot be denied. The homage paid to these celestials is doubtless the most salutary and propitious thing a human being can do. Priority is, however, given to Gaṇapati who is worshipped at the very commencement of a saṁskāra. Other deities though deemed as important as he, are worshipped next. The law-giver has directed all paṇḍits and purohitas to perform Gaṇeśa's pūjā with due reverence, concentration of mind, and ṣoḍaśopacāra—the sixteen modes of worship:

ध्यान– ॐ उद्यद्दिनेश्वररुचिं निजहस्तपद्मैः पाशाङ्कुशाभयवरान्दधतं गजास्यम् ।
रक्ताम्बरं सकलदुःखहरं गणेशं ध्यायेत् प्रसन्नमखिलाभरणाभिरामम् ।।

आसन– सुमुखाय नमस्तुभ्यं गणाधिपतये नमः ।
गृहाणासनमीश त्वं विघ्नपुञ्जं निवारय ।।

पाद्य– उमापुत्राय देवाय सिद्धवन्द्याय ते नमः ।
पाद्यं गृहाण देवेश विघ्नराज नमोऽस्तु ते ।।

अर्घ्य– एकदन्त महाकाय नागयज्ञोपवीतक ।
गणाधिदेव देवेश गृहाणार्घ्यं नमोऽस्तु ते ।।

पंचामृत– पयोदधिघृतक्षोद्रैः शर्करामिश्रितैः कृतम् ।
पंचामृतं गृहाणेदं स्नानार्थं विघ्नभंजन ।।

स्नानजल– नर्मदाचन्द्रभागादिगंगासंगमजैर्जलैः ।
स्नापितोऽसि मया देव विघ्नसंघं निवारय ।।

यज्ञोपवीत– सूर्यकोटिसमायाम नागयज्ञोपवीतक ।
स्वर्णमूलैः रचितं उपवीतं गृहाण मे ।।

वस्त्र– रक्ताम्बर धराघर्ष पाशांकुशधरेश्वर ।
वस्त्रयुग्मं मया दत्तं गृहाण मे परमेश्वर ।।

आचमनीय– सुगन्धमिश्रिततीर्थादिपूतं पानीयमुत्तमम् ।
आचम्यार्थं गृहाण त्वं विघ्नराज वरप्रद ।।

गन्ध-अक्षत– गन्धं गृहाण देवेश सर्वसौख्यं विवर्धय ।
रक्तचन्दनसंमिश्रैरक्षितैर्योजयाम्यहम् ।।

पुष्प– पाटलमल्लिकादूर्वाशतपत्राणि विघ्नहृत् ।
पुष्पाणि गृहाण देवेश विबुधप्रिय सर्वदा ।।

धूप-दीप– धूपं गृहाण देवेश विघ्नपुंजं निवारय ।
दीपं गृहाण देवेश शम्भुसूनो नमोऽस्तु ते ।।

नैवेद्य-जल– नानाविधं गृहाणेदं नैवेद्यं कृपया प्रभो ।
करानन विशुद्ध्यर्थं जलं एतद् गृहाण मे ।।

उपायन– हिरण्यं रजतं ताम्रं यत्किंचिदपि कल्पितम् ।
उपायनं गृहाणेदं सिद्धिबुद्धीश ते नमः ।।

स्तोत्र– ॐ नमस्ते गणपतये । त्वमेव प्रत्यक्षं त्वमसि । त्वमेव केवलं कर्त्तासि । त्वमेव केवलं धर्तासि । त्वमेव केवलं हर्तासि । त्वमेव सर्वं खल्विदं ब्रह्मासि । त्वं साक्षादात्मासि ।

नमस्कार– नमो वक्रतुण्डाय नमो गणपतये नमः । प्रथमपतये नमस्तेऽस्तु लम्बोदरायैकदन्ताय विघ्नविनाशिने शिवसुताय श्रीवरदमूर्तये नमो नमः ।।

dhyāna- *oṁ udyaddineśvararuciṁ nijahastapadmaiḥ pāśāṁkuśābhayavarāndadhataṁ gajāsyam* ।
raktāmbaraṁ sakaladuḥkhaharaṁ gaṇeśaṁ dhyāyet prasannamakhilābharaṇābhirāmam ॥

āsana- *sumukhāya namastubhyaṁ gaṇādhipataye namaḥ* ।
gṛhāṇāsanamīśa tvaṁ vighnapuṁjaṁ nivāraya ॥

pādya- *umāputrāya devāya siddhavandyāya te namaḥ* ।

pādyaṁ gṛhāṇa deveśa vighnarāja namo'stu te ||

arghya- *ekadanta mahākāya nāgayajñopavītaka* |
gaṇādhideva deveśa gṛhāṇārghyaṁ namo'stu te ||

paṁcāmṛta- *payodadhighṛtakṣodraiḥ śarkarāmiśritaiḥ kṛtam* |
paṁcāmṛtaṁ gṛhāṇedaṁ snānārthaṁ vighnabhaṁjana ||

snānajala- *narmadācandrabhāgādigaṁgāsaṁgamajairjalaiḥ* |
snāpito'si mayā deva vighnasaṁghaṁ nivāraya ||

yajñopavīta- *sūryakoṭisamāyāma nāgayajñopavītaka* |
svarṇamūlaiḥ racitaṁ upavītaṁ gṛhāṇa me ||

vastra- *raktāmbara dharāgharṣa pāśāṁkuśadhareśvara* |
vastrayugmaṁ mayā dattaṁ gṛhāṇa me parameśvara ||

ācamanīya- *sugandhamiśritatīrthādipūtaṁ pānīyamuttamam* |
ācamyārthaṁ gṛhāṇa tvaṁ vighnarāja varaprada ||

gandha- *gandhaṁ gṛhāṇa deveśa sarvasaukhyaṁ vivardhaya* |

akṣata- *raktacandanasaṁmiśrairakṣatairyojayāmyaham* ||

puṣpa- *pāṭalamallikādūrvāśatapatrāṇi vighnahṛt* |
puṣpāṇi gṛhāṇa deveśa vibudhapriya sarvadā ||

dhūpa-dīpa- *dhūpaṁ gṛhāṇa deveśa vighnapuṁjaṁ nivāraya* |
dīpaṁ gṛhāṇa deveśa śambhusūno namo'stu te ||

naivedya-jala- *nānāvidhaṁ gṛhāṇedaṁ naivedyaṁ kṛpayā prabho* |

	karānana viśuddhyartharn jalarn etad gṛhāṇa me ॥
upāyana-	*hiraṇyaṁ rajataṁ tāmraṁ yatkiṁcidapi kalpitam* । *upāyanaṁ gṛhāṇedaṁ siddhibuddhīśa te namaḥ* ॥
stotra-	*om namaste gaṇapataye* । *tvameva pratyakṣaṁ tvamasi* । *tvameva kevalaṁ karttāsi* । *tvameva kevalaṁ dhartāsi* । *tvameva kevalaṁ hartāsi* । *tvameva sarvaṁ khalvidaṁ brahmāsi* । *tvaṁ sākṣādātmāsi* ।
namaskāra-	*namo vakratuṇḍāya namo gaṇapataye namaḥ* । *prathamapataye namaste'stu lambodarāyaikadantāya vighnavināśine śivasutāya śrīvaradamūrtaye namo namaḥ* ॥

The Hindu devotion springs from liberal convictions and is rooted in a sensibility remarkably catholic, where so many gods are concerned. None of these is ignored. After Gaṇeśa is worshipped the Hindu attention turns to other devas, who, again, are worshipped with due sincerity and solemnity. The worshipper makes an offering of incense, raw rice, flowers, festal lamp, naivedya, clothes, etc. to them also and while doing so chants the following mantra:

ॐ गुरुर्ब्रह्मा गुरुर्विष्णुः गुरुर्देवो महेश्वरः ।
गुरुः साक्षात् परब्रह्म तस्मै श्रीगुरवे नमः ॥१॥
शुक्लाम्बरधरं देवं शशिवर्णं चतुर्भुजम् ।
प्रसन्नवदनं ध्यायेत्सर्वविघ्नोपशान्तये ॥२॥
सर्वदा सर्वकार्येषु नास्ति तेषाममङ्गलम् ।
येषां हृदिस्थो भगवान्मङ्गलायतनो हरिः ॥३॥
मङ्गलं भगवान् विष्णुर्मङ्गलं गरुडध्वजः ।
मङ्गलं पुण्डरीकाक्षो मङ्गलायतनो हरिः ॥४॥
त्वं वै चतुर्मुखो ब्रह्मा सत्यलोकपितामहः ।
आगच्छ मण्डले चास्मिन् मम सर्वार्थसिद्धये ॥५॥

विनायकं गुरुं भानुं ब्रह्मविष्णुमहेश्वरान् ।
सरस्वतीं प्रणम्यादौ शान्तिकार्यार्थसिद्धये ।। ६ ।।
ब्रह्मा मुरारिस्त्रिपुरन्तकारी भानुःशशी भूमिसुतो बुधश्च ।
गुरुश्च शुक्रः शनिराहुकेतवः सर्वे ग्रहाः शान्तिकरा भवन्तु ।। ७ ।।
आयातु वरदे देवि अक्षरे ब्रह्मवादिनि ।
गायत्रिच्छन्दसां माता ब्रह्मयोनिर्नमोऽस्तु ते ।। ८ ।।
सर्वमङ्गलमाङ्गल्ये शिवे सर्वार्थसाधिके ।
शरण्ये त्र्यम्बके गौरि नारायणि नमोऽस्तु ते ।। ९ ।।
हस्ते स्फाटिकमालिकां विदधतीं पद्मासने संस्थिताम् ।
वन्दे तां परमेश्वरीं भगवतीं बुद्धिप्रदां शारदाम् ।। १० ।।
गौरी पद्मा शची मेधा सावित्री विजया जया ।
देवसेना स्वधा स्वाहा मातरो लोकमातरः ।। ११ ।।
कीर्तिर्लक्ष्मीर्धृतिर्मेधा सिद्धिः प्रजा सरस्वती ।
माङ्गल्येषु प्रपूज्याश्च सप्तैता दिव्यमातरः ।। १२ ।।

सर्वदेव नमस्कार– ॐ सिद्धिबुद्धिसहिताय श्रीमन्महागणाधिपतये नमः ।
ॐ लक्ष्मीनारायणाभ्यां नमः ।
ॐ उमामहेश्वराभ्यां नमः ।
ॐ वाणीहिरण्यगर्भाभ्यां नमः ।
ॐ राधाकृष्णाभ्यां नमः ।
ॐ कुलदेवताभ्यो नमः ।
ॐ इष्टदेवताभ्यो नमः ।
ॐ ग्रामदेवताभ्यो नमः ।
ॐ स्थानदेवताभ्यो नमः ।
ॐ वास्तुदेवताभ्यो नमः ।
ॐ सर्वेभ्यो देवेभ्यो नमः ।
ॐ सर्वेभ्यो ब्राह्मणेभ्यो नमः ।
ॐ सर्वेभ्यो तीर्थेभ्यो नमः ।
ॐ गुरवे नमः ।
ॐ मातृपितृपदकमलेभ्यो नमः ।
ॐ गायत्रीदेव्यै नमः ।
ॐ महालक्ष्म्यै नमः ।

ॐ शिवायै नमः ।
ॐ शारदायै नमः ।
ॐ पुण्यं पुण्याहं दीर्घमायुरस्तु ।

om gururbrahmā gururviṣṇuḥ gururdevo maheśvaraḥ ।
guruḥ sākṣāt parabrahma tasmai śrīgurave namaḥ ॥ 1 ॥
śuklāmbaradharaṁ devaṁ śaśivarṇaṁ caturbhujam ।
prasannavadanaṁ dhyāyetsarvavighnopaśāntaye ॥ 2 ॥
sarvadā sarvakāryeṣu nāsti teṣāmamaṅgalam ।
yeṣāṁ hṛdistho bhagavānmaṅgalāyatano hariḥ ॥ 3 ॥
maṅgalaṁ bhagavān viṣṇurmaṅgalaṁ garuḍadhvajaḥ ।
maṅgalaṁ puṇḍarīkākṣo maṅgalāyatano hariḥ ॥ 4 ॥
tvaṁ vai caturmukho brahmā satyalokapitāmahaḥ ।
āgaccha maṇḍale cāsmin mama sarvārthasiddhaye ॥ 5 ॥
vināyakaṁ guruṁ bhānuṁ brahmaviṣṇumaheśvarān ।
sarasvatīm praṇamyādau śāntikāryārthasiddhaye ॥ 6 ॥
brahmā murāristripurantakārī bhānuḥśaśī bhūmisuto budhaśca ।
guruśca śukraḥ śanirāhuketavaḥ sarve grahāḥ śāntikarā bhavantu ॥ 7 ॥
āyātu varade devi akṣare brahmavādini ।
gāyatricchandasāṁ mātā brahmayonirnamo'stu te ॥ 8 ॥
sarvamaṅgalamāṅgalye śive sarvārthasādhike ।
śaraṇye tryambake gauri nārāyaṇi namo'stu te ॥ 9 ॥
haste sphāṭikamālikāṁ vidadhatīṁ padmāsane saṁsthitām ।
vande tāṁ parameśvarīṁ bhagavatīṁ buddhipradāṁ śaradām ॥ 10 ॥
gaurī padmā śacī medhā sāvitrī vijayā jayā ।
devasenā svadhā svāhā mātaro lokamātaraḥ ॥ 11 ॥
kīrtirlakṣmīrdhṛtirmedhā siddhiḥ prajā sarasvatī ।
māṅgalyeṣu prapūjyāśca saptaitā divyamātaraḥ ॥ 12 ॥

sarvadeva-namaskāra—

om siddhibuddhisahitāya śrīmanmahāgaṇādhipataye namaḥ ।
om lakṣmīnārāyaṇābhyāṁ namaḥ ।
om umāmaheśvarābhyāṁ namaḥ ।

om vāṇīhiraṇyagarbhābhyāṁ namaḥ ।
om rādhākṛṣṇābhyāṁ namaḥ ।
om kuladevatābhyo namaḥ ।
om iṣṭadevatābhyo namaḥ ।
om grāmadevatābhyo namaḥ ।
om sthānadevatābhyo namaḥ ।
om vāstudevatābhyo namaḥ ।
om sarvebhyo devebhyo namaḥ ।
om sarvebhyo brāhmaṇebhyo namaḥ ।
om sarvebhyo tīrthebhyo namaḥ ।
om gurave namaḥ ।
om mātṛpitṛpadakamalebhyo namaḥ ।
om gāyatrīdevyai namaḥ ।
om mahālakṣmyai namaḥ ।
om śivāyai namaḥ ।
om śāradāyai namaḥ ।
om puṇyaṁ puṇyāhaṃ dīrghamāyurastu ।

A luminous treatise on rituals, the *Nārada Purāṇa* begins with revealing the importance of oṁkāra and atha used by the purohitas and goes on to describe the essentials of the Hindu saṁskāras. The 'oṁkāra' and the word 'atha', says the book, are the two words formerly pierced through the throat of god Brahmā and came out. Hence these two are auspicious ones. He who has completed the rites mentioned and wishes to do the subsequent ones, shall utter the word 'atha'. It is sought for the purpose of endless benefits. Kuśa grass which is spread in a particular way is extolled for the rite of sprinkling water in the prescribed way round the fire. In the desired holy rite, the number of kuśa grass-blades should not be less or more, lest it should be fruitless.

The rite of parisamūhana is enjoined as a preventive action against worms, germs, insects, etc. that crawl and move about on the surface of the Earth. The three parallel lines that are enjoined, should be made equal. It has been laid down that they should not be made smaller or larger. It has been mentioned that the cowdung of certain types of cows should not be used in the holy rite of yajña—viz. the barren cow, the wicked or defiled cow, the cow with afflicted limbs and the cow whose calf is dead. The rite of proddharana (i.e. sprinkling of water upwards) is intended for the purpose of eradicating such terrible beings as moths, etc. that always roam about in the atmosphere. One should scrape or scratch the ground with sruva (sacrificial ladle or spoon) or the kuśa grass. It has been enjoined by Brahmā for the achievement of asthikaṇṭaka (bones and thorns?). The waters represent all the groups of devas and manes (pitṛs). Hence the sprinkling the altar with water has been laid down by sages who are experts in injunctions. It is mentioned that the sacrificial fire should be brought by women endowed with saubhāgya (good fortune, i.e. woman having her husband and sons alive) in an auspicious earthen pot. The fire should be placed in the earthen pot sprinkled with water. On observing the wastage (i.e. disappearance by being stolen away by demons) of the nectar, the fire latent in the sacrificial twigs has been placed on the altar by Brahmā and all other deities for its protection. Dānavas and others are standing in readiness to create trouble to the south of the yajña. For the sake of protection from them, one should establish god Brahmā in that direction. The vessels intended for consecration and cooking and all other vessels must be placed in the north; the yajamāna (the householder on whose behalf the yajña is being performed) sits to the west. All the brāhmaṇas sit to the east.

The Brahmā and the ācārya must be appointed from one's own śākhā (branch of Veda) in the course of the rite of yajña. There is no restriction in the case of the ṛtviks. They should be invited and honoured according to availability. The two *pavitras* (the kuśa grass twisted into a ring like loop with a tail) must be three *aṅgulas* in length. The *prokṣaṇī* (the vessel containing the holy water) must be four *aṅgulas* in length. The *ājyasthālī* (the vessel holding ghī) shall be three *aṅgulas* in length and the carusthālī (the vessel in which the caru, i.e. food offering is kept) must be six *aṅgulas* in length. The *upayamana* (the kuśa-grass ladle used at sacrifices) shall be two *aṅgulas* long; the *sammārjana* (that used for sweeping) shall be one *aṅgula* in length. The *sruva* (sacrificial ladle) is enjoined to be six *aṅgulas* long and *sruk* (sacrificial spoon) is said to be three and a half *aṅgulas* long. The sacrificial twigs are a span in length. The *praṇītā* vessel eight *aṅgulas* in length is placed to the north of the *prokṣaṇī* vessel. Whatever sacred water is there in the world as rivers and oceans is present in the *praṇītā* vessel. Hence it should be filled with water. The *vedikā* (sacrificial altar) is said to be naked and devoid of garments otherwise. Hence a wise man shall clothe it by means of the *darbha* grass.

The sprinkling must be done from the water taken from the *praṇītā* vessel. Thereby the holy rite becomes the yielder of great merit. It is glorified as very sacred. The *ājyasthālī* (the vessel holding ghī) shall be made with a *pala* weight of metal. The earthen pot shaped by the potter's wheel is remembered to be demoniac in character. The vessel *sthālī*, etc. shaped by means of the hand is said to be divine.

The auspiciousness or inauspiciousness of all rites depends on *sruva*. In order to make it sanctified it is warmed in the fire. When it is held at the tip there is no widowhood (?), if it is held in the middle deficiency of progeny or death of children is the result; if it is held at the root, the *hotṛ* dies. Hence it should be held after considering all this. The following six deities resort to the *sruva* at the interval of each *aṅgula* viz.—Agni, the sun, the moon, Viriñci (i.e. Brahmā), the wind god and Yama. Agni may lead to the destruction of objects of pleasure; the sun may cause sickness; the moon does not yield any special result; Viriñci is the bestower of all desired objects; the wind god is said to be the bestower of prosperity and Yama is considered to be the bestower of death. Hence the *sruva* should be held at the fourth or fifth *aṅgula*. The *sammārjana* and the *upayamana* are to be made with kuśa blades. The former one may be of all the branches(?) and the other of five branches or blades of *darbha* grass. In order to make *sruva* and *sruk*, it should be known that the trees, *śriparṇī, śamī, khadira, vikaṇṭaka* and *palāśa* are used. A *sruva*, a *hasta* (24 *aṅgulas* or about 18 inches) long is commendable, and a *sruk* of thirteen *aṅgulas* is also commendable. This is laid down for the Brāhmaṇas. In the case of others, it should be one *aṅgula* shorter. It is laid down in the *smṛtis* that the sprinkling of the vessels is for the destruction of defects (defilement) due to the glances of śūdras, the fallen ones and donkeys and other beings at them.

If the vessel is not filled up completely, there may be a loophole in the *yajña*. If it is filled completely, the *yajña* becomes full. When the time for *homa* has arrived, one shall not offer any seat anywhere. If it is offered, the fire may be excited and may give a terrible curse. Two *āghāras* (sprinklings or oblations of ghī) are said to be the two nostrils, the two oblations of *ājya*, two eyes, this is said to be the face of Prajāpati and the waist is formed out of the *vyāhṛtis*. The head, hands and the feet—these five are said to be the *homa* called Pañca-Varuṇa(?). What is sviṣṭakṛt (offering belonging to Agni) and the *pūrṇāhuti* (the final offering) are the two ears.

The physical body of the fire god should be conceived as follows: it has two faces, one heart, four ears, two noses, two heads, six eyes, tawny colour, and seven tongues. It has three hands on the left side and four hands on the right side. In the four right hands it holds the *sruk, sruva, akṣamālā* (rosary) and *sakti* (javelin). It has three girdles, three feet, a vessel for ghī and two chowries. Agni is seated on a ram. It has four horns and the lustre of the morning sun. It has a sacred thread and it is bedecked with ear-rings and has matted hair. One shall perform the rite of *homa* after conceiving the physical body of Agni thus. The brāhmaṇa who performs the homa rite by using mere hand for oblating milk, curds, ghī and any fried object becomes the slayer of a brāhmaṇa.

The food that a man eats, his deities also eat; but for the prosperous achievement of all desired objects, the gingelly seeds must be used more in the *havis* offered. In the course of *homas*, three *mudrās* (ritualistic gestures or symbolic representations by certain positions of fingers, etc.) should be shown,viz. what is designated as the hind, the she-swan, and the sow. While magic spells and incantations are used, the *mudrā* called the sow should be used and during the auspicious rites, the gestures of the hind and the she-swan shall be used. The ritualistic gesture called the female swine shall be by means of all the fingers; that of the she-swan shall be without the use of the small finger; the *mudrā* called the hind shall be by means of the three fingers, viz. the middle, the ring finger and the thumb. One shall perform the *homa* with gingelly seeds along with curds, honey and ghī the magnitude being the same as mentioned before, grasping these with all the five fingers. In all auspicious rites the kuśa grass-blades should be held closely to the ring finger.

Vināyaka (god Gaṇeśa) has been appointed as the controlling head of gaṇas. The nine planets are to be installed in the following order, viz. the Sun, Moon, Mars, Mercury, Jupiter, Venus, Saturn, Rahu and Ketu. For attaining auspiciousness, the replica or representation of the planets should be made of what follows respectively: copper, crystal, red-sandal-wood, two in gold and silver, iron, lead and bell-metal. Or they may be painted on the canvas-cloth in their respective colours or they may be represented by means of esoteric diagrams with coloured powders or pastes. Each planet should be worshipped by offering clothes, scents, or unguents and flowers according to the complexion of the planets. They should also be offered scents, *bali* (food-offerings), incense and *guggula* (a particular fragrant gum resin). For each presiding deity of the planets oblation of *caru* and *samidhās* be offered in the fire.

The sacrificial sticks special to each planet are as follows: the sun-plant (*arka*), *palāśa* (tree), *khadira* (*Acacia Catechu*), apāmārga (the Achyranthes Aspera), the *pippala, udumbara, dūrvā* and *kuśa* grass. To each of the planet one hundred eight or twenty-eight sacrificial sticks (that of the sun-plant for the sun, the *palāśa* twigs for the moon, etc.) smeared with honey or ghī or curds or milk should be oblated. The *naivedya* offered should consist of the following articles: rice cooked with jaggery, milk-pudding, haviṣya (food partakable to sages), ṣaṣṭikā grains cooked in milk, cooked rice with curds, havis (rice cooked in milk), *cūrṇa* (rice mixed with sesame), boiled rice of various colours due to its various components. These articles should be offered to each planet in due order. The wise person should feed the brāhmaṇas according to his financial ability and the availability of the foodstuffs. The food, etc. should be offered after duly honouring them by washing their feet, etc.

The following is the prescribed religious fee (dakṣiṇā) for the planets respectively: a cow, a conch, a strong bull, gold, yellow cloth, a white horse, a black tawny (?) coloured cow, iron (a weapon), a goat. The different articles offered as dakṣiṇā should be *pala* in weight. At the time of monetary gifts this should be said, "O Brāhmaṇa, boon has been granted by these: being worshipped (bless) them." Wealth, nobility, rise in position of leading men are controlled by planets. The existence and the non-existence of the universe depends on the planets. Hence, planets are highly adorable. If a person begins to worship planets without performance of *mātṛ-yāga* (a sacrifice in propitiation of Divine mothers), the mothers get angry with him and create impediments.

Those who seek auspiciousness should perform vasordhārā (a particular libation of ghī at the *agni-cayana*) by means of holy mantras of Vasu. Gaurī and other holy mothers should be propitiated by them on auspicious occasions. The mothers are sixteen in number viz.—Gaurī, Padmā, Śacī, Medhā, Sāvitrī, Vijayā, Jayā, Devasenā, Svadhā, Svāhā, Mātṛkā, Vaidhṛti, Dhṛti, Puṣṭi, Dṛṣṭi and Tuṣṭi—these sixteen should be worshipped for prosperity along with the

Ātmadevatā (the family deity). They are even superior to Gaṇeśa. All the necessary items in the worship should be followed: viz. the invocation, offering of *pādya* and arghya, ablution, sandal paste, *akṣatas* (raw rice grains), flowers, incense, burning light, fruits, *naivedya,* ācamanīya, betel leaves, areca nuts, showing of lights (nīrājana) and *dakṣiṇā.* All these must be offered for their satisfaction.

CHAPTER II

The Pūjās

Though the saṁskāras differ from one another on account of the purpose for which they are performed, certain ceremonial rites in most of them are essentially the same. No Hindu saṁskāra, for example, is performed without a family priest, whose role is that of an instructor and director, at whose bidding the ceremony begins and ends and who is expected to be an undisputed authority on the karmakāṇḍas. Certain pūjās are likewise common to most of the saṁskāras and are performed on a large number of festive occasions. The worship of the Vedic deities, for example, is all-pervasive and there is no sacrifice which dispenses with the worship of Agni or with fire oblation. And there is no mantra more sacrosanct than the Gāyatrī. Some of the rituals in sacrificial pūjās need to be understood and their modes defined before the actual ceremony of the upanayana is described.

Ṣoḍaśopacāra and Pañcopacāra

All ceremonial acts involve the *pūjā*[1] of gods. While some of

---

1. The term *pūjā* which literally means worship, is used to describe the various forms of worship in the home or in the temple. A *pūjā* is an act of reverence by a devotee towards a chosen representation of God, indicated by the presence of the *mūrti*. Strictly speaking, a pūjā is a formal mode of worship with its conventionally prescribed procedures or upacāras venerating the Lord as an honoured guest. The procedures are generally about fourteen in number. Among the important procedures of a *pūjā* are the initial invocation of the deity (āvāhana), the invitation to a seat (āsana), the washing of the feet (pādya), and acts of adoration through the offering of flowers, the burning of incense, the waving of light (dīpa) and the

the recognized authorities recommend five modes of worship, others speak of sixteen. The practice most in vogue is pañcopacāra, the adopter of which does homage in five ways. The sixteen modes of doing homage are adopted on special occasions when the ceremonies are performed elaborately and with great aplomb and fanfare. The word 'upacāra' is widely used in the sense of service, attendance, honouring, worshipping, etc. The sixteen ways of doing homage to a deity are thus enumerated:

आसनं स्वागतं पाद्यमर्घ्यमाचमनीयकम् ।
मधुपर्काचमनस्नानं वसनाभरणानि च ।
गंधपुष्पे धूपदीपौ नैवेद्यं वन्दनं तथा ।
āsanaṁ svāgataṁ pādyamarghyamācamanīyakam ।
madhuparkācamanasnānaṁ vasanābharaṇāni ca ।
gaṁdhapuṣpe dhūpadīpau naivedyaṁ vandanaṁ tathā ।

These are āvāhana (invocation), āsana (seat), pādya (relating or belonging to the foot), arghya (water offered at the respectful reception), ācamana (water used for purification or for sipping), snāna (bathing), vastra (clothes), upavīta (sacred thread), candana (sandal), puṣpa (flower), dhūpa (incense), dīpa (light), naivedya (offering of eatables), namaskāra (adoration or homage), pradakṣiṇā (circumambulation) and visarjana (concluding rite). Pañcopacāras are said to be of two kinds. In the first, the worshipper does the following five: dhyāna (meditation), āvāhana (invitation or invocation), naivedya (offering of eatables), āratī (waving lustral light) and praṇāma (bowing down). Those who express their devotion offer candana (sandal), puṣpa (flower),

---

consecration of food (naivedya). These acts are accompanied by the recitation of appropriate scriptural texts and forms of meditation. The *pūjā* ritual concludes with the distribution of prasāda, that is, food which has been ritually offered to the deity. The acceptance of prasāda is an acknowledgement of the Lord as the source of all that we enjoy. The word also means grace, and is symbolic of the blessings of the deity. A *pūjā*, therefore, is a total involvement of the body, speech, and mind in worship.

dhūpa (incense), dīpa (light), and naivedya (offering of eatables). These offerings which constitute the second kind of Pañcopacāra are widely known and made by the generality of worshippers. The word 'pādya' used above stands for water for washing the feet and 'arghya' for the same used for washing hands.

Invocation is a symbolical invitation to the deity presiding over the ceremony. This is done by meditating on and conjuring up an image of the deity and inviting him with raw rice grains and reciting ॐ सर्वेभ्यो देवेभ्यो नमः, आवाहयामि स्थापयामि (om sarvebhyo devebhyo namaḥ, āvāhayāmi sthāpayāmi). At the end of the invocation the rice grains are dropped on the place allotted to the god. Then, having assumed that he has responded, to the recitation of ॐ आसनं समर्पयामि (om āsanaṁ samarpayāmi). The seat offered consists of kuśa, dūrvā or blossoms. When he has taken his seat the devotee proceeds to wash his feet for which he has kept a special pot of water with dūrvā grass and sandal in it. With the recitation of ॐ पाद्यं समर्पयामि (om pādyaṁ samarpayāmi) he sprinkles this water where the god is installed. He is then welcomed with arghya, which is water in a vessel having sandal, raw rice, betel nut and flowers in it. These are offered with ॐ अर्घ्यं समर्पयामि (om arghyaṁ samarpayāmi). In another water jar keep some water taken from the sacred rivers, Gaṅgā or Yamunā; in case this sacred water is not available, any river or well-water will be a good substitute if it is pure. Drop it with mango or betel leaves or with a natural ladle on the symbolical god with ॐ आचमनं समर्पयामि (om ācamanaṁ samarpayāmi). The god is next bathed with ॐ स्नानं समर्पयामि (oṁ snānaṁ samarpayāmi) and made to wear new clothes with ॐ वस्त्रं समर्पयामि (om vastraṁ samarpayāmi). Imagining that you are doing so, keep the clothes either where the deity is or on his image. The next mode of worship is the offer of the sacred thread with ॐ यज्ञोपवीतं समर्पयामि (om yajñopavītaṁ samarpayāmi). Having thus adored him now mark him with sandal or rolī (red fragrant powder), for which the appropriate mantra is ॐ गन्धं समर्पयामि (om gandhaṁ samarpayāmi). The devotee then adores the god with the offer of flowers he likes most. He avoids offering ketaka blossom to Śiva and āka blossom to Viṣṇu. Śiva's favourite flower, however, is āka. The flower offering is made with the mantra ॐ पुष्पं समर्पयामि (om puṣpaṁ samarpayāmi). For incense one can have it from the *Bazar* and offer it with the mantra ॐ धूपं दर्शयामि (om dhūpaṁ darśayāmi). The same procedure is followed when offering light, food, betel and sacrificial fee with the following mantras:

ॐ दीपं दर्शयामि
ॐ नैवेद्यं निवेदयामि
ॐ ताम्बूलपूगफलानि समर्पयामि
ॐ दक्षिणां समर्पयामि ।।
om dīpaṁ darśayāmi
om naivedyaṁ nivedayāmi
om tāmbūlapūgaphalāni samarpayāmi
om dakṣiṇāṁ samarpayāmi ॥

The sixteen modes of worship end with the devotee going around the symbolical deity with a sense of complete surrender to him. The god whom the devotee circumambulates is on his right side. When performing a pūjā, one must not be oblivious of one's own means nor must one deem it obligatory to perform all the pūjās at once. Selection may be made in accordance with one's own capacity and means to perform them. If any ceremonial material is not available all one can do is to offer it *in absentia*, assuming that he is offering it.

Śrautas and Smārttas

The three broad kinds of ceremonial performances are nitya, naimittika, and kāmya. The nitya ceremonies are sandhyopāsana, agnihotra, etc. which are always performed from the investiture of the sacred thread to death. The naimittikas are performed on child birth and death, called jātakarma and antyeṣṭi respectively. The performance of śrāddha and satiation of deceased persons in the dark half in the Gauṇa Āśvina (pitṛpakṣa) by presenting to them libations of water (tarpaṇa) are naimittikas, for they are performed on special occasions and for special purposes, not every day. The sacrifice performed to obtain male children or one performed at the time of adoption (putreṣṭi) or the pilgrimage to holy places are kāmyas. Desire (kāma or kāmanā) for fruit is the underlying motive of all such ceremonies as belong to this last category. If no such desire for male children exists, then there is no need for the sacrifices called putreṣṭi. The other two kinds of ceremonies—the nityas and the naimittikas—have to be performed, no matter whether there is any desire for any fruit or not. The rites performed for atonement and expiation belong to the class of kāmyas which are in fact and at bottom only naimittikas because desire for fruit underlies both the categories. Viewed thus, there are only two kinds of ceremonies, the nityas and naimittikas, of which, again, there are two kinds known as śrauta and smārtta. Śrauta karmas are vaitānika and the smārttas are gṛhya and āvasathya. The words gṛha and āvasathya stand for home and it is common knowledge that a home without a housewife is of no account and desolate. As the housewife is the ever-present spirit of the house, she is called 'gṛha'. The sacrificial fire in which the gṛhya ceremonies are performed has no less than six names—smārtta, gṛhya, āvasathya, śālāgni, aupāsana and vaivāhika. The rule which governs the installation of this fire is that the festal fire in which oblation is made during the nuptial is brought from the pavilion and established according to rule in a pit dug for the purpose. There are three occasions on which the gṛhya agni is installed: they are marriage, death of the father and separation of brothers from one another. Even if these three occasions do not make this installation possible, another auspicious occasion may be used for this purpose. Marriage and investiture of the sacred thread and other ceremonies are called smārtta because we find them elaborately dealt with in the smṛtis. The scriptures, including histories, mythologies and other religious books apart from the Vedas are all included in the smṛtis, which is the reason why the ceremonies dealt with in them are called smārttas. When however the scriptures and the Purāṇas come into conflict, it is the former that is regarded as more authoritative. On such occasions the word smṛti becomes synonymous with Manu and the law-giver of that ilk.

Maṇḍapa

Such acts as *havana*[1] cannot be completed unhindered without a *maṇḍapa* or pavilion. The reason is that crows, cats, dogs, etc. may by their very touch defile the sacrificial objects or the festal ground where the materials collected for the sacraments have also to be protected from gales and rains. Strong winds laden with sparks may cause devastation and rains may extinguish the sacrificial fire. If the pavilion, however, cannot be erected, efforts should be made to have at least some shade in its place. Care should also be taken to erect the *maṇḍapa* on a piece of land which is slightly elevated and to so raise it that its length is equal to its width.

The materials commonly used in ceremonial worship and performance of the saṁskāras are: pañcagavya, madhuparka, pañcāmṛta, pañcapallava, sarvagandha, sarvauṣadhi, saptadhātu, pañcaratna, dhūpa, saptadhānya, saptamṛttikā, kalaśa, abhāva dravya, etc.

pañcagavya—the five products of the cow (viz. milk, coagulated or sour milk, butter, and the liquid and solid excreta).

pañcāmṛta—the five kinds of divine food (viz. milk, coagulated or sour milk, butter, honey, and sugar).

1. Defined by Monier Williams as a hole made in the ground for the sacrificial fire which is to receive a burnt oblation, offering of an oblation with fire, sacrifice.

यज्ञ-मण्डप
(Yajña-maṇḍapa)

pañcapallava—the aggregate of five springs or shoots of the āmra, vaṭa, pīpara, gūlara, and pākari.
pañcaratna—a collection of five jewels or precious stones (viz. gold, diamond, sapphire, ruby, and pearl).
saptadhātu—a collection of seven metals (viz. gold, silver, copper, brass, iron, zinc, and lead).
saptadhānya—the seven kinds of grains [viz. barley, wheat, sesamum, penicum frumentaceum (a kind of cultivated millet), kaṁganī (a kind of corn), green lentil, and gram].
madhutraya—the mixture of butter, milk, and honey.
sarvagandha—camphor, sandal, musk, and saffron.
sarvauṣadhi—the different herbs like *kūṭa, jaṭāmāṁsī, haldī,*

dāru haldī, morabela, candana, vaca, śilājīta, campaka, and *mothā.*

saptamṛttikā—seven earths collected from seven places.

kalaśa—a jar made of any of the following metals: gold, silver, and copper. If the host cannot provide a kalaśa made of any of these metals, it can be substituted by an earthen pot.

abhāva dravya—in the absence or non-availability of any of the materials recommended for use, any other material, preferably of the same value or kind, may be used.

agnināma—the richness and multiplicity of synonyms for the word 'agni' need not cause any confusion, for each ceremony has its own appropriate name for the sacrificial fire. In the garbhādhāna ceremony, for example, the fire god is not Agni but Māruta; in the puṁsavana, he is Pāvamāna; in the sīmantonnayana, he is Maṁgala; in the jātakarma, he is called Prabala, in the christening ceremony, he is called Pārthiva; in the annaprāśana Śuci; in the tonsure ceremony Śuci; in the initiation Samudbhava; in the shaving of beard (keśānta) Sūrya and in the nuptial Yojaka. The list of synonyms for 'agni' does not end here. In āvasthyādhāna, he is called Dvija, in penance Viṭa, in a domestic or simple sacrifice Pāvaka, in pūrṇāhuti Mṛḍa, in udara (stomach) Vaiśvānara, in vaiśvadeva homa Rukma, in agnihotra Gārhapatya, Āhavanīya and Dakṣiṇāgni, etc. It is incumbent on the host as well as the officiating priest to remember Agni's name for the ceremony being conducted.

Each ceremony has its own presiding deity. The garbhādhāna, for example, is presided over by Brahmā, the puṁsavana by Prajāpati, the sīmantonnayana by Dhātā, the jātakarma, niṣkramaṇa and annaprāśana by Savitā, the nāmakaraṇa, the cūḍākaraṇa and keśānta by Prajāpati, the upanayana by Indra, the Vedārambha by Pāvaka, the sacred ceremonial acts by Śraddhā, the nuptials by Prajāpati. The nāndīśrāddha as an integral part of the garbhādhāna etc. is presided over by Viśvedeva called Kratudakṣa or elsewhere by Viśvedeva called Satyavasu. Agni, Sūrya, and Prajāpati are the presiding gods of aupāsana homa, while Agnigarbha is the god who presides over sthālīpāka. It is supremely beneficial to mutter to oṁkāra at the beginning of each ceremony.

Before a ceremonial act is begun it is incumbent on the performer to start with what is called svastivācana. The first step in nuptial ceremonies, for example, is to resolve to perform them before the actual ceremonies begin to be performed. Such a resolve is the performer's commitment not to abandon the ceremony midway or give it up in the face of hurdles. When uttering the saṁkalpa, the person making the resolution holds sesamum, kuśa grass (preferably three kuśa blades), barley or rice grains, betel-nut and water in his hand. A few copper coins are also added to them these days, though this practice does not find any mention in books on the saṁskāras or in the scriptures. While making the resolution, the person concerned mentions his native place, time, month, date, day, asterism, etc. and then his own name and at the end the name of the ceremony which he is about to perform. The resolution ends when the maker of it utters the word 'करिष्ये' (kariṣye) and drops the kuśas, barley or raw rice grains, etc. on the ground. Only the day on which the ceremony is being performed, its month, whether bright half or dark, the lunar day, asterism, etc. should be uttered. But even before these one should resolve to worship Ganeśa for the unhindered completion of the ceremony and keep him on the place or on the altar especially designed for him. This special homage to Gaṇeśa should be done according to the sixteen modes of worship (ṣoḍaśopacāra). The custom widely prevalent is to recall the family deity, the chosen tutelary deity, and Viṣṇu while reverencing Gaṇeśa.

After paying due obeisance to Gaṇeśa the principal saṁkalpa is to be uttered, followed by svastivācana and puṇyāhavācana, which again should be followed by mātṛkāpūjana and nāndīśrāddha. In the performance of the puṇyāhavācana four brāhmaṇas, duly reverenced with incense, betel leaves, sacrificial fee, etc. are engaged to conduct it. The host along with his wife takes his seat facing the north of the brāhmaṇa. Alternatively, if the brāhmaṇas are seated facing the north, the host and his wife should sit facing the east. The host with his knees resting on the ground should keep both hands on his head like a lotus in full bloom.

Svastivācana

It consists in taking a beautiful unleaking earthen (or metallic) vessel, free from all loopholes and apertures and touching the ground where it is to be kept with the mantra:

ॐ मही द्यौः पृथिवी च न इमं यज्ञं मिमिक्षताम् ।
पिपृतां नो भरीमभिः ।। १ ।।
om mahī dyauḥ pṛthivī ca na imaṁ yajñaṁ mimikṣatām ।
pipṛtāṁ no bharīmabhiḥ ॥ 1 ॥

The second step is to make a little ball of rice with the recitation of the following mantra:

ॐ ओषधयः समवदन्त सोमेन सह राज्ञा ।
यस्मै कृणोति ब्राह्मणस्तं राजन् पारयामसि ।। २ ।।
om oṣadhayaḥ samavadanta somena saha rājñā ।
yasmai kṛṇoti brāhmaṇastaṁ rājan pārayāmasi ॥ 2 ॥

The third and the fourth steps are, respectively, keeping the vessel on the heap of rice and filling it with water with the recitation of the next two mantras:

ॐ आ जिघ्र कलशं मह्या त्वा विशन्त्विन्दवः ।
पुनरूर्जा निवर्त्तस्व सा नः सहस्रं धुक्ष्वोरुधारा पयस्वती पुनर्माविशताद्रयिः ।।३ ।।
ॐ इमं मे वरुण श्रुधि हवमद्या च मृडय ।
त्वामवस्युराचके ।। ४ ।।
om ā jigrha kalaśaṁ mahyā tvā viśantvindavaḥ ।
punarūrjā nivarttasva sā naḥ sahasraṁ dhukṣvorudhārā
payasvatī punarmāviśatādrayiḥ ॥ 3 ॥

om imaṁ me varuṇa śrudhi havamadyā ca mṛḍaya ।
tvāmavasyurācake ॥ 4 ॥

Then draw a svastika (a kind of mystical cross or mark made on persons or things to denote good luck) on the vessel. Drop a little khasa root (a fragrant grass used for cooling purposes) or any fragrant object into the vessel, smear it with sandal paste and with the recitation of the first mantra put sarvauṣadhi into it. Barley grains and dūrvā grass are to be dropped into it with the recitation of the second and third mantra respectively:

ॐ गन्धद्वारां दुराधर्षां नित्यपुष्टां करीषिणीम् ।
ईश्वरीं सर्वभूतानां तामिहोपह्वये श्रियम् ।। १ ।।
ॐ या औषधीः पूर्वा जाता देवेभ्यस्त्रियुगं पुरा ।
मनै नु बभ्रूणामहं शतं धामानि सप्त च ।। २ ।।
ॐ काण्डात्काण्डात्प्ररोहन्ती परुषः परुषस्परि ।
एवानो दूर्वे प्र तनु सहस्रेण शतेन च ।। ३ ।।
om gandhadvārāṁ durādharṣāṁ nityapuṣṭāṁ karīṣiṇīm ।
īśvarīṁ sarvabhūtānāṁ tāmihopahvaye śriyam ॥ 1 ॥
om yā auṣadhīḥ pūrvā jātā devebhyastriyugaṁ purā ।
manai nu babhrūṇāmahaṁ śataṁ dhāmāni sapta ca ॥ 2 ॥
om kāṇḍātkāṇḍātprarohantī paruṣaḥ paruṣaspari ।
evāno dūrve pra tanu sahasreṇa śatena ca ॥ 3 ॥

The svastivācana continues with dropping into it the pañcapallavas with the recitation of the first mantra and the saptamṛttikās with the second:

ॐ अश्वत्थे वो निषदनं पर्णे वो वसतिष्कृता ।
गोभाज इत्किलासथ यत्सनवथ पूरुषम् ।। १ ।।
ॐ स्योना पृथिवि नो भवानृक्षरा निवेशनी ।
यच्छा नः शर्म सप्रथः ।। २ ।।
om aśvatthe vo niṣadanaṁ parṇe vo vasatiṣkṛtā ।
gobhāja itkilāsatha yatsanavatha pūruṣam ॥ 1 ॥
om syonā pṛthivi no bhavānṛkṣarā niveśanī ।
yacchā naḥ śarma saprathaḥ ॥ 2 ॥

Having done this now put pure fruits into it with the first mantra and pañcaratna with the second. The texts enjoin that a piece of gold should be dropped into the vessel with the muttering of the third mantra. If, however, the kalaśa is made of gold no such action is recommended:

ॐ याः फलिनीर्या अफला अपुष्पा याश्च पुष्पिणीः ।
बृहस्पतिप्रसूतास्ता नो मुञ्चन्त्वंहसः ॥ १ ॥
ॐ परिवाजपतिः कविरग्निर्हव्यान्यक्रमीत् ।
दधद्रत्नानि दाशुषे ॥ २ ॥
ॐ हिरण्यगर्भः समवर्त्तताग्रे भूतस्यजातः पतिरेक आसीत् ।
स दाधार पृथिवीं द्यामुतेमां कस्मै देवाय हविषा विधेम ॥ ३ ॥

om yāḥ phalinīryā aphalā apuṣpā yāśca puṣpiṇīḥ ।
bṛhaspatiprasūtāstā no muñcantvaṁhasaḥ ॥ 1 ॥
om parivājapatiḥ kaviragnirhavyānyakramīt ।
dadhadratnāni dāśuṣe ॥ 2 ॥
om hiraṇyagarbhaḥ samavarttatāgre bhūtasyajātaḥ patireka āsīt ।
sa dādhāra pṛthivīṁ dyāmutemāṁ kasmai devāya haviṣā vidhema ॥ 3 ॥

Then with the citation of the following mantra wrap the vessel with a piece of new saffron coloured cloth:

ॐ युवा सुवासाः परिवीत आगात् स उश्रेयान् भवति जायमानः ।
तं धीरासः कवय उन्नयन्ति स्वाध्यो मनसा देवयन्तः ॥

om yuvā suvāsāḥ parivīta āgāt sa uśreyān bhavati jāyamānaḥ ।
taṁ dhīrāsaḥ kavaya unnayanti svādhyo manasā devayantaḥ ॥

Recite the following mantra while keeping an earthen plate filled with rice grains on top of the sacrificial vessel (kalaśa).

ॐ पूर्णा दर्वि परापत सुपूर्णा पुनरापत ।
वस्नेव विक्रीणावहा इषमूर्जं शतक्रतो ॥

om pūrṇā darvi parāpata supūrṇā punarāpata ।
vasneva vikrīṇāvahā iṣamūrjaṁ śatakrato ॥

Varuṇa should be invoked with the following mantra:

ॐ तत्त्वा यामि ब्रह्मणा वन्दमानस्तदाशास्ते यजमानो
हविर्भिः अहेडमानो वरुणेह बोध्युरुशंसमा न आयुः प्रमोषीः ।
om tattvā yāmi brahmaṇā vandamānastadāśāste yajamāno havirbhiḥ aheḍamāno varuṇeha bodhyuruśaṁsamā na āyuḥ pramoṣīḥ ।

Then adore him with all the sixteen modes of worship as you keep on reciting:

ॐ भूर्भुवः स्वः अपांपतये वरुणाय नमः ।
om bhūrbhuvaḥ svaḥ apāṁpataye varuṇāya namaḥ ।

The Gaṅgā, the sacred rivers and the tīrthas should be invoked with the following mantra:

ॐ सर्वे समुद्राः सरितस्तीर्थानि जलदा नदाः ।
आयान्तु मम शान्त्यर्थं दुरितक्षयकारकाः ।।
om sarve samudrāḥ saritastīrthāni jaladā nadāḥ ।
āyāntu mama śāntyarthaṁ duritakṣayakārkāḥ ॥

Then touch the vessel with your right-hand ring finger while reciting the following mantras:

कलशस्य मुखे विष्णुः कण्ठे रुद्रः समाश्रितः ।
मूले तस्य स्थितो ब्रह्मा मध्ये मातृगणाः स्मृताः ।।
कुक्षौ तु सागराः सप्त सप्तद्वीपा वसुन्धरा ।
ऋग्वेदाऽथ यजुर्वेदः सामवेदो ह्यथर्वणः ।।
अंगैश्च सहिताः सर्वे कलशन्तु समाश्रिताः ।
देवदानवसंवादे मथ्यमाने महोदधौ ।
उत्पन्नोऽसि तदा कुम्भ विधृतो विष्णुना स्वयम् ।।
त्वत्तोये सर्वतीर्थानि देवाः सर्वे त्वयिस्थिताः ।
त्वयि तिष्ठन्ति भूतानि त्वयि प्राणाः प्रतिष्ठिताः ।।
शिवः स्वयं त्वमेवासि विष्णुस्त्वं च प्रजापतिः ।

आदित्या वसवो रुद्रा विश्वेदेवाः सपैतृकाः ।।
त्वयि तिष्ठन्ति सर्वेऽपि यतः कामफलप्रदाः ।
सान्निध्यं कुरु मे देव प्रसन्नो भव सर्वदा ।।

kalaśasya mukhe viṣṇuḥ kaṇṭhe rudraḥ samāśritaḥ ।
mūle tasya sthito brahmā madhye mātṛgaṇāḥ smṛtāḥ ॥
kukṣau tu sāgarāḥ sapta saptadvīpā vasundharā ।
ṛgvedā'tha yajurvedaḥ sāmavedo hyatharvaṇaḥ ॥
aṁgaiśca sahitāḥ sarve kalaśantu samāśritāḥ ।
devadānavasaṁvāde mathyamāne mahodadhau ॥
utpanno'si tadā kumbha vidhṛto viṣṇunā svayam ।
tvattoye sarvatīrthāni devāḥ sarve tvayisthitāḥ ।
tvayi tiṣṭhanti bhūtāni tvayi prāṇāḥ pratiṣṭhitāḥ ॥
śivaḥ svayaṁ tvamevāsi viṣṇustvaṁ ca prajāpatiḥ ।
ādityā vasavo rudrā viśvedevāḥ sapaitṛkāḥ ॥
tvayi tiṣṭhanti sarve'pi yataḥ kāmaphalapradāḥ ।
sānnidhyaṁ kuru me deva prasanno bhava sarvadā ॥

***Puṇyāhavācana*[1]**

Having hymned this prayer let your knees touch the ground as you keep your hands, lotus-like with palms open, on your head. The officiating priest should hold the kalaśa with his right hand while the host recites the following mantra:

ॐ त्रीणि पदा विचक्रमे विष्णुर्गोपा अदाभ्यः ।
अतो धर्माणि धारयन् ।।

om trīṇi padā vicakrame viṣṇurgopā adābhyaḥ ।
ato dharmāṇi dhārayan ॥

Then should Puṇyāhavācana begin with the repetition of 'तेनायुष्प्रमाणेन पुण्यं पुण्याहं दीर्घमायुरस्त्विति' (tenāyuṣpramāṇena puṇyaṁ puṇyāhaṁ dīrghamāyurastviti). The brāhmaṇas should bless the host saying tathāstu (amen). Uttering 'suprokṣitamastu' the host should sprinkle water on the

1. Literally proclaiming or wishing an auspicious day; repeating 'this is an auspicious day' three times at the commencement of a religious ceremony.

hands of the brāhmaṇas, after which they shall take out a few drops from the vessel and with the repetition of the following mantra sprinkle them on the host and his wife.

ॐ शं त आपो धन्वन्याः शं ते सन्त्वनूप्याः ।
शं ते खनित्रिमा आपः शं याः कुम्भेभिराभृता ।।
om śaṁ te āpo dhanvanyāḥ śaṁ te santvanūpyāḥ ।
śaṁ te khanitrimā āpaḥ śaṁ yāḥ kumbhebhirābhṛtā ॥

To the host's 'सौमनस्यमस्तु' (saumanasyamastu) the brāhmaṇas would reply by saying 'अस्तु सौमनस्यम्' (astu saumanasyam). Thereupon the host would mutter 'अक्षतं चास्तु मे पुण्यं दीर्घमायुर्यशो बलम् । यद्यच्श्रेयस्करं लोके तत्तदस्तु सदा मम ।' (akṣataṁ cāstu me puṇyaṁ dīrghamāyuryaśo balam । yadyacśr-eyaskaraṁ loke tattadastu sadā mama), to which the brāhmaṇas would reply by saying 'अस्त्वक्षतमरिष्टं च' (astvakṣatamariṣṭaṁ ca) which means: "May not your merit perish and may not any disaster befall thee!" The host should thus entreat 'गन्धाः पान्तु सौमंगल्यम्' (gandhāḥ pāntu saumaṁgalyam), which should evoke 'इति भवन्तु' (iti bhavantu) or 'amen' from the brāhmaṇas who should also pronounce the following benediction:

त्र्यम्बकं यजामहे सुगन्धिं पुष्टिवर्द्धनम् ।
उर्वारुकमिव बन्धनान्मृत्योर्मुक्षीय मामृतात् ।।
tryambakaṁ yajāmahe sugandhiṁ puṣṭivarddhanam ।
urvārukamiva bandhanānmṛtyormukṣīya māmṛtāt ॥

Then shall the brāhmaṇas say 'ॐ पान्तु गन्धा अस्तु सौमंगल्यं च' (om pāntu gandhā astu saumaṁgalyaṁ ca). This is followed by a dialogue between the host and the brāhmaṇas:

यजमान	—	**अक्षताः पान्तु आयुष्यमस्तु ।**
ब्राह्मणाः	—	**ॐ पान्त्वक्षता अस्तु आयुष्यम् ।**
यजमान	—	**पुष्पाणि पान्तु सौश्रियमस्तु ।**
ब्राह्मणाः	—	**ॐ पान्तु पुष्पाणि अस्तु सौश्रियम् ।**

यजमान	—	ताम्बूलानि पान्तु ऐश्वर्यमस्तु ।
ब्राह्मणाः	—	ॐ पान्तु ताम्बूलानि अस्त्वैश्वर्यम् ।
यजमान	—	दक्षिणाः पान्तु बहुदेवत्वं चास्तु ।
ब्राह्मणाः	—	ॐ पान्तु दक्षिणा अस्तु बहुदेवत्वम् ।
यजमान	—	शांतिः पुष्टिस्तुष्टिः श्रीर्यशो विद्या विनयो वित्तं बहुपुत्रत्वं चायुष्यं चास्तु ।
ब्राह्मणाः	—	ॐ अस्तु शान्तिः पुष्टिस्तुष्टिः श्रीर्यशोविद्याविनयो वित्तं बहुपुत्रत्वं चायुष्यं च ।
यजमान	—	यं कृत्वा सर्ववेदयज्ञक्रियाकरणकर्मारम्भाः शुभाः शोभनाः प्रवर्तन्ते तमहमोंकारमादिं कृत्वा ऋग्यजुः सामाथर्वणा शीर्वचनं बह्वृषिसम्मतं समनुज्ञातं भवद्भिरनुज्ञातः पुण्यं पुण्याहं वाचयिष्ये ।
ब्राह्मणाः	—	ॐ वाच्यताम् ।
yajamāna	—	*akṣatāḥ pāntu āyuṣyamastu* ।
brāhmaṇas	—	*om pāntvakṣatā astu āyuṣyam* ।
yajamāna	—	*puspāṇi pāntu sauśriyamastu* ।
brāhmaṇas	—	*om pāntu puṣpāṇi astu sauśriyam* ।
yajamāna	—	*tāmbūlāni pāntu aiśvaryamastu* ।
brāhmaṇas	—	*om pāntu tāmbūlāni astvaiśvaryam* ।
yajamāna	—	*dakṣiṇāḥ pāntu bahudevatvaṁ cāstu* ।
brāhmaṇas	—	*om pāntu dakṣiṇā astu bahudevatvam* ।
yajamāna	—	*śāṁtiḥ puṣṭistuṣṭiḥ śrīryaśo vidyā vinayo vittaṁ bahuputratvaṁ cāyuṣyaṁ cāstu* ।
brāhmaṇas	—	*om astuśāntiḥ puṣṭistuṣṭiḥ śrīryaśo-vidyā vinayo vittaṁ bahuputratvaṁ cāyuṣyaṁ ca* ।
yajamāna	—	*yaṁ kṛtvā sarvavedayajñakriyākaraṇa-karmārambhāḥ śubhāḥ śobhanāḥ pravartante tamahamoṁkāramādiṁ kṛtvā ṛgyujaḥ sāmātharvaṇā śīrvacanaṁ bahvṛṣisammataṁ samanujñātaṁ bhavadbhiranujñātaḥ puṇyaṁ puṇyā-haṁ vācayiṣye* ।
brāhmaṇas	—	*om vācyatām* ।

Having received the brāhmaṇas' acceptance, the host shall give them barley or rice and receive their blessings:

ॐ भद्रं कर्णेभिः शृणुयाम देवा भद्रं पश्येमाक्षभिर्यजत्राः ।
स्थिरैरंगैस्तुष्टुवा ᳬ सस्तनूभिर्व्यशेमहि देवहितं यदायुः ॥ १ ॥
देवानां भद्रा सुमतिर्ऋजूयतां देवाना ᳬ रातिरभि नो निवर्तताम् ।
देवाना ᳬ सख्यमुपसेदिमा वयं देवा न आयुः प्रतिरन्तु जीवसे ॥ २ ॥
न तद्रक्षा ᳬ सि न पिशाचास्तरन्ति देवानामोजः प्रथमजं ह्येतत् ।
योबिभर्ति दाक्षायण ᳬ हिरण्य ᳬ स देवेषु कृणुते दीर्घमायुः स मनुष्येषु
कृणुते दीर्घमायुः ॥ ३ ॥
दीर्घायुस्त ओषधे खनिता यस्मै च त्वा खनाम्यहम् ।
अथो त्वं दीर्घायुर्भूत्वा शतवल्शा विरोहतात् ॥ ४ ॥
ॐ द्रविणोदा द्रविणसस्तुरस्य द्रविणोदाः सनरस्य प्रय ᳬ सत् ।
द्रविणोदा वीरवतीमिषन्नो द्रविणोदा रासते दीर्घमायुः ॥ ५ ॥
ॐ सविता पश्चात्सविता पुरस्तात् सवितोत्तरात्तात्सविताऽधरात्ताद् ।
सविता नः सुवतु सर्वतातिं सविता नो रासतां दीर्घमायुः ॥ ६ ॥
नवो नवो भवति जायमानोऽह्नां केतुरुषसामेत्यग्रम् ।
भागं देवेभ्यो विदधात्यायन प्रचन्द्रमास्तिरते दीर्घमायुः ॥ ७ ॥
ॐ उच्चा दिवि दक्षिणावन्तो अस्थुर्ये अश्वदाः सहते सूर्येण ।
हिरण्यदा अमृतत्वं भजन्ते वासोदाः सोम प्रतिरन्त आयुः ॥ ८ ॥
आप उन्दन्तु जीवसे दीर्घायुत्वाय वर्चसे ।
यस्त्वाहृदा कीरिणा मन्यमानोऽमर्त्यं मर्त्यो जोहवीमि ॥ ९ ॥
जातवेदो यशोऽअस्मासु धेहि प्रजाभिरग्ने अमृतत्वमश्याम् ।
यस्मै त्वं सुकृते जातवेद उ लोकमग्ने कृणवः स्योनम् ॥ १० ॥
अश्विनं स पुत्रिणं वीरवन्तं गोमन्तं रयिं नशते स्वस्ति ॥ ११ ॥

om bhadraṁ karṇebhiḥ śṛṇuyāma devā bhadraṁ pas'yemākṣaabhiryajatrāḥ ।
sthirairaṁgaistuṣṭvāṁ sastanūbhirvyaśemahi devahitaṁ yadāyuḥ ॥ 1 ॥
devānāṁ bhadrāsumatirṛjūyatāṁ devānāṁ rātirabhi no nivartatām ।
devānāṁ sakhyamupasedimā vayaṁ devā na āyuḥ pratirantu jīvase ॥ 2 ॥

na tadrakṣāṁsi na piśācāstaranti devānāmojaḥ
prathamajaṁ hyetat ।
yo bibharti dākṣāyaṇaṁ hiraṇyaṁ sa deveṣu kṛṇute
dīrghamāyuḥ sa manuṣyeṣu kṛṇute dīrghamāyuḥ ॥ 3 ॥
dīrghāyusta oṣadhe khanitā yasmai ca tvā khanāmyaham ।
atho tvaṁ dīrghāyurbhūtvā śatavalśā virohatāt ॥ 4 ॥
om draviṇodā draviṇasasturasya draviṇodāḥ sanarasya
prayaṁ sat ।
draviṇodā vīravatīmiṣanno draviṇodā rāsate
dīrghamāyuḥ ॥ 5 ॥
om savitā paścātsavitā purastāt savitottarāttātsavitā'-
dharāttād ।
savitā naḥ suvatu sarvatātiṁ savitā no rāsatāṁ
dīrghamāyuḥ ॥ 6 ॥
navo navo bhavati jāyamāno'nhāṁ keturuṣasāmetya-
gram । *bhāgaṁ devebhyo vidadhātyāyan*
pracandramāstirate dīrghamāyuḥ ॥ 7 ॥
om uccā divi dakṣiṇāvanto asthurye aśvadāḥ sahate
sūryeṇa ।
hiraṇyadā amṛtatvaṁ bhajante vāsodāḥ soma pratiranta
āyuḥ ॥ 8 ॥
āpa undantu jīvase dīrghāyutvāya varcase ।
yastvāhṛdā kīriṇā manyamāno'martyaṁ martyo
johavīmi ॥ 9 ॥
jātavedo yaśo'asmāsu dhehi prajābhiragne
amṛtatvamaśyām ।
yasmai tvaṁ sukṛte jātaveda u lokamagne kṛnavaḥ
syonam ॥ 10 ॥
aśvinaṁ sa putriṇaṁ vīravantaṁ gomantaṁ rayiṁ naśate
svasti ॥ 11 ॥

Responding to these blessings, the host shall say 'व्रतनियमजप तपःस्वाध्याय क्रतुशमदमदयादानविशिष्टानां सर्वेषां ब्राह्मणानां मनः समाधीयताम् । (vrataniyamajapa tapaḥsvādhyāya kratuśamadamadayādānaviśiṣṭānāṁ sarveṣāṁ brāhmaṇānāṁ manaḥ samādhīyatām). The brāhmaṇas shall reply by saying समाहित-

मनसः स्मः (samāhitamanasaḥ smaḥ). To the host's words प्रसीदन्तु भवन्तः (prasīdantu bhavantaḥ), the brāhmaṇas shall thus reply: प्रसन्नाः स्मः (prasannāḥ smaḥ). Then the host shall say:

ॐ शांतिरस्तु । ॐ पुष्टिरस्तु । ॐ तुष्टिरस्तु । ॐ वृद्धिरस्तु । ॐ अविघ्नमस्तु । ॐ आयुष्यमस्तु । ॐ आरोग्यमस्तु । ॐ शिवं कर्मास्तु । ॐ कर्मसमृद्धिरस्तु । ॐ वेदसमृद्धिरस्तु । ॐ शास्त्रसमृद्धिरस्तु । ॐ इष्टसम्पदस्तु । ॐ अरिष्टनिरसनमस्तु । ॐ यत्पापमनारोग्यमशुभकल्याणं तत्प्रतिहतमस्तु । ॐ यच्छ्रेयस्तदस्तु । ॐ उत्तरे कर्मण्यविघ्नमस्तु । ॐ उत्तरोत्तरं महरहरभिवृद्धिरस्तु । ॐ उत्तरोत्तराः क्रियाः शुभाः शोभना सम्पद्यन्ताम् । ॐ तिथिकरणमुहूर्त्तनक्षत्रग्रहलग्नसम्पदस्तु । (उदकसिंचनम्) ॐ तिथिकरणमुहूर्त्तनक्षत्रग्रहलग्नाधिदेवताः प्रीयन्ताम् । ॐ तिथिकरणे समुहूर्त्ते सनक्षत्रे संग्रहे साधिदैवते प्रीयेताम् । ॐ दुर्गापांचाल्यौ प्रीयेताम् । ॐ अग्निपुरोगा विश्वेदेवाः प्रीयन्ताम् । ॐ इन्द्रपुरोगा मरुद्गणाः प्रीयन्ताम् । ॐ माहेश्वरी पुरोगा उमामातरः प्रीयन्ताम् । ॐ अरुन्धतीपुरोगाः पतिव्रताः प्रीयन्ताम् । ॐ विष्णुपुरोगाः सर्वे देवाः प्रीयंताम् । ॐ ब्रह्मपुरोगाः सर्वे वेदाः प्रीयन्ताम् । ॐ ब्रह्म च ब्राह्मणाश्च प्रीयन्ताम् । ॐ श्रीसरस्वत्यौ प्रीयेताम् । ॐ श्रद्धामेधे प्रीयेताम् । ॐ भगवती कात्यायनी प्रीयताम् । ॐ भगवती माहेश्वरी प्रीयताम् । ॐ भगवती ऋद्धिकरी प्रीयताम् । ॐ भगवती पुष्टिकरी प्रीयताम् । ॐ भगवती तुष्टिकरी प्रीयताम् । ॐ भगवन्तौ विघ्नविनायकौ प्रीयेताम् । ॐ सर्वाः कुलदेवताः प्रीयन्ताम् । ॐ सर्वा ग्रामदेवताः प्रीयन्ताम्।

ॐ हताश्च ब्रह्मविद्विषो हताश्च परिपन्थिनो हताअस्य कर्मणो विघ्नकर्तारः शत्रवः पराभवं यान्तु । ॐ शाम्यन्तु घोराणि । ॐ शाम्यन्तु पापानि । शाम्यन्त्वी तयः शुभानि वर्द्धन्ताम् । ॐ शिवा आपः सन्तु । ॐ शिवा ऋतवः सन्तु । ॐ शिवा अग्नयः सन्तु । ॐ शिवा आहुतयः सन्तु । ॐ शिवा ओषधयः सन्तु । ॐ शिवा वनस्पतयः सन्तु । ॐ शिवा अतिथयः सन्तु । ॐ अहोरात्रे शिवे स्याताम् । ॐ निकामे निकामे नः पर्जन्यो वर्षतु फलवत्यो न ओषधयः पच्यन्तां योगक्षेमो नः कल्पताम् ।

ॐ शुक्रांगारकबुधबृहस्पतिशनैश्चरराहुकेतुसोमसहिता आदित्यपुरोगाः सर्वे ग्रहाः प्रीयन्ताम् । ॐ भगवान् महासेनः प्रीयताम् ।

om śāṁtirastu । *om puṣṭirastu* । *om tuṣṭirastu* । *om*

vṛddhirastu । *om avighnamastu* । *om āyuṣyamastu* । *om ārogyamastu* । *om śivaṁ karmāstu* । *om karmasamṛddhirastu* । *om vedasamṛddhirastu* । *om śāstrasamṛddhirastu* । *om iṣṭasampadastu* । *om ariṣṭanirasanamastu* । *om yatpāpamanārogyamaśubhakalyāṇaṁ tatpratihatamastu* । *om yacchreyastadastu* । *om uttre karmaṇyavighnamastu* । *om uttarottara maharaharabhivṛddhirastu* । *om uttarottarāḥ kriyāḥ śubhāḥ śobhanā sampadyantām* । *om tithikaraṇamuhūrttanakṣatragrahalagnasampadastu* । (*udakasiṁcanam*) *om tithikaraṇamuhūrttanakṣatragrahalagnādhidevatāḥ prīyantām* । *om tithikaraṇe samuhūrtte sanakṣatre saṁgrahe sādhidaivate prīyetām* । *om durgāpāṁcālyau prīyetām* । *om agnipurogā viśvedevāḥ prīyantām* । *om indrapurogā marudgaṇāḥ prīyantām* । *om māheśvarī purogā umāmātaraḥ prīyantām* । *om arundhatīpurogāḥ pativratāḥ prīyantām* । *om viṣṇupurogāḥ sarve devāḥ prīyaṁtām* । *om brahma-purogāḥ sarve vedāḥ prīyantām* । *om brahma ca brāhmaṇāśca prīyantām* । *om śrīsarasvatyau prīyetām* । *om śraddhāmedhe prīyetām* । *om bhagavatī kātyāyanī prīyatām* । *om bhagavatī māheśvarī prīyatām* । *om bhagavatī ṛddhikarī prīyatām* । *om bhagavatī puṣṭikarī prīyatām* । *om bhagavatī tuṣṭikarī prīyatām* । *om bhagavantau vighnavināyakau prīyetām* । *om sarvāḥ kuladevatāḥ prīyantām* । *om sarvā grāmadevatāḥ prīyantām* ।

om hatāśca brahmavidviṣo hatāśca paripanthino hatāasya karmaṇo vighnakartāraḥ śatravaḥ parābhavaṁ yāntu । *om śāmyantu ghorāṇi* । *om śāmyantu pāpāni* । *śāmyantvī tayaḥ śubhāni varddhantām* । *om śivā āpaḥ santu* । *om śivā ṛtavaḥ santu* । *om śivā agnayaḥ santu* । *om śivā āhutayaḥ santu* । *om śivā oṣadhayaḥ santu* । *om śivā vanaspatayaḥ santu* । *om śivā atithayaḥ santu* । *om ahorātre śive syātām* । *om nikāme nikāme naḥ parjanyo varṣatu phalavatyo na oṣadhayaḥ pacyantāṁ yogakṣemo naḥ kalpatām* ।

om śukrāṁgārakabudhabṛhaspatiśanaiścararāhuketusomasahitā ādityapurogāḥ sarve grahāḥ prīyantām । *om bhagavān mahāsenaḥ prīyatām* ।

Then the host shall say 'ॐ पुण्याहकालान् वाचयिष्ये' (om puṇyāhakālān vācayiṣye). Replying, the brāhmaṇas shall say 'ॐ वाच्यताम्' (om vācyatām) and recite the following mantra:

ॐ उद्गातेव शकुने साम गायसि ब्रह्मपुत्र इव सवनेषु शंससि ।
वृषेव वाजी शिशुमतीरपीत्य सर्वतो नः शकुने भद्रमावद विश्वतो नः शकुने पुण्यमावद ।।

om udgāteva śakune sāma gāyasi brahmaputra iva savaneṣu śaṁsasi ।
vṛṣeva vājī śiśumatīrapītya sarvato naḥ śakune bhadramāvada viśvato naḥ śakune puṇyamāvada ॥

In a feeble voice the host will thus speak: 'भो ब्राह्मणाः मम गृहे अस्य क्रियमाणस्य कर्मणः पुण्याहं भवन्तो ब्रुवन्तु' (bho brāhmaṇāḥ mama gṛhe asya kriyamāṇasya karmaṇaḥ puṇyāhaṁ bhavanto bruvantu). The brāhmaṇas will just utter 'ॐ पुण्याहम्' (om puṇyāham). The host will repeat 'भो ब्राह्मणाः. . .' (bho brāhmaṇāḥ . . .) twice or three times in a rather low tone and receive the brāhmaṇas' reply in the same words. After all this the host will make the following submission:

ब्राह्मं पुण्यमहर्यच्च सृष्ट्युत्पालनकारकम् ।
वेदवृक्षोद्भवं नित्यं तत्पुण्याहं ब्रुवन्तु नः ।।

brāhmam puṇyamaharyacca sṛṣṭyutpālanakārakam ।
vedavṛkṣodbhavaṁ nityaṁ tatpuṇyāhaṁ bruvantu naḥ ॥

and recite these words:

ॐ पुनन्तु मा देवजनाः पुनन्तु मनसा धियः
पुनन्तु विश्वा भूतानि जातवेदः पुनीहि मा ।।

om punantu mā devajanāḥ punantu manasā dhiyaḥ
punantu viśvā bhūtāni jātavedaḥ punīhi mā ॥

Now let the host say 'भो ब्राह्मणाः सकुटुम्बस्य, सपरिवारस्य मम गृहे क्रियमाणस्यामुककर्मणः कल्याणं भवन्तो ब्रुवन्तु ।' (bho brāhmaṇāḥ sakuṭumbasya, saparivārasya mama gṛhe kriyamāṇas-yāmukakarmaṇaḥ kalyāṇaṁ bhavanto bruvantu). The brāhmaṇas shall bless the host, saying 'ॐ कल्याणम्' (om kalyāṇam). Then they shall recite this mantra:

ॐ यथेमां वाचं कल्याणीमावदानि जनेभ्यः ।
ब्रह्मराजन्याभ्यां शूद्राय चार्याय च स्वाय चारणाय च ।
प्रियो देवानां दक्षिणायै दातुरिह भूयासमयं मे कामः
समृद्ध्यतामुपमादो नमतु ।।
om yathemāṁ vācaṁ kalyāṇīmāvadāni janebhyaḥ ।
brahmarājanyābhyāṁ śūdrāya cāryāya ca svāya cārṇāya ca ।
priyo devānāṁ dakṣiṇāyai dāturiha bhūyāsamayaṁ me kāmaḥ
samṛddhyatāmupamādo namatu ॥

Host: 'भो ब्राह्मणाः सकुटुम्बस्य मम गृहे क्रियमाणस्यामुककर्मणः ऋद्धिं भवन्तो ब्रुवन्तु' (bho brāhmaṇāḥ sakuṭumbasya mama gṛhe kriyamāṇasyāmukakarmaṇaḥ ṛddhiṁ bhavanto bruvantu).

Brāhmaṇas: 'ऋध्यताम्' (ṛdhyatām).

ॐ सत्रस्य ऋद्धिरस्यगन्म ज्योतिरमृता अभूम ।
दिवं पृथिव्या अध्यारुहामाविदाम देवान्स्वर्ज्योतिः ।।
om satrasya ṛddhirasyaganma jyotiramṛtā abhūma ।
divaṁ pṛthivyā adhyāruhāmāvidāma devānsvarjyotiḥ ॥

Host: 'भो ब्राह्मणाः सकुटुम्बस्य सपरिवारस्य मम गृहे क्रियमाणस्यामुककर्मणः स्वस्तिं भवन्तो ब्रुवन्तु' (bho brāhmaṇāḥ sakuṭumbasya saparivārasya mama gṛhe kriyamāṇasyāmukakarmaṇaḥ svastiṁ bhavanto bruvantu).

Brāhmaṇas: 'ॐ स्वस्ति न इन्द्रो वृद्धश्रवाः स्वस्ति नः पूषा विश्ववेदाः ।स्वस्ति नस्ताक्ष्योऽअरिष्टनेमिः स्वस्ति नो बृहस्पतिर्दधातु ।।' (om svasti na indro vṛddhaśravāḥ svasti naḥ pūṣā viśvavedāḥ । svasti nastārkṣyo'ariṣṭanemiḥ svasti no bṛhaspatirdadhātu ॥)

Host: 'भो ब्राह्मणाः मम सकुटुम्बस्य गृहे क्रियमाणस्यामुककर्मणः श्रियं भवन्तो

ब्रुवन्तु' (bho brāhmaṇāḥ mama sakuṭumbasya gṛhe kriyamāṇasyāmukakarmaṇaḥ śriyaṁ bhavanto bruvantu).

Brāhmaṇas: 'अस्तु श्रीः' (astu śrīḥ) three times:

ॐ श्रीश्च ते लक्ष्मीश्च पत्न्यावहोरात्रे पार्श्वे नक्षत्राणि रूपमश्विनौ व्यात्तम् ।
इष्णन्निषाणामुम्म इषाण सर्वलोकं म इषाण ।। १ ।।

om śrīśca te lakṣmīśca patnyāvahorātre pārśve nakṣatrāṇi rūpamaśvinau vyāttam ।
iṣṇannisāṇāmumma iṣāṇa sarvalokaṁ ma iṣāṇa ॥ 1 ॥

ॐ शतमिन्नु शरदोऽअन्तिदेवा यत्रा नश्चक्राजरसन्तनूनाम् ।
पुत्रासो यत्र पितरो भवन्ति मा नो मध्या रीरिषतायुर्गन्तोः ।। २ ।।

om śataminnu śarado'antidevā yatrā naścakrājara-santanūnām ।
putrāso yatra pitaro bhavanti mā no madhyā rīriṣtāyur-gantoḥ ॥ 2 ॥

मनसः काममाकूतिं वाचः सत्यमशीय ।
पशूनां रूपमन्नस्य रसो यशः श्रीः श्रयतां मयि ।।३ ।।

manasaḥ kāmamākūtiṁ vācaḥ satyamaśīya ।
paśūnāṁ rūpamannasya raso yaśaḥ śrīḥ śrayatāṁ mayi ॥ 3 ॥

प्रजापतिर्लोकपालो धाता ब्रह्मा च देवराट् ।
भगवान् शाश्वतो नित्यः स नो रक्षतु सर्वतः ।।

prajāpatirlokapālo dhātā brahmā ca devarāṭ ।
bhagavān śāśvato nityaḥ sa no rakṣatu sarvataḥ ॥

The brāhmaṇas should recite the following mantra after muttering 'भगवान् प्रजापतिः प्रीयताम्' (bhagavān prajāpatiḥ prīyatām):

ॐ प्रजापते न त्वदेतान्यन्य विश्वा रूपाणि परितो बभूव ।
यत्कामास्ते जुहुमस्तन्नो अस्तु वयं स्याम पतयो रयीणाम् ।।

om prajāpate na tvadetānyanya viśvā rūpāṇi parito babhūva ।
yatkāmāste juhumastanno astu vayaṁ syāma patayo rayīṇām ॥

After reciting the above mantra the brāhmaṇas should say

आयुष्मते स्वस्ति (āyuṣmate svasti) three times. The following mantra should be muttered in continuation:

ॐ प्रतिपन्थामपद्महि स्वस्तिगामनेहसम् ।
येन विश्वाः परिद्विषो वृणक्ति विन्दते वसु ।।
om pratipanthāmapadmahi svastigāmanehasam ।
yena viśvāḥ paridviṣo vṛṇakti vindate vasu ॥

Then the host will thus speak: 'अस्मिन्पुण्याहवाचने न्यूनातिरिक्तो यो विधिः स तु ब्राह्मणानी वचनात् श्रीमहागणपतिप्रसादाच्च परिपूर्णोऽस्तु' (asminpuṇyāhavācane nyūnātirikto yo vidiḥ sa tu brāhmaṇāni vacanāt śrīmahāgaṇapatiprasādācca paripūrṇo'stu).

The brāhmaṇas should reply by saying ॐ अस्तु परिपूर्णः (om astu paripūrṇaḥ).

Having done all this the brāhmaṇas, all well-versed in the Vedas, will consecrate the host and his wife by sprinkling water from the sacrificial vessel on them. During this ritual the hostess shall take her seat on the left side of her husband. Then the brāhmaṇas shall carefully take out the dūrvā blades and mango leaves from the vessel and wetting them again and again consecrate the couple with each of the following mantras:

ॐ पयः पृथिव्यां पय ओषधीषु पयो दिव्यन्तरिक्षेपयोधाः ।
पयस्वतीः प्रदिशः सन्तु मह्यम् ।।
ॐ पंच नद्यः सरस्वतीमपियन्ति स्रोतसः ।
सरस्वती तु पंचधा सो देशेऽभवत्सरित् ।।
ॐ पुनन्तु मा देवजनाः पुनन्तु मनसा धियः ।
पुनंतु विश्वा भूतानि जातवेदः पुनीहि मा ।।
ॐ देवस्य त्वा सवितुः प्रसवेऽश्विनोर्बाहुभ्यां पूष्णो हस्ताभ्याम् ।
सरस्वत्यै वाचो यन्तुर्यन्त्रिये दधामि बृहस्पतेष्ट्वा साम्राज्येनाभिषिञ्चामि . . .
ॐ देवस्य त्वा सवितुः प्रसवेऽश्विनोर्बाहुभ्यां पूष्णो हस्ताभ्याम् ।
सरस्वत्यै वाचो यन्तुर्यन्त्रेणाग्नेः साम्राज्येनाभिषिञ्चामि . . .
ॐ देवस्य त्वा सवितुः प्रसवेऽश्विनोर्बाहुभ्यां पूष्णो हस्ताभ्याम् ।

अश्विनोर्भैषज्येन तेजसे ब्रह्मवर्चसायाभिषिञ्चामि . . .

ॐ देवस्य त्वा सवितुः प्रसवेऽश्विनोर्बाहुभ्यां पूष्णो हस्ताभ्याम् ।

सरस्वत्यै भैषज्येन वीर्यायान्नाद्यायाभिषिञ्चामि . . . .

ॐ देवस्य त्वा सवितुः प्रसवेऽश्विनोर्बाहुभ्यां पूष्णो हस्ताभ्याम् ।

इन्द्रस्येन्द्रियेण बलाय श्रियै यशसेऽभिषिञ्चामि . . .

om payaḥ pṛthivyāṁ paya oṣadhīṣu payo divyantarikṣe-payodhāḥ ।
payasvatīḥ pradiśaḥ santu mahyam ॥
om paṁca nadyaḥ sarasvatīmapiyanti srotasaḥ ।
sarasvatī tu paṁcadhā so deśe'bhavatsarit ॥
om punantu mā devajanāḥ punantu manasā dhiyaḥ ।
punaṁtu viśvā bhūtāni jātavedaḥ punīhi mā ॥
om devasya tvā savituḥ prasave'śvinorbāhubhyāṁ pūṣṇo hastābhyām ।
sarasvatyai vāco yanturyantriye dadhāmi bṛhaspateṣṭvā sāmrājyenābhiṣiñcāmi . . . .
om devasya tvā savituḥ prasave'śvinorbāhubhyāṁ pūṣṇo hastābhyām ।
sarasvatyai vāco yanturyantreṇāgneḥ sāmrājyenābhiṣiñcāmi . . .
om devasya tvā savituḥ prasave'śvinorbāhubhyāṁ pūṣṇo hastābhyām ।
aśvinorbhaiṣajyena tejase brahmavarcasāyābhiṣiñcāmi. . .
om devasya tvā savituḥ prasave'śvinorbāhubhyāṁ pūṣṇo hastābhyām ।
sarasvatyai bhaiṣajyena vīryāyānnādyāyābhiṣiñcāmi . . .
om devasya tvā savituḥ prasave'śvinorbāhubhyāṁ pūṣṇo hastābhyām ।
indrasyendriyeṇa balāya śriyai yaśase'bhiṣiñcāmi . . .

Fill in the blanks indicated in the last five mantras by pronouncing the host's name. Then should the following mantras be repeated:

ॐ विश्वानि देव सवितर्दुरितानि परासुव ।
यद्भद्रं तन्न आसुव ।।

ॐ धामच्छदग्निरिन्द्रो ब्रह्मा देवो बृहस्पतिः ।
सुचेतसो विश्वेदेवा यज्ञं प्रावन्तु नः शुभे ।।
ॐ त्वं यविष्ठ दाशुषो नृंः पाहि शृणुधी गिरः ।
रक्षा तोकमुत त्मना ।।
ॐ अन्नपतेऽन्नस्य नो देह्यनमीवस्य शुष्मिणः ।
प्रप्रदातारन्तारिष ऊर्जं नो धेहि द्विपदे शं चतुष्पदे ।।
ॐ द्यौः शान्तिरन्तरिक्ष ँ शांतिः पृथिवी शांतिरापः शांतिरोषधयः शांतिः ।
वनस्पतयः शांतिर्विश्वेदेवाः शांतिर्ब्रह्म शांतिः सर्व ँ शांतिः शांतिरेव शांतिः
सा मा शांतिरेधि ।।
ॐ यतो यतः समीहसे ततो नो अभयं कुरु ।
शन्नः कुरु प्रजाभ्योऽअभयं नः पशुभ्यः ।
अमृताभिषेकोऽस्तु शांति शांतिः सुशांतिर्भवतु ।।

om viśvāni deva savitarduritāni parāsuva ।
yadbhadraṁ tanna āsuva ।
om dhāmacchadagnirindro brahmā devo bṛhaspatiḥ ।
sucetaso viśvedevā yajñaṁ prāvantu naḥ śubhe ॥
om tvaṁ yaviṣṭha dāśuṣo nṝṁḥ pāhi śṛṇudhī giraḥ ।
rakṣā tokamuta tmanā ॥
om annapate'nnasya no dehyanamīvasya śuṣmiṇaḥ
prapradātārantāriṣa ūrjaṁ no dhehi dvipade śaṁ catuṣpade ॥
om dyauḥ śāntirantarikṣaṁ śāṁtiḥ pṛthivī śāṁtirāpaḥ śāṁtiroṣadhayaḥ śāṁtiḥ ।
vanaspatayaḥ śāṁtirviśvedevāḥ śāṁtirbrahma śāṁtiḥ sarvaṁ śāṁtiḥ śāṁtireva śāṁtiḥ sā mā śāṁtiredhi ॥
om yato yataḥ samīhase tato no abhayaṁ kuru ।
śannaḥ kuru prajābhyo'abhayaṁ naḥ paśubhyaḥ ।
amṛtābhiṣeko'stu śāṁti śāṁtiḥ suśāṁtirbhavatu ॥

Among the penultimate rites is the waving of the lustral light around the host and his wife by four unwidowed women who are blessed with children. When they are thus engaged the brāhmaṇas shall chant the mantra:

ॐ अनाधृष्टा पुरस्तादग्नेराधिपत्यऽआयुर्मे दाः ।

पुत्रवती दक्षिणत इन्द्रस्याधिपत्ये प्रजां मे दाः ।
सुषदा पश्चाद्देवस्य सवितुराधिपत्ये चक्षुर्मे दाः ।
आश्रुतिरुत्तरतो धातुराधिपत्ये रायस्पोषं मे दाः ।
विधृतिरुपरिष्टाद् बृहस्पतेराधिपत्यऽओजो मे दाः ।
विश्वाभ्यो मा नाष्ट्राभ्यः पाहि मनोरश्वासि ।।

om anādhṛṣṭā purastādagnerādhipatya'āyurme dāḥ ।
putravatī dakṣiṇata indrasyādhipatye prajāṁ me dāḥ ।
suṣadā paścāddevasya saviturādhipatye cakṣurme dāḥ ।
āśrutiruttarato dhāturādhipatye rāyaspoṣaṁ me dāḥ ।
vidhṛtiruparişṭād bṛhaspaterādhipatya'ojo me dāḥ ।
viśvābhyo mā nāṣṭrābhyaḥ pāhi manoraśvāsi ॥

Ṣoḍaśamātṛkā-pūjana

An important constituent of the Hindu saṁskāras and one that is given a place of pride in all ceremonial performances is ṣoḍaśamātṛkā-pūjana or worship of the mātṛkās whose number varies from fourteen to sixteen. The fourteen mātṛkās or divine mothers are Gaurī, Padmā, Śacī, Medhā, Sāvitrī, Vijayā, Jayā, Devasenā, Svadhā, Svāhā, Dhṛti, Puṣṭi, Tuṣṭi and the family deity. To these are also added the cosmic mother and the mother of the revealers of the śāstras, though these are but the adjectives of Gaurī. Thus the number of the divine mothers swells to sixteen.

Of all the deities reverenced by the devotees, the topmost rank goes to Gaṇeśa. Even the worshippers of the divine mothers attach considerable importance to Gaṇeśa and hold, with the author of the *Brahma Purāṇa,* that:

गणेशः क्रियमाणानां मातृभ्यः पूजनं सकृत् ।
सकृदेव भवेच्छ्राद्धमादौ न पृथगादिषु ।।
कुड्यलग्ना वसोर्धाराः पंचधारा घृतेन तु ।
कारयेत्सप्त वा धारा नातिनीचा न चोच्छ्रिताः ।।

gaṇeśaḥ kriyamāṇānāṁ mātṛbhyaḥ pūjanaṁ sakṛt ।
sakṛdeva bhavecchrāddhamādau na pṛthagādiṣu ॥
kuḍyalagnā vasordhārāḥ paṁcadhārā ghṛtena tu ।
kārayetsapta vā dhārā nātinīcā na cocchṛtāḥ ॥

If a number of ceremonies have to be performed at the same time, then in that case prayer for peace, homage to Gaṇapati, svastivācana, puṇyāhavācana, vasordhārā, paṁcadhārā, mātṛkāpūjā should all be done only once at the very outset and not separately.

On a wall plastered with cowdung drop five or seven streams of clarified butter. They should neither be too high nor too low. The host, having bathed himself, should take a comfortable seat facing the east, and with his wife on the right and his son, for whom the ceremony is being performed, on the right of his mother. He should then have some kuśa blades, water and barley grains in his hand before uttering the following saṁkalpa:

अद्य शुभपुण्यतिथावमुककर्मांगतया
गणपतिसहितगौर्यादिचतुर्दशमातृकापूजनमहं करिष्ये ।

adya śubhapuṇyatithāvamukakarmāṁgatayā gaṇapati-sahitagauryādicaturdaśamātṛkāpūjanamahaṁ kariṣye ।

The saṁkalpa is to be followed by the invocation:

ॐ गणपतये नमः, गणपतिमावाहयामि स्थापयामि ।
ॐ गौर्यै नमः, गौरीमावाहयामि स्थापयामि ।
ॐ पद्मायै नमः, पद्मामावाहयामि स्थापयामि ।
ॐ शच्यै नमः, शचीमावाहयामि स्थापयामि ।
ॐ मेधायै नमः, मेधामावाहयामि स्थापयामि ।
ॐ सावित्र्यै नमः, सावित्रीमावाहयामि स्थापयामि ।
ॐ विजयायै नमः, विजयामावाहयामि स्थापयामि ।
ॐ जयायै नमः, जयामावाहयामि स्थापयामि ।
ॐ देवसेनायै नमः, देवसेनामावाहयामि स्थापयामि ।
ॐ स्वधायै नमः, स्वधामावाहयामि स्थापयामि ।
ॐ स्वाहायै नमः, स्वाहामावाहयामि स्थापयामि ।
ॐ धृत्यै नमः, धृतिमावाहयामि स्थापयामि ।
ॐ पुष्ट्यै नमः, पुष्टिमावाहयामि स्थापयामि ।
ॐ तुष्ट्यै नमः, तुष्टिमावाहयामि स्थापयामि ।

ॐ आत्मकुलदेवतायै नमः, आत्मकुलदेवतामावाहयामि स्थापयामि ।

om gaṇapataye namaḥ, gaṇapatimāvāhayāmi sthāpayāmi ।
om gauryai namaḥ, gaurīmāvāhayāmi sthāpayāmi ।
om padmāyai namaḥ, padmāmāvāhayāmi sthāpayāmi ।
om śacyai namaḥ, śacīmāvāhayāmi sthāpayāmi ।
om medhāyai namaḥ, medhāmāvāhayāmi sthāpayāmi ।
om sāvitryai namaḥ, sāvitrīmāvāhayāmi sthāpayāmi ।
om vijayāyai namaḥ, vijayāmāvāhayāmi sthāpayāmi ।
om jayāyai namaḥ, jayāmāvāhayāmi sthāpayāmi ।
om devasenāyai namaḥ, devasenāmāvāhayāmi sthāpayāmi ।
om svadhāyai namaḥ, svadhāmāvāhayāmi sthāpayāmi ।
om svāhāyai namaḥ, svāhāmāvāhayāmi sthāpayāmi ।
om dhṛtyai namaḥ, dhṛtimāvāhayāmi sthāpayāmi ।
om puṣṭyai namaḥ, puṣṭimāvāhayāmi sthāpayāmi ।
om tuṣṭyai namaḥ, tuṣṭimāvāhayāmi sthāpayāmi ।
om ātmakuladevatāyai namaḥ, ātmakuladevatāmāvāhayāmi sthāpayāmi ।

Those who believe the number of the divine mothers to be sixteen shall also include two more invocations as follows:

ॐ मातृभ्यो नमः, मातर्रींवाहयामि स्थापयामि ।
ॐ लोकमातृभ्यो नमः, लोकमातर्रींवाहयामि स्थापयामि ।।

om mātṛbhyo namaḥ, mātṝrāvāhayāmi sthāpayāmi ।
om lokamātṛbhyo namaḥ, lokamātṝrāvāhayāmi sthāpayāmi ॥

On a wooden board spread with plain cloth keep handfuls of yellow rice at fifteen or seventeen places separately for doing homage to Gaṇeśa and other divinities. It is on these spots (where the coloured grains are kept) that the gods are to be invoked. Let them be installed there with the following mantra:

ॐ मनोजूतिर्जुषतामाज्यस्य बृहस्पतिर्यज्ञमिमं तनोतु ।
अरिष्टं यज्ञ ㆑ं समिमं दधातु विश्वेदेवास इह मादयन्तामों ३ प्रतिष्ठा ।।

om manojūtirjuṣatāmājyasya bṛhaspatiryajñamimaṁ tanotu ।
ariṣṭaṁ yajñaṁ samimaṁ dadhātu viśvedevāsa iha mādayantāmoṁ 3 pratiṣṭhā ॥

Homage done to the mātṛkās according to the sixteen modes of worship—āvāhana, āsana, pādya, arghya, ācamana, snāna, vastra, yajñopavīta, gandha, puṣpa, dhūpa, dīpa, naivedya, tāmbūla, pradakṣiṇā and puṣpāṁjali—is mātṛkāpūjana. Each mode of worship adopted should be named before the devotee pays obeisance and while repeating 'samarpayāmi'.

On a wall duly plastered with cowdung (or washed clean) let there be seven streams of clarified butter dropped on it with the recitation of the following mantra:

ॐ वसोः पवित्रमसि शतधारं वसोः पवित्रमसि सहस्रधारम् ।
देवं त्वा सविता पुनातु वसोः पवित्रेण शतधारेण सुप्वा कामधुक्षः ।।
om vasoḥ pavitramasi śatadhāraṁ vasoḥ pavitramasi sahasradhāram ।
devaṁ tvā savitā punātu vasoḥ pavitreṇa śatadhāreṇa supvā kāmadhukṣaḥ ॥

Then utter 'ॐ वसोर्धारादेवताभ्यो नमः' (om vasordhārādevatābhyo namaḥ) and offer incense, flower, festal light, etc. with the utterance of the following:

गन्धं समर्पयामि, पुष्पाणि समर्पयामि, धूपं समर्पयामि, दीपं समर्पयामि, नैवेद्यं समर्पयामि ।
gandhaṁ samarpayāmi, puṣpāṇi samarpayāmi, dhūpaṁ samarpayāmi, dīpam samarpayāmi, naivedyaṁ samarpayāmi ।

Having paid obeisance in this manner the following āyuṣya (giving long life) mantras should be muttered:

ॐ आयुष्यं वर्चस्य छं रायस्पोषमौद्भिदम् ।
इद छं हिरण्यं वर्चस्वज्जैत्रायाविशतादु माम् ।। १ ।।

ॐ न तद्रक्षा ँ सि न पिशाचास्तरन्ति देवानामोजः प्रथमज ँ ह्येतत् ।
यो बिभर्ति दाक्षायण ँ हिरण्य ँ स देवेषु कृणुते दीर्घमायुः स मनुष्येषु
कृणुते दीर्घमायुः ॥ २ ॥
ॐ यदाबध्नन् दाक्षायणाः हिरण्य ँ शतानीकाय सुमनस्यमानाः ।
तन्न आबध्नामि शतशारदा या युष्मान् जरदष्टिर्यथासम् ॥ ३ ॥
ॐ भद्रं कर्णेभिः शृणुयाम देवा भद्रं पश्येमाक्षभिर्यजत्राः ।
स्थिरैरंगैस्तुष्टुवांसस्तनूभिर्व्यशेम हि देवहितं यदायुः ॥ ४ ॥
ॐ शतमिन्नु शरदोऽअन्ति देवा यत्रा नश्चक्राजरसं तनूनाम् ।
पुत्रासो यत्र पितरो भवन्ति मा नो मध्या रीरिषतायुर्गन्तोः ॥ ५ ॥

om āyuṣyaṁ varcasyaṁ rāyaspoṣamaudbhidam ।
idaṁ hiraṇyaṁ varcasvajjaitrāyāviśatādu mām ॥ 1 ॥
om na tadrakṣāṁsi na piśācāstaranti devānāmojaḥ prathamajaṁ hyetat ।
yo bibharti dākṣāyaṇaṁ hiraṇyaṁ sa deveṣu kṛṇute dīrghamāyuḥ sa manuṣyeṣu kṛṇute dīrghamāyuḥ ॥ 2 ॥
om yadābadhnan dākṣāyaṇāḥ hiraṇyaṁ śatānīkāya sumanasyamānāḥ ।
tanna ābadhnāmi śataśāradā yā yuṣmān jaradaṣṭiryathāsam ॥ 3 ॥
om bhadraṁ karṇebhiḥ śṛṇuyāma devā bhadraṁ paśyemākṣabhiryajatrāḥ sthirairaṁgaistuṣṭuvāṁsastanūbhirvyaśema hi devahitaṁ yadāyuḥ ॥ 4 ॥
om śataminnu śarado'anti devā yatrā naścakrājarasaṁ tanūnām ।
putrāso yatra pitaro bhavanti mā no madhyā rīriṣṭāyurgantoḥ ॥ 5 ॥

Nāndī Śrāddha

Śrāddha is a ceremony in honour and for the benefit of dead relatives observed with great strictness at various fixed periods and on occasions of rejoicing as well as mourning by the surviving relatives to three paternal or three maternal forefathers, i.e. to father, grandfather, and great grandfather. It should be borne in mind that a śrāddha is not a funeral ceremony (antyeṣṭi) but a supplement to such a ceremony. It is an act of reverential homage to a deceased person performed by relatives, and is moreover supposed to supply the dead with strengthening nutriment after the performance of the previous funeral ceremonies has endowed them with ethereal bodies. It is not until the first śrāddha has taken place that he attains a position among the pitṛs or Divine Fathers in their blissful abode called pitṛ-loka, and the śrāddha is most desirable and efficacious when performed by a son.

Because of its importance and many facets, all of which stress its centrality, nāndī śrāddha has come to acquire many names, of which ābhyudayika and vṛddhiśrāddha are not less well known. Dwelling on the time when this rite is performed Hemādri has opined that the mātṛśrāddha be performed in the forenoon, the pitṛśrāddha at noon and the śrāddha offered to the grandparents like the maternal grandfather should be performed at the end. If all these rites cannot be performed separately at different times, their performance altogether at the same time prior to the actual ceremony before which the last rites are to be performed has been permitted. This derives its legality from the older Manu. According to Kātyāyana mātṛśrāddha performed separately from pitṛśrāddha is forbidden. It is desirable to perform obsequies with the muttering of āyuṣya mantras for the peace of the last six manes. Nowhere does Kātyāyana in his śrāddhasūtras recommend performance of matṛśrāddha separately.

These obsequies should be performed according to the rules based on or produced by the doer's will or imagination. He should perform each and every rite except samantraka āvāhana,[1] arghyadāna,[2] agnikaraṇa,[3] piṇḍadāna,[4] vikira,[5]

---

1. Invocation with mantras possessing charms or spells.
2. Water libation.
3. Kindling or feeding the sacrificial fire with clarified butter.
4. The offerings of balls of rice.
5. Scattering a portion of rice offered to conciliate beings hostile to sacrifice.

akṣayya svadhāvācana,[1] and praśna.[2] The saṁkalpas uttered for all propitious rites should also be used in it but it is desirable that it should use sentences ending with the prathamā vibhakti (the first or nominative case and its terminations), not with the ṣaṣṭhī.

The nāndīśrāddha requires the performer to keep wearing his sacred thread in the customary manner, i.e. from the left shoulder to the right side. That is the savya[3] manner of wearing it. In the apasavya manner the sacred string is worn in the reverse manner, i.e. from right to left. Use of sesamum seeds (*tila*) is also forbidden because these rites are both divine (daivata) and auspicious, not to be repeated except on the occasion of coronation and son's birth. In case the performer's father is alive, then the śrāddha of the mother and grandmother should be performed. If the mother is alive, then the maternal grandfather's obsequies should be completed. Care should be taken not to perform these rites if father, mother and maternal grandfather are all alive. If the performer's father is alive on such occasions as second marriage, installation of sacrificial fire, sacrifices performed to obtain male children and one performed at the time of adoption, performance of rites to propitiate the Soma and the Nāgas, the son should perform all those rites in the names of those for whom the father performs the śrāddha. If, however, the performer's mother and maternal grandfather are not alive and if his father still lives, he should perform the nāndīśrāddha along with his wife in the names of grandmother, great grandmother, grandfather, great grandfather, his father's great grandmother, great-great grandmother. Here, again, the śāstras strike a note of warning and forbid the performance of the śrāddha for the mother's maternal

1. The sacrificial offering due to each god, especially the food or libation, or refreshing drink offered to the pitṛs or spirits of deceased ancestors. The exclamation or benediction used on presenting (or as a substitute for) the above oblation or libation to the gods or departed ancestors.
2. A task or lesson in Vedic recitation.
3. The sacred thread worn over the left shoulder.

grandfather. One should not perform the nāndīśrāddha also for her living father and grandfather.

In the samāvartana saṁskāras the performer is a bachelor and consequently debarred from performing this śrāddha; it is performed instead by his father. If the latter is survived by his elder son, or brother, etc. he should perform the rites, which means that during the performance of samāvartana saṁskāras the father himself should perform the ābhyudayika (nāndī) śrāddha for his pitṛs. Enlarging upon the conditions laid down in the law books for performing the śrāddha during the samāvartana, the institutors of the law forbid paying this homage to the manes if the grandfather is alive. This applies also to the marital saṁskāras, as it does to the samāvartana.

In the event of the father's demise, such saṁskāras as the tonsure, the initiation, etc. are performed by the elder brother, uncle, maternal uncle, et al. Satya and Vasu are the two of the glad-faced presiding Viśvedevas in this śrāddha, which should begin with the appropriate saṁkalpa. Have eight small altars constructed and a leaf of the ḍhāka tree (*Butea frondoza*) spread over each. Then place kuśas for two Viśvedevas and six pitṛs upon them. The prescribed rules now enjoin the householder to take his seat facing the east and perform the ācamana and the prāṇāyāma. Having performed these preliminaries, he should utter the following saṁkalpa, mentioning his country and time:

अद्य शुभपुण्यतिथौ (अमुक) संस्कारांगत्वेन सांकल्पिकेन विधिना ब्राह्मणयुग्मभोजनपर्याप्तान्ननिष्क्रयीभूतयथाशक्तिहिरण्येन नान्दीश्राद्धमहं करिष्ये ।

adya śubhapuṇyatithau (amuka) saṁskārāṁgatvena sāṁkalpikena vidhinā brāhmaṇayugmabhojanaparyāptānnaniṣkrayībhūtayathāśaktihiraṇyena nāndīśrāddhamahaṁ kariṣye ।

The saṁkalpa should then be followed by doing obeisance, according as one wills, to the Viśvedevas, father and other elders, grandmother, etc. They should also be given footwear, seats, perfumes, etc., properly fed and given monetary gifts. After each saṁkalpa offer, while making pādyadāna, milk, barley and water with your hand. Having made such an offering, sprinkle water on the two palāśa or ḍhāka leaves lying on the two Viśvedevas and mutter the following mantra:

ॐ नान्दीमुखाः सत्यवसुसंज्ञकाः विश्वेदेवाः ।
ॐ भूर्भुवः स्वः इदं वः पाद्यं पादावनेजनं पादप्रक्षालनं वृद्धिः ।।
om nāndimukhāḥ satyavasusaṁjñakāḥ viśvedevāḥ ।
om bhūrbhuvaḥ svaḥ idaṁ vaḥ pādyaṁ pādāvanejanaṁ pādaprakṣālanaṁ vṛddhiḥ ॥

Then mutter the following while making water oblation to the next three palāśa leaves one after another for your father and others:

ॐ स्वगोत्राः पितृपितामहप्रपितामहाः सपत्नीकाः नान्दीमुखाः ।
ॐ भूर्भुवः स्वः इदं वः पाद्यं पादावनेजनं पादप्रक्षालनं वृद्धिः ।।
om svagotrāḥ pitṛpitāmahaprapitāmahāḥ sapatnīkāḥ nāndīmukhāḥ ।
om bhūrbhuvaḥ svaḥ idaṁ vaḥ pādyaṁ pādāvanejanaṁ pādaprakṣālanaṁ vṛddhiḥ ॥

The next act of offering oblation to the remaining three leaves is performed for the grandmother and the rest in proper order with the following mantra:

ॐ द्वितीयगोत्राः मातामहप्रमातामहवृद्धप्रमातामहाः सपत्नीकाः नान्दीमुखाः ।
ॐ भूर्भुवः स्वः इदं वः पाद्यं पादावनेजनं पादप्रक्षालनं वृद्धिः ।।
om dvitīyagotrāḥ mātāmahapramātāmahavṛddhapramātāmahāḥ sapatnīkāḥ nāndīmukhāḥ ।
om bhūrbhuvaḥ svaḥ idaṁ vaḥ pādyaṁ pādāvanejanaṁ pādaprakṣālanaṁ vṛddhiḥ ॥

Now place one after another two kuśa blades on the two leaves kept on Viśvedevas, three on the three leaves kept on the father and the rest and three more on the three leaves kept on the grandmother and others and recite the following:

ॐ सत्यवसुसंज्ञकानां विश्वेषां देवानां नान्दीमुखानाम् ।
ॐ भूर्भुवः स्वः इदमासनं सुखासनं
नान्दीश्राद्धे क्षणौ क्रियेताम् तथा
प्रान्पुंसां भवन्तौ प्राप्नुतः ।

om satyavasusaṁjñakānāṁ viśveṣāṁ devānāṁ nāndīmukhānāṁ ।
om bhūrbhuvaḥ svaḥ idamāsanaṁ sukhāsanaṁ
nāndīśrāddhe kṣaṇau kriyetām tathā
prānpuṁsāṁ bhavantau prāpnutaḥ ।

Having offered seats to the Viśvedevas with this mantra let the father and others be seated with the following:

स्वगोत्राणां पितृपितामहप्रपितामहानां सपत्नीकानां नान्दीमुखानां ।
ॐ भूर्भुवः स्वः (आदि पूर्ववत्) ।

svagotrāṇāṁ pitṛpitāmahaprapitāmahānāṁ sapatnīkānāṁ nāndīmukhānāṁ ।
om bhūrbhuvaḥ svaḥ . . . .

While offering seats to the maternal grandfather and others on the remaining three leaves, mutter the following mantra:

द्वितीयगोत्राणां मातामहप्रमातामहवृद्धप्रमातामहानां सपत्नीकानां नान्दीमुखानां ।
ॐ भूर्भुवः स्वः (आदि पूर्ववत्) ।

dvitīyagotrāṇāṁ mātāmahapramātāmahavṛddhapramātāmahānāṁ sapatnīkānāṁ nāndīmukhānāṁ ।
om bhūrbhuvaḥ svaḥ . . .

Other offerings, such as those of flowers and aromatics, should be made with the recitation of the following mantras. The first mantra is for the offerings to the Viśvedevas, the second to the father and others and the third to the grandmother and the rest:

ॐ सत्यवसुसंज्ञेभ्यो विश्वेभ्यो देवेभ्यो नान्दीमुखेभ्यः
इदं गन्धाद्यर्चनं स्वाहा संपद्यतां वृद्धिः ॥ १ ॥
ॐ स्वगोत्रेभ्यो पितृपितामहप्रपितामहेभ्यः सपत्नीकेभ्यो नान्दीमुखेभ्यः इदं गन्धाद्यर्चनं स्वाहा सम्पद्यतां वृद्धिः ॥ २ ॥
ॐ द्वितीयगोत्रेभ्यो मातामहप्रमातामहवृद्धप्रमातामहेभ्यः सपत्नीकेभ्यो नान्दी-मुखेभ्यः इदं गन्धाद्यर्चनं स्वाहा सम्पद्यतां वृद्धिः ॥ ३ ॥

om satyavasusaṁjñebhyo viśvebhyo devebhyo nāndīmukhebhyaḥ idaṁ gandhādyarcanaṁ svāhā saṁpadyatāṁ vṛddhiḥ ॥ 1 ॥
om svagotrebhyo pitṛpitāmahaprapitāmahebhyaḥ sapatnīkebhyo nāndīmukhebhyaḥ idaṁ gandhādyar-canaṁ svāhā sampadyatāṁ vṛddhiḥ ॥ 2 ॥
om dvitīyagotrebhyo mātāmahapramātāmahavṛddha-pramātāmahebhyaḥ sapatnīkebhyo nāndīmukhebhyaḥ idaṁ gandhādyarcanaṁ svāhā sampadyatāṁ vṛddhiḥ ॥ 3 ॥

Offer foodgrains adequate enough to satiate a brāhmaṇa. Either raw rice or gold can also be offered instead of foodgrains. If even these are lacking, offer whatever fee you are capable of giving. The following mantras should be muttered when making gifts of foodgrains, etc. to the Viśvedevas, father, grandmother, etc. in the given order:

ॐ सत्यवसुसंज्ञकेभ्यो विश्वेभ्यो देवेभ्यो नांदीमुखेभ्यो ब्राह्मणयुग्म-भोजनपर्याप्तमन्नं तन्निष्क्रयीभूतं किंचिद्धिरण्यं दत्तममृतरूपेण स्वाहा संपद्यतां वृद्धिः ॥ १ ॥
ॐ स्वगोत्रेभ्यो पितृपितामहप्रपितामहेभ्य सपत्नीकेभ्यो नान्दीमुखेभ्यो ब्राह्मणयुग्म (इत्यादि पूर्ववत्) ॥ २ ॥
ॐ द्वितीयगोत्रेभ्यो मातामहप्रमातामहवृद्धप्रमातामहेभ्यः सपत्नीकेभ्यो नान्दीमुखेभ्यो ब्राह्मणयुग्म (इत्यादि पूर्ववत्) ॥ ३ ॥

om satyavasusaṁjñakebhyo viśvebhyo devebhyo nāṁdīmukhebhyo brāhmaṇayugmabhojanaparyā-ptamannaṁ tanniṣkrayībhūtaṁ kiṁciddhiraṇyaṁ dattamamṛtarūpeṇa svāhā saṁpadyatāṁ vṛddhiḥ ॥ 1 ॥
om svagotrebhyo pitṛpitāmahaprapitāmahebhya

sapatnīkebhyo nāndīmukhebhyo brāhmaṇayugma. . . ॥2॥
om dvitīyagotrebhyo mātāmahapramātāmahavṛddha-pramātāmahebhyaḥ sapatnīkebhyo nāndīmukhebhyo brāhmaṇayugma . . . ॥3॥

Having spoken these mantras, mutter the following while offering barley, milk and water to the Viśvedevas, father, grandfather and the rest in due order:

ॐ नान्दीमुखाः सत्यवसुसंज्ञकाः विश्वेदेवाः प्रीयन्ताम् ।।१।।
ॐ स्वगोत्राः पितृपितामहप्रपितामहाः सपत्नीकाः नान्दीमुखाः प्रीयन्ताम् ।।२।।
ॐ द्वितीयगोत्राः मातामहप्रमातामहवृद्धप्रमातामहाः सपत्नीकाः नान्दीमुखाः प्रीयन्ताम् ।।३।।

om nāndīmukhāḥ satyavasusaṁjñakāḥ viśvedevāḥ prīyantām ॥1॥
om svagotrāḥ pitṛpitāmahaprapitāmahāḥ sapatnīkāḥ nāndīmukhāḥ prīyantām ॥2॥
om dvitīyagotrāḥ mātāmahapramātāmahavṛddha-pramātāmahāḥ sapatnīkāḥ nāndīmukhāḥ prīyantām ॥3॥

The next step in the ceremony brings it to the last stage when the householder seeks the blessings of the brāhmaṇas. Here, again, no departure from the prescribed rule is permitted. His conversation with the brāhmaṇas should follow the following pattern:

यजमान	ब्राह्मण
१. गोत्रं नो वर्द्धताम् ।	१. वर्द्धताम् वो गोत्रम् ।
२. दातारो नो वर्द्धन्ताम् ।	२. अभिवर्द्धन्तां वो दातारः ।
३. वेदाश्च नो वर्द्धन्ताम् ।	३. वर्द्धन्तां वो वेदाः ।
४. संततिर्नोऽभिवर्द्धताम्।	४. वर्द्धतां वः संततिः ।
५. श्रद्धाच नो मा व्यगमत् ।	५. मा व्यगमद वः श्रद्धा ।
६. बहुदेवाश्च नः सन्तु ।	६. सन्तु वो बहुदेवाः ।
७. अन्नं च नो बहु भवेत् ।	७. भवेदन्नं वो बहु ।
८. अतिथींश्च लभामहै ।	८. लभध्वमतिथीन् ।

९. याचितारश्च नः संतु ।	९. संतु वो याचितारः ।
१०. एता आशिषः सत्याः संतु ।	१०. सन्त्वेत्ता आशिषः सत्याः ।
yajamāna	*brāhmaṇa*
1. *gotraṁ no varddhatām* ǀ	1. *varddhatām vo gotram* ǀ
2. *dātāro no varddhantām* ǀ	2. *abhivarddhantāṁ vo dātāraḥ* ǀ
3. *vedāśca no varddhantām* ǀ	3. *varddhantāṁ vo vedāḥ* ǀ
4. *saṁtatirno'bhivarddhatām* ǀ	4. *varddhatāṁ vaḥ saṁtatiḥ* ǀ
5. *śraddhāca no mā vyagamat* ǀ	5. *mā vyagamad vaḥ śraddhā* ǀ
6. *bahudevāśca naḥ santu* ǀ	6. *santu vo bahudevāḥ* ǀ
7. *annaṁ ca no bahu bhavet* ǀ	7. *bhavedannaṁ vo bahu* ǀ
8. *atithīṁśca labhāmahai* ǀ	8. *labhadhvamatithīn* ǀ
9. *yācitāraśca naḥ saṁtu* ǀ	9. *saṁtu vo yācitāraḥ* ǀ
10. *etā āśiṣaḥ satyāḥ saṁtu* ǀ	10. *santvetā āśiṣaḥ satyāḥ* ǀ

At the conclusion of this dialogue, the householder should resolve to offer the sacrificial fee separately to the three—viz. the viśvedevas, father, grandmother, etc.—in the following manner:

ॐ सत्यवसुसंज्ञकेभ्यो विश्वेभ्यो देवेभ्यो नान्दीमुखेभ्यः कृतस्य नान्दीश्राद्धस्य फलप्रतिष्ठासिद्ध्यर्थं द्राक्षामलकयवमूलनिष्क्रयीभूतां दक्षिणां दातु-महमुत्सृजे ।। १ ।।

ॐ स्वगोत्रेभ्यः पितृपितामहप्रपितामहेभ्यः सपत्नीकेभ्यो नांदीमुखेभ्यः कृतस्य (इत्यादि पूर्ववत्) ।। २ ।।

ॐ द्वितीयगोत्रेभ्यो मातामहप्रमातामहवृद्धप्रमातामहेभ्यः सपत्नीकेभ्यः नान्दीमुखेभ्यः कृतस्य (इत्यादि पूर्ववत्) ।। ३ ।।

om satyavasusaṁjñakebhyo viśvebhyo devebhyo nāndīmukhebhyaḥ kṛtasya nāndīśrāddhasya phala-pratiṣṭhāsiddhyarthaṁ drākṣāmalakayavamūla-niṣkrayībhūtāṁ dakṣiṇāṁ dātumahamutsṛje ‖ 1 ‖
om svagotrebhyaḥ pitṛpitāmahaprapitāmahebhyaḥ sapātnīkebhyo nāṁdīmukhebhyaḥ kṛtasya . . . ‖ 2 ‖
om dvitīyagotrebhyo mātāmahapramātāmahavṛddha-

pramātāmahebhyaḥ sapatnīkebhyaḥ nāndīmukhebhyaḥ kṛtasya . . . ॥ 3 ॥

The brāhmaṇas shall say 'susampannam' after the fee has been paid. The function should end with the following mantra:

ॐ वाजे वाजे वत वाजिनो धनेषु विप्रा अमृता ऋतज्ञाः ।
अस्य मध्वः पिबत मादयध्वं तृप्ता यात पथिभिर्देवयानैः ॥
om vāje vāje vata vājino dhaneṣu viprā amṛtā ṛtajñāḥ ।
asya madhvaḥ pibata mādayadhvaṁ tṛptā yāta pathibhirdevayānaiḥ ॥

Let the householder then entreat the brāhmaṇas to declare the ceremony closed with their own blessings and those of the manes. Let the brāhmaṇas declare 'अस्तु परिपूर्णः' (astu paripūrṇaḥ) and mutter the following verses to mark the end of the rites:

प्रमादात् कुर्वतां कर्म प्रच्यवेताध्वरेषु यत् ।
स्मरणादेव तद्विष्णोः सम्पूर्णं स्यादिति स्थितिः ॥ १ ॥
यस्य स्मृत्या च नामोक्त्या तपोयज्ञक्रियादिषु ।
न्यूनं सम्पूर्णतां याति सद्यो वन्दे तमच्युतम् ॥ २ ॥
pramādāt kurvatāṁ karma pracyavetādhvareṣu yat ।
smaraṇādeva tadviṣṇoḥ sampūrṇaṁ syāditi sthitiḥ ॥ 1 ॥
yasya samṛtyā ca nāmoktyā tapoyajñakriyādiṣu ।
nyūnaṁ sampūrṇatāṁ yāti sadyo vande tamacyutam ॥ 2 ॥

The curtain drops with the householder concentrating on the Lord, so that his shortcomings evident in the performance of the rites may be condoned:

ॐ विष्णवे नमः विष्णवे नमः विष्णवे नमः ।
om viṣṇave namaḥ viṣṇave namaḥ viṣṇave namaḥ ।

Pradhānakalaśasthāpana

Other ceremonies next in importance to nāndiśrāddha are the main kalaśasthāpana and grahapūjā. They derive their importance from the fact that such ceremonies as those of marriage and initiation begin with them. Those who know their importance do not, therefore, ignore them. Just as mātṛkāpūjā has almost disappeared today, giving rise to a custom by which the living mother is worshipped, and just as the nāndīśrāddha has given way to the ritual observed by women who invite the manes and sing festive songs, especially mentioning the names of their ancestors of the last four generations, so have kalaśasthāpana and grahapūjā suffered eclipse. This, according to the scriptures, is reprehensible. There must be a main kalaśa (pitcher or urn) on a festive occasion and it is in the fitness of things that it be installed thereon. The law givers go to the extent of enjoining that even if hundreds of sacrificial pitchers have been installed in the past or are likely to be installed in the future, a pitcher, altogether new for a new ceremony, should be installed. First have an altar made for the nine planets and draw upon it a

नवग्रहमण्डल कमलाकार
(Navagrahamaṇḍala Kamalākāra)

नवग्रहमंडल चतुष्कोण
(Navagrahamaṇḍala Catuṣkoṇa)

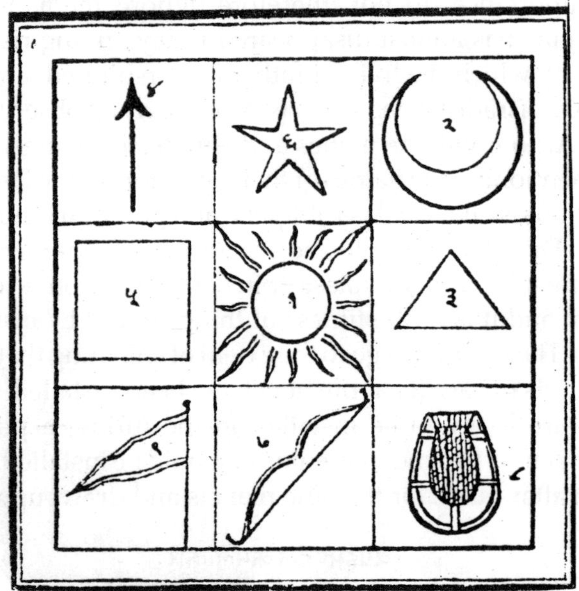

circle or the planetary sphere with coloured powder (*rolī*) or rice. Install the sacred pitcher to the north-eastern quarter of it. We give here two such pictures of the planetary orbs which should act as models.

The installation of the sacrificial urn should be preceded by the appropriate saṁkalpa:

ॐ अद्य यथोक्तपुण्यतिथौ प्रधानकलशस्थापनं तत्र वरुणादिदेवतावाहनपूजनं च करिष्ये ।

om adya yathoktapuṇyatithau pradhānakalaśasthāpanaṁ tatra varuṇādidevatāvāhanapūjanaṁ ca kariṣye ।

The ceremony of the installation of the sacrificial pitcher should follow all the instructions laid down in the scriptures for the puṇyāhavācana ceremony. Install two pitchers in the south and north. Touch the ground with your hands as you descant the following mantra:

ओं मही द्यौः पृथिवी च न इमं यज्ञं मिमिक्षताम् ।
पिपृतां नो भरीमभिः ।।
om mahī dyauḥ pṛthivī ca na imaṁ yajñaṁ mimikṣatām ।
pipṛtāṁ no bharīmabhiḥ ॥

and keep in the south and north a quantity of saptadhānya, barley or rice grains with the recitation of the following scriptural verses:

ओं ओषधयः समवदन्त सोमेन सह राज्ञा ।
यस्मै कृणोति ब्राह्मणस्तं राजन् पारयामसि ।।
om oṣadhayaḥ samavadanta somena saha rājñā ।
yasmai kṛṇoti brāhmaṇastaṁ rājan pārayāmasi ॥

The mantra to be muttered while keeping the pitchers in the south and north in succession is as follows:

ओं आजिघ्र कलशं मह्या त्वा विशन्त्विन्दवः ।
पुनरूर्जा निर्वत्तस्व सा नः सहस्त्रं धुक्ष्वोरुधारा पयस्वती पुनर्मा विशताद्रयिः ।।
om ājighra kalaśaṁ mahyā tvā viśantvindavaḥ ।
punarūrjā nirvattasva sā naḥ sahasraṁ dhukṣvorudhārā payasvatī punarmā viśatādrayiḥ ॥

All other rituals should be performed in this order. Now fill the pitchers with water with the recitation of the following mantra:

ओं वरुणस्योत्तम्भनमसि वरुणस्य ऋतसदन्यसि
वरुणस्य ऋतसदनमसि वरुणस्य ऋतसदनमासीद ।
om varuṇasyottambhanamasi varuṇasya ṛtasadanyasi varuṇasya ṛtasadanamasi varuṇasya ṛtasadanamāsīda ।

Now drop a little sandal into the water as you intone this mantra:

ओं गन्धद्वारां दुराधर्षां नित्यपुष्टां करीषिणीम् ।
ईश्वरीं सर्वभूतानां तामिहोपह्वये श्रियम् ।।
om gandhadvārāṁ durādharṣāṁ nityapuṣṭāṁ karīṣiṇīm ।

īśvarīṁ sarvabhūtānāṁ tāmihopahvaye śriyam ॥

Continue to drop one thing or another in the following order:

First drop ten auspicious herbs with the mantra:

ओं या औषधीः पूर्वा जाता देवेभ्यस्त्रियुगं पुरा ।
मनै नु बभ्रूणामहं शतं धामानि सप्त च ॥
om yā auṣadhīḥ pūrvā jātā devebhyastriyugaṁ purā ।
manai nu babhrūṇāmahaṁ śataṁ dhāmāni sapta ca ॥

Then drop a few blades of dūrvā grass with another mantra:

ओं काण्डात्काण्डात्प्ररोहन्ती परुषः परुषस्परि ।
एवा नो दूर्वे प्र तनु सहस्रेण शतेन च ॥
om kāṇḍātkāṇḍātprarohantī paruṣaḥ paruṣaspari ।
evā no dūrve pra tanu sahasreṇa śatena ca ॥

Next, drop a bunch of five leaves of āmra, vaṭa, pīpara, gūlara and pākari with

ओं अश्वत्थे वो निषदनं पर्णे वो वसतिष्कृता ।
गोभाज इत्किलासथ यत्सनवथ पूरुषम् ॥
om aśvatthe vo niṣadanaṁ parṇe vo vasatiṣkṛtā ।
gobhāja itkilāsatha yatsanavatha pūruṣam ॥

Drop earth collected from seven places with

ओं स्योना पृथिवि नो भवानृक्षरा निवेशनी ।
यच्छा नः शर्म सप्रथः ॥
om syonā pṛthivi no bhavānṛkṣarā niveśanī ।
yacchā naḥ śarma saprathaḥ ॥

betel-nut and other fruits with

ओं याः फलिनीर्या अफला अपुष्पा याश्च पुष्पिणीः ।
बृहस्पतिः प्रसूतस्ता नो मुञ्चन्त्वꣳ हसः ॥
om yāḥ phalinīryā aphalā apuṣpā yāśca puṣpiṇīḥ ।

bṛhaspatiḥ prasūtastā ṅo muñcantvaṁ hasaḥ ।

betel leaves with

ओं प्राणाय स्वाहाऽपानाय स्वाहा ।
om prāṇāya svāhā'pānāya svāhā ।

five jewels such as diamond, ruby, sapphire, etc. with

ओं परिवाजपतिः कविरग्निर्हव्यान्यक्रमीत ।
दधद्रत्नानि दाशुषे ।।
om parivājapatiḥ kaviragnirhavyānyakramīt ।
dadhadratnāni dāśuṣe ॥

and, finally, a little gold with:

ओं हिरण्यगर्भः समवर्त्तताग्रे भूतस्य जातः पतिरेक आसीत् ।
स दाधार पृथिवीं द्यामुतेमां कस्मै देवाय हविषा विधेम ।।
om hiraṇyagarbhaḥ samavarttatāgre bhūtasya jātaḥ pati-reka āsīt ।
sa dādhāra pṛthivīṁ dyāmutemāṁ kasmai devāya haviṣā vidhema ॥

The following mantra should be muttered while letting a piece of cloth or cotton threads in double folds to be wound round each of the sacrificial pitchers:

ओं युवा सुवासाः परिवीत आगात् स उ श्रेयान्भवति जायमानः ।
तं धीरासः कवय उन्नयन्ति स्वाध्यो मनसा देवयन्तः ।।
om yuvā suvāsāḥ parivīta āgāt sa u śreyānbhavati jāyamānaḥ ।
taṁ dhīrāsaḥ kavaya unnayanti svādhyo manasā devayantaḥ ॥

Here is the mantra to be cited while putting a small bowl filled with grains on each pitcher:

ओं पूर्णा दर्वि परापत सुपूर्णा पुनरापत ।
वस्नेव विक्रीणावहा इषमूर्जं शतक्रतो ।।

om pūrṇā darvi parāpata supūrṇā punarāpata ।
vasneva vikrīṇāvahā iṣamūrjaṁ śatakrato ।

Having accomplished this part of the ceremony, take a little raw rice and invoke Varuṇa:

ओं तत्त्वा यामि ब्रह्मणा वन्दमानस्तदाशास्ते यजमानो हविर्भिः ।
अहेडमानो वरुणेह बोध्युरुशं समा न आयुः प्रमोषीः ।
ओं वरुणाय नमः भूर्भुवः स्वः वरुणमावाहयामि ।
om tattvā yāmi brahmaṇā vandamānastadāśāste yajamāno havirbhiḥ ।
ahedamāno varuṇeha bodhyuruśaṁ samā na āyuḥ pramoṣīḥ ।
om varuṇāya namaḥ bhūrbhuvaḥ svaḥ varuṇamā-vāhayāmi ।

Make obeisance to him in the fivefold or sixteenfold manner of worshipping a deity. Reciting 'om tattvā yāmi . . .' etc., offer floral oblation and, praying, mutter this verse:

ॐ अनया पूजया वरुणः प्रीयताम् ।।
om anayā pūjayā varuṇaḥ prīyatām ॥

The invocation and worship of Varuṇa should be done in the sacrificial pitchers first in the southern and then in the northern quarter. The process of invocation continues a little longer when into the pitchers the sacred rivers, such as the Gaṅgā, are invoked with the mantra:

ओं सर्वे समुद्राः सरितस्तीर्थानि जलदा नदाः ।
आयान्तु यजमानस्य दुरितक्षयकारकाः ।।
om sarve samudrāḥ saritastīrthāni jaladā nadāḥ ।
āyāntu yajamānasya duritakṣayakārakāḥ ॥

Then, touching the pitchers with the tip of your ring finger, consecrate them with the following:

ओं कलशस्यमुखे विष्णुः कण्ठे रुद्रः समाश्रितः ।

मूले तस्य स्थितो ब्रह्मा मध्ये मातृगणाः स्मृताः ।। १ ।।
कुक्षौ तु सागराः सप्त सप्तद्वीपा वसुन्धरा ।
ऋग्वेदोऽथ यजुर्वेदः सामवेदो ह्यथर्वणः ।।
अंगैश्च सहिताः सर्वे कलशं तु समाश्रिताः ।। २ ।।
अत्र गायत्री सावित्री शान्तिः पुष्टिकरी तथा ।
आयान्तु मम शान्त्यर्थं दुरितक्षयकारिकाः ।। ३ ।।

om kalaśasyamukhe viṣṇuḥ kaṇṭhe rudraḥ samāśritaḥ ।
mūle tasya sthito brahmā madhye mātṛgaṇāḥ smṛtāḥ ॥1॥
kukṣau tu sāgarāḥ sapta saptadvīpā vasundharā ।
ṛgvedo'tha yajurvedaḥ sāmavedo hyatharvaṇaḥ ॥
aṁgaiśca sahitāḥ sarve kalaśaṁ tu samāśritāḥ ॥2॥
atra gāyatrī sāvitrī śāntiḥ puṣṭikarī tathā ।
āyāntu mama śāntyarthaṁ duritakṣayakārikāḥ ॥3॥

Then make obeisance to them:

ॐ देवदानवसंवादे मथ्यमाने महोदधौ ।
उत्पन्नोऽसि तदा कुम्भ विधृतो विष्णुना स्वयम् ।। १ ।।
त्वत्तोये सर्वतीर्थानि देवाः सर्वे त्वयि स्थिताः ।
त्वयि तिष्ठन्ति भूतानि त्वयि प्राणाः प्रतिष्ठिताः ।। २ ।।
शिवः स्वयं त्वमेवासि विष्णुस्त्वं च प्रजापतिः ।
आदित्या वसवो रुद्राः विश्वेदेवाः सपैतृकाः ।। ३ ।।
त्वयि तिष्ठन्ति सर्वेऽपि यतः कामफलप्रदाः ।। ४ ।।
त्वत्प्रसादादिमं यज्ञं कर्त्तुमीहे जलोद्भव ।
सांनिध्यं कुरु मे देव प्रसन्नो भव सर्वदा ।। ५ ।।

om devadānavasaṁvāde mathyamāne mahodadhau ।
utapanno'si tadā kumbha vidhṛto viṣṇunā svayam ॥1॥
tvattoye sarvatīrthāni devāḥ sarve tvayi sthitāḥ ।
tvayi tiṣṭhanti bhūtāni tvayi prāṇāḥ pratiṣṭhitāḥ ॥2॥
śivaḥ svayaṁ tvamevāsi viṣṇustvaṁ ca prajāpatiḥ ।
ādityā vasavo rudrāḥ viśvedevāḥ sapaitṛkāḥ ॥3॥
tvayi tiṣṭhanti sarve'pi yataḥ kāmaphalapradāḥ ॥4॥
tvatprasādādimaṁ yajñaṁ karttumīhe jalodbhava ।
sānnidhyaṁ kuru me deva prasanno bhava sarvadā ॥5॥

This is how the sacred ceremonial pitchers are installed. Some carping adherents to another school, however, would question the legitimacy of the omissions and gaps in the description of the ceremony described above. They advocate a slightly different ritual when they with considerable vehemence recommend dropping of a little milk, clarified butter, curd, the Brahmā made of kuśa grass, etc., into the pitcher in addition to the objects mentioned above. The divergence between their attitude to this ritual and the one described above becomes all the more glaring when they prescribe smearing the pitchers with cowdung. Yet some other schools of karmakāṇḍas incorporate into their system the lighting of an earthen lamp near the pitchers. Needless to say, the ritualists adhering to a separate school would have us chant the following mantras when dropping milk, butter, etc., into the pitcher. First, drop the kuśa symbolizing the Brahmā with the following mantra:

ओं पवित्रे स्थो वैष्णव्यौ सवितुर्वः प्रसव उत्पुनाम्यच्छिद्रेण पवित्रेण सूर्यस्य रश्मिभिः ।

om pavitre stho vaiṣṇavyau saviturvaḥ prasava utpunāmyacchidreṇa pavitreṇa sūryasya raśmibhiḥ ।

The mantras accompanying the dropping of the remaining objects are as follows:

(for milk)

ॐ पयः पृथिव्यां पय ओषधीषु पयो दिव्यन्तरिक्षे पयोधाः ।
पयस्वतीः प्रदिशः सन्तु मह्यम् ।।

om payaḥ pṛthivyāṁ paya oṣadhīṣu payo divyantarikṣe payodhāḥ ।
payasvatīḥ pradiśaḥ santu mahyam ।

(for curd)

ॐ दधिक्राव्णो अकारिषं जिष्णोरश्वस्य वाजिनः ।
सुरभि नो मुखा करत् प्र ण आयूंषि तारिषत् ।।

om dadhikrāvṇo akāriṣaṁ jiṣṇoraśvasya vājinaḥ ।
surabhi no mukhā karat pra ṇa āyūṁṣi tāriṣat ॥

(for clarified butter)

ॐ घृतवती भुवनानामभिश्रियोर्वी पृथ्वी मधुदुघे सुपेशसा ।
द्यावापृथिवी वरुणस्य धर्म्मणा विष्कभिते अजरे भूरिरेतसा ।।

om ghṛtavatī bhuvanānāmabhiśriyorvī pṛthvī madhudughe supeśasā ।
dyāvāpṛthivī varuṇasya dharmmaṇā viṣkabhite ajare bhūriretasā ॥

(for smearing cowdung)

ओं मा नस्तोके तनये मा न आयुषि मा नो गोषु मा नो अश्वेषु रीरिषः।
मा नो वीरान् रुद्र भामिनो वधीर्हविष्मन्तः सदमित्त्वां हवामहे ।।

om mā nastoke tanaye mā na āyuṣi mā no goṣu mā no aśveṣu rīriṣaḥ ।
mā no vīrān rudra bhāmino vadhīrhaviṣmantaḥ sadamittvā havāmahe ॥

Grahapūjā

Grahapūjā, as the name indicates, is the devotee's act of worship in order to propitiate the planets which to all Hindus exercise considerable influence, sometimes propitious and at other times evil, upon our lives. In this worship again imagination and symbolism play a vital role. The planets are brought down to the terrestrial plane, installed wherever necessary and worshipped. The devotee invokes them often in the sacrificial pitcher itself and worships them in the manner they are invoked—

ओं भूर्भुवः स्वः आदित्याय साधिदैवतप्रत्यधिदैवताय नमः ।
ओं भूर्भुवः स्वः चन्द्राय साधिदैवतप्रत्यधिदैवताय नमः ।।

om bhūrbhuvaḥ svaḥ ādityāya sādhidaivatapratya-dhidaivatāya namaḥ ।
om bhūrbhuvaḥ svaḥ candrāya sādhidaivatapratyadhi-daivatāya namaḥ ॥

These are only illustrative. The devotee should, while chanting the mantra, name each of the planetary gods separately invoked in the pitcher. If the number of altars made is proportioned to the number of these gods, it is desirable to invoke them on each of the altars separately.

The pūjā of these celestial bodies begins as usual with the worshipper's saṁkalpa:

ओं अद्य यथोक्तविशेषणविशिष्टायां शुभपुण्यतिथौ अमुककर्मणः निर्विघ्नसमाप्तये तदंगतया आदित्यादिनवग्रहाणामधिदैवतप्रत्यधिदैवत-लोकपालदिक्पालसहितानामावाहनपूजनादि करिष्ये ।

om adya yathoktaviśeṣaṇaviśiṣṭāyāṁ śubhapuṇyatithau amukakarmaṇaḥ nirvighnasamāptaye tadaṁgatayā ādityādinavagrahāṇāmadhidaivatapratyadhidaivata-lokapāladikpālasahitānāmāvāhanapūjanādi kariṣye ।

With a red flower and raw rice in one hand and a white one in the other, he should invoke in the centre of the heavenly orb the Sun and all his tutelary gods:

ॐ सप्तम्यां विशाखान्वितायां कलिंगे जातं कश्यपगोत्रं लोहितवर्णं वर्त्तुलाकृतिं मण्डलमध्यस्थं प्राङ्मुखं द्विभुजं पद्महस्तं सप्ताश्वरथवाहनं क्षत्रियाधिपतिमीश्वराधिदैवताग्निप्रत्यधिदैवतसहितं सूर्यमावाहयामि ॐ भूर्भुवः स्वः ईश्वराग्निसहितसूर्याय नमः । इहागच्छ । ओं आकृष्णेन रजसा वर्त्तमानो निवेशयन्नमृतं मर्त्त्यं च । हिरण्ययेन सविता रथेना देवो याति भुवनानि पश्यन् । ईश्वराग्निसहितसूर्य इह तिष्ठ इमं यज्ञमभिरक्ष ।

om saptamyāṁ viśākhānvitāyāṁ kaliṁge jātaṁ kaśyapagotraṁ lohitavarṇaṁ varttulākṛtiṁ maṇḍala-madhyasthaṁ prāṅmukhaṁ dvibhujaṁ padmahastaṁ saptāśvarathavāhanaṁ kṣatriyādhipatimīśvarādhidaivat-āgnipratyadhidaivatasahitaṁ sūryamāvāhayāmi om bhūrbhuvaḥ svaḥ īśvarāgnisahitasūryāya namaḥ । *ihāgaccha* । *om ākṛṣṇena rajasā varttamāno niveśayanna-mṛtaṁ marttyaṁ ca* । *hiraṇyayena savitā rathenā devo yāti bhuvanāni paśyan* । *īśvarāgnisahitasūrya iha tiṣṭha imaṁ yajñamabhirakṣa* ।

Having read this, drop red flowers and raw rice grains on the solar orb. This done, drop white flowers and raw rice grains on the right-hand side of the solar maṇḍala for Īśvara and on its left-hand side for Agni. When making the invocation keep the red and white flowers separately in both hands. In like manner continue to keep the white one in one of your hands. The reason is that the propitiatory rites demand the retention of a white flower for the chosen tutelary gods. Then with white flower and raw rice in your hands invoke the Moon and his chosen goddess Umā and the tutelary god Water on the south-east quarter of the Sun:

ॐ चतुर्दश्यां कृत्तिकान्वितायां समुद्रे जातमत्रिगोत्रं श्वेतवर्णं चतुरस्राकृतिमर्द्धचन्द्राकृतिं वा मण्डलात्पूर्वदक्षिणदिक्स्थं पश्चिमाभिमुखं दशाश्वरथवाहनं विशांपतिमुमाधिदैवतजलप्रत्यधिदैवतसहितं चन्द्रमावाहयामि । ओं भूर्भुवः स्वः उमाजलसहितचन्द्राय नमः । इहागच्छ । ॐ इमं देवा असपत्नं सुबध्वं महते क्षत्राय महते ज्यैष्ठयाय महते जानराज्यायेन्द्रस्येन्द्रियाय । इमममुष्य पुत्रमस्यै विश एष वोऽमी राजा सोमोऽस्माकं ब्राह्मणानां राजा । उमाजलसहितचन्द्र इह तिष्ठ इमं यज्ञमभिरक्ष ।

om caturdaśyāṁ kṛttikānvitāyāṁ samudre jātamatrigotraṁ śvetavarṇaṁ caturasrākṛtimarddhacandrākṛtiṁ vā maṇḍalātpūrvadakṣiṇadiksthaṁ paścimābhimukhaṁ daśāśvarathavāhanaṁ viśāṁpatimumādhidaivatajalapratyadhidaivatasahitaṁ candramāvāhayāmi । om bhūrbhuvaḥ svaḥ umājalasahitacandrāya namaḥ । ihāgaccha । om imaṁ devā asapatnaṁ subadhvaṁ mahate kṣatrāya mahate jyaiṣṭhyāya mahate jānarājyāyendrasyendriyāya । imamamuṣya putramasyai viśa eṣa vo'mī rājā somo'smākaṁ brāhmaṇānāṁ rājā । umājalasahitacandra iha tiṣṭha imaṁ yajñamabhirakṣa ।

Intoning this mantra, drop the flower and rice grains first on the Moon, then on Umā on the right and on the Water on the left. For all chosen and tutelary gods should one keep white rice grains, betel-nut or flower and invoke the gods on it, as has been pointed out elsewhere. Then with red and white flowers separately in your hands coupled with raw rice grains, invoke Mars or Maṁgala with his chosen god Skanda and tutelary Pṛthivī on the right of the Sun:

ओं दशम्यां पूर्वाषाढ़ान्वितायामवन्त्यां जातं भारद्वाजगोत्रं रक्तवर्णं त्रिकोणं मण्डलाद् दक्षिणदिग्विभागस्थं उत्तराभिमुखं मेषवाहनं क्षत्रियाधिपतिं स्कन्दाधिदैवतक्षितिप्रत्यधिदैवतसहितं भौममावाहयामि ओं भूर्भुवः स्वः स्कन्दक्षितिसहितभौमाय नमः इहागच्छ । ओं अग्निर्मूर्द्धा दिवः ककुत्पतिः पृथिव्या अयम् । अपां रेतांसि जिन्वति ।

om daśamyāṁ pūrvāṣāḍhānvitāyāmavantyāṁ jātaṁ bhāradvājagotraṁ raktavarṇaṁ trikoṇaṁ maṇḍalād dakṣiṇadigvibhāgasthaṁ uttarābhimukhaṁ meṣavāhanaṁ kṣatriyādhipatiṁ skandādhidaivatakṣitipratyadhidaivatasahitaṁ bhaumamāvāhayāmi om bhūrbhuvaḥ svaḥ skandakṣitisahitabhaumāya namaḥ ihāgaccha । *om agnirmūrddhā divaḥ kakutpatiḥ pṛthivyā ayam* । *apāṁ retāṁsi jinvati* ।

Having recited this mantra put red flowers on Mars and the white ones and raw rice grains on the left and right of it. The next graha to be invoked is Mercury, his chosen god Nārāyaṇa and tutelary Viṣṇu. Put the yellow or green and white flowers and raw rice grains on the north-east quarter of the Sun:

ओं द्वादश्यां धनिष्ठान्वितायां मगधदेशे जातमत्रिगोत्रं हरिद्वर्णं पीतवर्णं वा बाणाकृतिं मण्डलात् पूर्वोत्तरस्थं सूर्याभिमुखं शूद्राधिपतिं नारायणाधिदैवतविष्णुप्रत्यधिदैवतसहितं बुधमावाहयामि ओं भूर्भुवः स्वः नारायणविष्णुसहितबुधाय नमः । इहागच्छ । ओं उद्बुध्यस्वाग्ने प्रतिजागृहि त्वमिष्टापूर्त्ते संसृजेथामयं च । अस्मिन् सधस्थे अध्युत्तरस्मिान् विश्वेदेवा यजमानश्च सीदत । नारायणविष्णुसहितबुध इह तिष्ठ इमं यज्ञमभिरक्ष ।

om dvādaśyāṁ dhaniṣṭhānvitāyāṁ magadhadeśe jātamatrigotraṁ haridvarṇaṁ pītavarṇaṁ vā bāṇākṛtiṁ maṇḍalāt pūrvottarasthaṁ sūryābhimukhaṁ śūdrādhipatiṁ nārāyaṇādhidaivataviṣṇupratyadhidaivatasahitaṁ budhamāvāhayāmi om bhūrbhuvaḥ svaḥ nārāyaṇaviṣṇusahitabudhāya namaḥ । *ihāgaccha* । *om udbudhyasvāgne pratijāgṛhi tvamiṣṭāpūrtte saṁsṛjethāmayaṁ ca* । *asmin sadhasthe adhyuttarasmān viśvedevā yajamānaśca sīdata* । *nārāyaṇaviṣṇusahitabudha iha tiṣṭha imaṁ yajñamabhirakṣa* ।

With this mantra, duly recited, place the yellow or green flowers on Mercury and the white flowers and raw rice grains on the left and right of it. Jupiter should be invoked thus:

ओं एकादश्यामुत्तराफाल्गुनीयुतायां सिन्धुदेशे जातमांगिरसगोत्रं गोरोचनाभं दीर्घचतुष्कोणाकृतिं मण्डलादुत्तरस्थितं सूर्याभिमुखम् सिंहवाहनं ब्रह्माधिदैवतेन्द्रप्रत्यधिदैवतसहितं गुरुमावाहयामि ओं भूर्भुवः स्वः ब्रह्मेन्द्रसहितगुरवे नमः । इहागच्छ । ओं बृहस्पते अति यदर्यो अर्हाद् द्युमद्विभाति क्रतुमज्जनेषु । यद्दीदयच्छवस ऋतप्रजात तदस्मासु द्रविणं धेहि चित्रम् । ब्रह्मेन्द्रसहितगुरो इह तिष्ठ इमं यज्ञमभिरक्ष ।

om ekādaśyāmuttarāphālgunīyutāyāṁ sindhudeśe jātamāṁgirasagotraṁ gorocanābhaṁ dīrghacatuṣkoṇākṛtiṁ maṇḍalāduttarasthitaṁ sūryābhimukham siṁhavāhanaṁ brahmādhidaivatendrapratyadhidaivatasahitaṁ gurumāvāhayāmi om bhūrbhuvaḥ svaḥ brahmendrasahitagurave namaḥ । *ihāgaccha* । *om bṛhaspate ati yadaryo arhād dyumadvibhāti kratumajjaneṣu* । *yaddīdayacchavasa ṛtaprajāta tadasmāsu draviṇaṁ dhehi citram* । *brahmendrasahitaguro iha tiṣṭha imaṁ yajñamabhirakṣa* ।

Jupiter is invoked with the chosen Brahmā and the tutelary Indra on the north of the Sun with yellow and white flowers and raw rice grains. Keep the yellow flowers on Jupiter and the white ones and raw rice grains on the right and left of it. The invocation to Venus requires the following verses:

ओं नवम्यां पुष्ययुतायां भोजकटे जातं भार्गवगोत्रं शुक्लवर्णं पञ्चकोणं मण्डलात्पूर्वदिक्स्थं सूर्याभिमुखं श्वेताश्ववाहनमिंद्राधिदैवतेन्द्राणीप्रत्यधि-

दैवतसहितं शुक्रमावाहयामि ।ओं भूर्भुवः स्वः इन्द्रेन्द्राणीसहितशुक्रायनमः । भगवन् इहागच्छ । ओं अन्नात्परिस्त्रुतो रसं ब्रह्मणा व्यपिबत्क्षत्रं पयः सोमं प्रजापतिः । ऋतेन सत्यमिन्द्रियं विपानंशुक्रमन्धस इन्द्रस्येन्द्रियमिदं पयोऽमृतम्मधु ।इन्द्रेन्द्राणीसहितशुक्र इह तिष्ठ इमं यज्ञमभिरक्ष ।

om navamyāṁ puṣyayutāyāṁ bhojakaṭe jātaṁ bhārgavagotraṁ śuklavarṇaṁ pañcakoṇaṁ maṇḍalātpūrvadiksthaṁ sūryābhimukhaṁ śvetāśvavāhanamiṁdrādhidaivatendrāṇīpratyadhidaivatasahitaṁ śukramāvāhayāmi । om bhūrbhuvaḥ svaḥ indrendrāṇīsahitaśukrāya namaḥ । bhagavan ihāgaccha । om annātparisruto rasaṁ brahmaṇā vyapibatkṣatraṁ payaḥ somaṁ prajāpatiḥ । ṛtena satyamindriyaṁ vipānaṁśukramandhasa indrasyendriyamidaṁ payo'mṛtammadhu । indrendrāṇīsahitaśukra iha tiṣṭha imaṁ yajñamabhirakṣa ।

The chosen god Indra and the tutelary Indrāṇī are both invoked along with Venus on the east of the Sun with white flowers and raw rice grains. Having read this mantra put the flowers and rice grains on Venus, Indra and Indrāṇī. On the western side of the Sun invoke Saturn and his chosen god Yama and his tutelary Prajāpati with black bilva leaves, white blossoms and raw rice grains:

ओं अष्टम्यां रेवतीयुतायां सौराष्ट्रे जातं काश्यपगोत्रं लोहवर्णं धनुराकृतिं मण्डलात्पश्चिमस्थं सूर्याभिमुखं गृध्रवाहनं संकरजातिं यमाधिदैवत-प्रजापतिप्रत्यधिदैवतसहितं शनिमावाहयामि । ओं भूर्भुवः स्वः यमप्रजापतिसहितशनये नमः ।भगवन्निहागच्छ ।ओं शन्नोदेवीरभिष्ट्य आपो भवन्तु पीतये । शंयोरभिस्त्रवन्तु नः । यमप्रजापतिसहितशने इह तिष्ठ इमं यज्ञमभिरक्ष ।

om aṣṭamyāṁ revatīyutāyāṁ saurāṣṭre jātaṁ kāśyapagotraṁ lohavarṇaṁ dhanurākṛtiṁ maṇḍalātpaścimasthaṁ sūryābhimukhaṁ gṛdhravāhanaṁ saṁkarajātiṁ yamādhidaivataprajāpatipratyadhidaivatasahitaṁ śanimāvāhayāmi । om bhūrbhuvaḥ svaḥ yamaprajāpatisahitaśanaye namaḥ । bhagavannihāgaccha ।

om śannodevīrabhiṣṭaya āpo bhavantu pītaye । saṁyorabhisravantu naḥ । yamaprajāpatisahitaśane iha tiṣṭha imaṁ yajñamabhirakṣa ।

Follow the reading of this mantra by placing black bilva leaves, rice grains and blossoms on Saturn and the white one on Yama and Prajāpati. Taking black-white blossoms and raw rice invoke Rāhu[1] along with Kāla and Sarpa, his chosen and tutelary gods, to the south-west of the Sun:

ओं पौर्णमास्यां भरणीयुतायां बर्बरे जातं पैठीनसिगोत्रं कृष्णवर्णं शूर्पाकृतिं मण्डलात्पश्चिमदक्षिणदिक्स्थं सूर्याभिमुखं शूद्राधिपतिं कालाधिदैवत-सर्पप्रत्यधिदैवतसहितं राहुमावाहयामि । ओं भूर्भुवः स्वः कालसर्पसहितराहवेनमः । भगवन्निहागच्छ । ओं कया नश्चित्र आभुवदूती सदावृधः सखा । कया शचिष्ठया वृता । कालसर्पसहितराहो इह तिष्ठ इमं यज्ञमभिरक्ष ।

om paurṇamāsyāṁ bharaṇīyutāyāṁ barbare jātaṁ paiṭhīnasigotraṁ kṛṣṇavarṇaṁ śūrpākṛtiṁ maṇḍalāt-paścimadakṣiṇadiksthaṁ sūryābhimukhaṁ śūdrādhi-patiṁ kālādhidaivatasarpapratyadhidaivatasahitaṁ rāhumāvāhayāmi । om bhūrbhuvaḥ svaḥ kālasarpa-sahitarāhavenamaḥ । bhagavannihāgaccha । om kayā naścitra ābhuvadūtī sadāvṛdhaḥ sakhā । kayā śaciṣṭhayā vṛtā । kālasarpasahitarāho iha tiṣṭha imaṁ yajñama-bhirakṣa ।

Keep the black rice on Rāhu and the white rice on Kāla. Continuing, take blue and white blossoms and raw rice and, keeping them in your hands, invoke Ketu, considered in astronomy the ninth planet, to the north-west of the Sun. If blue blossoms are not available the black ones will do. Remember that Ketu's *adhidaivata* is Citragupta and *pratyadhidaivata* is Brahmā. The invocatory mantra is this:

---

1. One of the nine principal planets; name of a Daitya or demon who is supposed to seize the sun and the moon and thus cause eclipses.

ॐ अमावस्यायामाश्लेषान्वितायामन्तर्वेद्यां जातं जैमिनिगोत्रं धूम्रवर्णं ध्वजाकृतिं कपोतवाहनमंत्यजाधिपतिं मण्डलात्पश्चिमोत्तरस्थं सूर्याभिमुखं चित्रगुप्ताधिदैवतब्रह्मप्रत्यधिदैवतसहितकेतुमावाहयामि ॐ भूर्भुवः स्वः चित्रगुप्तब्रह्मसहितकेतवे नमः । केतो इहागच्छ । ओं केतुं कृण्वन्नकेतवे पेशो मर्या अपेशसे । समुषद्भिरजायथाः । चित्रगुप्तब्रह्मसहितकेतो इह तिष्ठ इमं यज्ञमभिरक्ष ।

om amāvasyāyāmāśleṣānvitāyāmantarvedyāṁ jātaṁ jaiminigotraṁ dhūmravarṇaṁ dhvajākṛtiṁ kapotavāhanamaṁtyajādhipatiṁ maṇḍalātpaścimottarasthaṁ sūryābhimukhaṁ citraguptādhidaivatabrahmapratyadhidaivatasahitaket umāvāhayāmi । *om bhūrbhuvaḥ svaḥ citraguptabrahmasahitaketave namaḥ* । *keto ihāgaccha* । *om ketuṁ kṛṇvannaketave peśo maryā apeśase* । *samuṣadbhirajāyathāḥ* । *citraguptabrahmasahitaketo iha tiṣṭha imaṁ yajñamabhirakṣa* ।

Place the blue rice grains on Ketu and the white on Citragupta and Brahmā.

With this end these planetary invocations. But the *pūjā* of the grahas includes paying obeisance to many more deities, among whom the most outstanding are: Vināyaka, Durgā, Vāyu, Ākāśa, Aśvinīkumāras, Vāstoṣpati, Kṣetrādhipati, etc.

No other grahamaṇḍala (planetary circle) is required for the invocation of the Pañcalokapālas like Vināyaka or of Vāstoṣpati and Kṣetrapāla. They should be invoked in the maṇḍala described above. With raw rice, betel nut and blossoms in your hand invoke Vināyaka to the north of Rāhu. The relevant mantra here is:

ओं गणानां त्वा गणपतिं हवामहे प्रियाणां त्वा प्रियपतिं हवामहे निधीनां त्वा निधिपतिं हवामहे वसो मम ।

आहमजानिगर्भधमा त्वमजासि गर्भधम् । ओं भूर्भुवः स्वः विनायकाय नमः । विनायक इहागच्छ इह तिष्ठ इमं यज्ञमभिरक्ष ।।

om gaṇānāṁ tvā gaṇapatiṁ havāmahe priyāṇāṁ tvā

priyapatiṁ havāmahe nidhīnāṁ tvā nidhipatiṁ havāmahe vaso mama ।
āhamajānigarbhadhamā tvamajāsi garbhadham । *om bhūrbhuvaḥ svaḥ vināyakāya namaḥ* । *vināyaka ihāgaccha iha tiṣṭha imaṁ yajñamabhirakṣa* ।

Next, invoke Durgā to the north of Saturn with the incantation of the following mantra:

ओं अम्बे अम्बिके अम्बालिके न मा नयति कश्चन ।
ससस्त्यश्वकः सुभद्रिकां काम्पीलवासिनीम् ।
ओं भूर्भुवः स्वः दुर्गायै नमः ।
दुर्गे इहागच्छ इह तिष्ठ इमं यज्ञमभिरक्ष ।।
om ambe ambike ambālike na mā nayati kaścana ।
sasastyaśvakaḥ subhadrikāṁ kāmpīlavāsinīm ।
om bhūrbhuvaḥ svaḥ durgāyai namaḥ ।
durge ihāgaccha iha tiṣṭha imaṁ yajñamabhirakṣa ।

Invoke Vāyu to the north of the Sun with the following:

ॐ वातो वा मनो वा गन्धर्वाः सप्तविंशतिः ।
ते अग्रे अश्वमयुञ्जजँस्ते अस्मिञ्जवमादधुः ।
ओं भूर्भुवः स्वः वायवे नमः ।
वायो इहागच्छ इह तिष्ठ इमं यज्ञमभिरक्ष ।।
om vāto vā mano vā gandharvāḥ saptaviṁśatiḥ ।
te agre aśvamayuñjaṁste asmiñjavamādadhuḥ ।
om bhūrbhuvaḥ svaḥ vāyave namaḥ ।
vāyo ihāgaccha iha tiṣṭha imaṁ yajñambhirakṣa ॥

Invoke Ākāśa (celestial sphere) to the south of Rāhu with:

ओं ऊर्ध्वा अस्य समिधो भवन्त्यूर्ध्वा शुक्रा शोचींष्यग्नः ।
द्युमत्तमा सुप्रतीकस्य सूनोः ।
ॐ भूर्भुवः स्वः आकाशाय नमः ।
आकाश इहागच्छ इह तिष्ठ इमं यज्ञमभिरक्ष ।।४।।
om ūrdhvā asya samidho bhavantyūrdhvā śukrā

śocīṁṣyagnaḥ ।
dyumattamā supratīkasya sūnoḥ ।
om bhūrbhuvaḥ svaḥ ākāśāya namaḥ ।
ākāśa ihāgaccha iha tiṣṭha imaṁ yajñamabhirakṣa ॥

The Aśvinīkumāras should be invoked to the south of Ketu with:

ॐ या वां कशा मधुमत्यश्विना सूनृतावती ।
तया यज्ञं मिमिक्षतम् ।
ओं भूर्भुवः स्वः अश्विभ्यां नमः ।
अश्विनौ इहागच्छतम् इह तिष्ठतम् इमं यज्ञमभिरक्षतम् ।।
om yā vāṁ kaśā madhumatyaśvinā sūnṛtāvatī ।
tayā yajñaṁ mimikṣatam ।
om bhūrbhuvaḥ svaḥ aśvibhyāṁ namaḥ ।
aśvinau ihāgacchatam iha tiṣṭhatam imaṁ yajñamabhira-kṣatam ॥

Vāstoṣpati needs to be invoked to the north of the Jupiter with:

ओं वास्तोष्पते प्रतिजानीह्यस्मान् स्वावेशो अनमीवो भवा नः ।
यत्त्वेमहे प्रति तन्नो जुषस्व शन्नो भव द्विपदे शं चतुष्पदे ।
ओं भूर्भुवः स्वः वास्तोष्पतये नमः ।
वास्तोष्पते इहागच्छ इह तिष्ठ इमं यज्ञमभिरक्ष ।।
om vāstoṣpate pratijānīhyasmān svāveśo anamīvo bhavā naḥ ।
yattvemahe prati tanno juṣasva śanno bhava dvipade śaṁ catuṣpade ।
om bhūrbhuvaḥ svaḥ vāstoṣpataye namaḥ ।
vāstoṣpate ihāgaccha iha tiṣṭha imaṁ yajñamabhirakṣa ।

Kṣetrādhipati is invoked to the north of Vāstoṣpati with the following incantatory verse:

ओं भूर्भुवः स्वः क्षेत्राधिपतये नमः ।
क्षेत्राधिपते इहागच्छ इह तिष्ठ इमं यज्ञमभिरक्ष ।।

om bhūrbhuvaḥ svaḥ kṣetrādhipataye namaḥ ।
kṣetrādhipate ihāgaccha iha tiṣṭha imaṁ yajñamabhirakṣa ॥

All these gods, including the elements, should be invoked and worshipped with white blossoms and raw rice grains. This would apply to the worship of other deities to be mentioned hereafter.

Upon the line drawn on the altar all around the grahamaṇḍala all the ten protecting deities of all the ten quarters (*dikpālas*) should be invoked with flowers and raw rice. Indra prefers being invoked in the east with the following mantra:

ओं त्रातारमिंद्रमवितारमिन्द्रम् हवे हवे सुहवं शूरमिन्द्रम् ।
ह्वयामि शक्रं पुरुहूतमिन्द्रम् स्वस्ति नो मधवा दधात्विन्द्रः ।
ओं भूर्भुवः स्वः इन्द्राय नमः ।
इन्द्र इहागच्छ इह तिष्ठ इमं यज्ञमभिरक्ष ।।

om trātāramiṁdramavitāramindraṁ have have suhavaṁ śūramindram ।
hvayāmi śakraṁ puruhūtamindraṁ svasti no madhavā dadhātvindraḥ ।
om bhūrbhuvaḥ svaḥ indrāya namaḥ ।
indra ihāgaccha iha tiṣṭha imaṁ yajñamabhirakṣa ॥

Agni, the god of fire, should be invoked in the south-east quarter called Agnikoṇa with the following mantra:

ॐ अग्नि दूतं पुरो दधे हव्यवाहमुपब्रुवे ।
देवाँ आसादयादिह ।
ॐ भूर्भुवः स्वः अग्नये नमः ।
अग्ने इहागच्छ इह तिष्ठ इमं यज्ञमभिरक्ष ।।

om agniṁ dūtaṁ puro dadhe havyavāhamupabruve ।
devām̐ āsādayādiha ।
om bhūrbhuvaḥ svaḥ agnaye namaḥ ।
agne ihāgaccha iha tiṣṭha imaṁ yajñamabhirakṣa ॥

Yama, of whom mortals are so afraid, should be invoked in

the south. His propitiatory verses are:

ॐ असि यमो अस्यादित्योऽअर्वन्नसि त्रितो गुह्येन व्रतेन ।
असि सोमेन समया विपृक्त आहुस्ते त्रीणि दिवि बन्धनानि ।
ओं भूर्भुवः स्वः यमाय नमः ।
यम इहागच्छ इह तिष्ठ इमं यज्ञमभिरक्ष ।।
om asi yamo asyādityo'arvannasi trito guhyena vratena ।
asi somena samayā viprkta āhuste trīṇi divi bandhanāni ।
om bhūrbhuvaḥ svaḥ yamāya namaḥ ।
yama ihāgaccha iha tiṣṭha imaṁ yajñamabhirakṣa ॥

The scriptures advise invoking Nairṛti in the south-west quarter with:

ॐ एष ते निर्ऋते भागस्तं जुषस्व ।
ओं भूर्भुवः स्वः निर्ऋतये नमः ।
निर्ऋते इहागच्छ इह तिष्ठ इमं यज्ञमभिरक्ष ।।
om eṣa te nirṛte bhāgastaṁ juṣasva ।
om bhūrbhuvaḥ svaḥ nirṛtaye namaḥ ।
nirṛte ihāgaccha iha tiṣṭha imaṁ yajñamabhirakṣa ॥

Varuṇa is invoked in the west with the following mantra:

ओं इमं मे वरुण श्रुधि हवमद्या च मृडय ।
त्वामवस्युराचके ।
ओं भूर्भुवः स्वः वरुणाय नमः ।
वरुण इहागच्छ इह तिष्ठ इमं यज्ञमभिरक्ष ।।
om imaṁ me varuṇa śrudhi havamadyā ca mṛḍaya ।
tvāmavasyurācake ।
om bhūrbhuvaḥ svaḥ varuṇāya namaḥ ।
varuṇa ihāgaccha iha tiṣṭha imaṁ yajñamabhirakṣa ॥

The wind god, Vāyu, should be invoked in the north-west by chanting:

ओं वातो वा मनो वा गन्धर्वाः सप्तविं शतिः ।
ते अग्रे अश्वमयुञ्जँस्ते अस्मिन् जवमादधुः ।

ॐ भूर्भुवः स्वः वायवे नमः ।
वायो इहागच्छ इह तिष्ठ इमं यज्ञमभिरक्ष ।।
om vāto vā mano vā gandharvāḥ saptaviṁ śatiḥ ।
te agre aśvamayuñjaṁste asmin javamādadhuḥ ।
om bhūrbhuvaḥ svaḥ vāyave namaḥ ।
vāyo ihāgaccha iha tiṣṭha imaṁ yajñamabhirakṣa ॥

Kubera or Soma is, as the śāstras enjoin, invoked in the north, for which the sacred formula is:

ओं वयं सोम व्रते तव मनस्तनूषु बिभ्रतः ।
प्रजावन्तः सचेमहि ।
ओं भूर्भुवः स्वः कुबेराय नमः ।
कुबेर इहागच्छ इह तिष्ठ इमं यज्ञमभिरक्ष ।।
om vayaṁ soma vrate tava manastanūṣu bibhrataḥ ।
prajāvantaḥ sacemahi ।
om bhūrbhuvaḥ svaḥ kuberāya namaḥ ।
kubera ihāgaccha iha tiṣṭha imaṁ yajñamabhirakṣa ॥

Īśa or Mahādeva is invoked in the north-east quarter with the following mantra:

ओं तमीशानं जगतस्तस्थुषस्पतिं धियंजिन्वमवसे हूमहे वयम् ।
पूषा नो यथा वेदसामसद्वृधे रक्षिता पायुरदब्धः स्वस्तये ।
ओं भूर्भुवः स्वः ईशाय नमः ।
ईश इहागच्छ इह तिष्ठ इमं यज्ञमभिरक्ष ।।
om tamīśānaṁ jagatastasthuṣaspatiṁ dhiyaṁjinvamavase hūmahe vayam ।
pūṣā no yathā vedasāmasadvṛdhe rakṣitā pāyuradabdhaḥ svastaye ।
om bhūrbhuvaḥ svaḥ īśāya namaḥ ।
īśa ihāgaccha iha tiṣṭha imaṁ yajñamabhirakṣa ॥

The next deity to be invoked is Brahmā, who should be invited between the east and the north-east by intoning:

ओं ब्रह्म जज्ञानं प्रथमं पुरस्ताद्विसीमतः सुरुचो वेन आवः ।
स बुध्न्या उपमा अस्य विष्ठाः सतश्चयोनिमसतश्च विवः ।

ओं भूर्भुवः स्वः ब्रह्मणे नमः ।
ब्रह्मन् इहागच्छ इह तिष्ठ इमं यज्ञमभिरक्ष ।।
om brahma jajñānaṁ prathamaṁ purastādvisīmataḥ suruco vena āvaḥ ।
sa budhnyā upamā asya viṣṭhāḥ sataścayonimasataśca vivaḥ ।
om bhūrbhuvaḥ svaḥ brahmaṇe namaḥ ।
brahman ihagaccha ihatiṣṭha imaṁ yajñamabhirakṣa ॥

Now invoke Ananta between the west and the south-west with another mantra, which is as follows:

ओं नमोऽस्तु सर्पेभ्यो ये के च पृथिवीमनु ।
ये अन्तरिक्षे ये दिवि तेभ्यः सर्प्पेभ्यो नमः ।
ओं भूर्भुवः स्वः अनन्त
इहागच्छ इह तिष्ठ इमं यज्ञमभिरक्ष ।।
om namo'stu sarpebhyo ye ke ca pṛthivīmanu ।
ye antarikṣe ye divi tebhyaḥ sarppebhyo namaḥ ।
om bhūrbhuvaḥ svaḥ ananta
ihāgaccha iha tiṣṭha imaṁ yajñamabhirakṣa ॥

Thus having invoked all the nine planets (*navagrahas*) and the protecting deities of the quarters (*dikpālas*) consecrate them all at once with raw rice grains, muttering the following mantras:

ओं एतन्ते देव सवितर्यज्ञं प्राहुर्बृहस्पतये ब्रह्मणे ।
तेन यज्ञमव तेन यज्ञपतिं तेन मामव ।
मनोजूतिर्जुषतामाज्यस्य बृहस्पतिर्यज्ञमिमं तनोत्वरिष्टं यज्ञं समिमं दधातु ।
विश्वेदेवास इह मादयन्तामोम्प्रतिष्ठ ।
ओं भूर्भुवः स्वः आदित्यादिनवग्रहाः सांगाः सपरिवाराः सवाहना अधिदेवताप्रत्यधिदेवताविनायकादिपञ्चलोक पालवास्तोष्पतिक्षेत्रा-धिपतीन्द्रादिदशदिक्पालसहिताः सुप्रतिष्ठिता वरदा भवन्तु ।
om etante deva savitaryajñaṁ prāhurbṛhaspataye brahmaṇe ।
tena yajñamava tena yajñapatiṁ tena māmava ।

manojūtirjuṣatāmājyasya bṛhaspatiryajñamimaṁ
tanotvariṣṭaṁ yajñaṁ samimaṁ dadhātu ।
viśvedevāsa iha mādayantāmompratiṣṭha ।
om bhūrbhuvaḥ svaḥ ādityādinavagrahāḥ sāṁgāḥ saparivārāḥ savāhanā adhidevatāpratyadhidevatā-vināyakādipañcaloka pālavāstoṣpatikṣetrādhipatīndrā-didaśadikpālasahitāḥ supratiṣṭhitā varadā bhavantu ।

This should be followed by concentrating your attention on all the nine planets with the following mantra:

ओं पद्मासनः पद्मकरो द्विबाहुः पद्मद्युतिः सप्ततुरंगवाहनः ।
दिवाकरो लोकगुरुः किरीटी मयि प्रसादं विदधातु देवः ।। १ ।।
ओं श्वेताम्बरः श्वेतविभूषणश्च श्वेतद्युतिर्दण्डधरो द्विबाहुः ।
चन्द्रोऽमृतात्मा वरदः किरीटी श्रेयांसि मह्यं विदधातु देवः ।। २ ।।
ओं रक्ताम्बरो रक्तवपुः किरीटी चतुर्भुजो मेषगमो गदाभृत् ।
धरासुतः शक्तिधरश्च शूली सदा मम स्याद्वरदः प्रशान्तः ।। ३ ।।
ओं पीताम्बरः पीतवपुः किरीटी चतुर्भुजो दण्डधरश्च हारी ।
चर्मासिभृत्सोमसुतः सदा मे सिंहाधिरूढो वरदो बुधोऽस्तु ।। ४ ।।
ओं पीताम्बरः पीतवपुः किरीटी चतुर्भुजो देवगुरुः प्रशान्तः ।
दधाति दण्डं च कमण्डलुं च तथाऽक्षसूत्रं वरदोऽस्तु मह्यम् ।। ५ ।।
ओं श्वेताम्बरः श्वेतवपुः किरीटी चतुर्भुजो दैत्यगुरुः प्रशान्तः ।
तथाक्षसूत्रं च कमण्डलुं च दण्डं च बिभ्रद्वरदोऽस्तु मह्यम् ।। ६ ।।
ओं नीलद्युतिः शूलधरः किरीटी गृध्रस्थितस्त्रासकरो धनुष्मान् ।
चतुर्भुजः सूर्यसुतः प्रशान्तः सदास्तु मह्यं वरदो मन्दगामी ।। ७ ।।
ओं नीलाम्बरो नीलवपुः किरीटी करालवक्त्रः करवालशूली ।
चतुर्भुजश्चर्मधरश्च राहुः सिंहाधिरूढो वरदोऽस्तु मह्यम् ।। ८ ।।
ओं धूम्रो द्विबाहुर्वरदो गदाभृत् गृध्रासनस्थो विकृताननश्च ।
किरीटकेयूरविभूषितांगः सदास्तु मे केतुगणः प्रशान्तः ।। ९ ।।

om padmāsanaḥ padmakaro dvibāhuḥ padmadyutiḥ
saptaturaṁgavāhanaḥ ।
divākaro lokaguruḥ kirīṭī mayi prasādaṁ vidadhātu
devaḥ ॥ 1 ॥
om śvetāmbaraḥ śvetavibhūṣaṇaśca śvetadyutirdaṇḍa-

dharo dvibāhuḥ ।
candro'mṛtātmā varadaḥ kirīṭī śreyāṁsi mahyaṁ
vidadhātu devaḥ ॥ 2 ॥
om raktāmbaro raktavapuḥ kirīṭī caturbhujo meṣagamo
gadābhṛt ।
dharāsutaḥ śaktidharaśca śūlī sadā mama syādvaradaḥ
praśāntaḥ ॥ 3 ॥
om pītāmbaraḥ pītavapuḥ kirīṭī caturbhujo daṇḍadharaśca
hārī ।
carmāsibhṛtsomasutaḥ sadā me siṁhādhirūḍho
varado budho'stu ॥ 4 ॥
om pītāmbaraḥ pītavapuḥ kirīṭī caturbhujo devaguruḥ
praśāntaḥ ।
dadhāti daṇḍaṁ ca kamaṇḍaluṁ ca tathā'kṣasūtraṁ
varado'stu mahyam ॥ 5 ॥
om śvetāmbaraḥ śvetavapuḥ kirīṭī caturbhujo daityaguruḥ
praśāntaḥ ।
tathākṣasūtraṁ ca kamaṇḍaluṁ ca daṇḍaṁ ca
bibhradvarado'stu mahyam ॥ 6 ॥
om nīladyutiḥ śūladharaḥ kirīṭī gṛdhrasthitastrāsakaro
dhanuṣmān ।
caturbhujaḥ sūryasutaḥ praśāntaḥ sadāstu mahyaṁ
varado mandagāmī ॥ 7 ॥
om nīlāmbaro nīlavapuḥ kirīṭī karālavaktraḥ karavālaśūlī
caturbhujaścarmadharaśca rāhuḥ siṁhādhirūḍho
varado'stu mahyam ॥ 8 ॥
om dhūmro dvibāhurvarado gadābhṛt gṛdhrāsanastho
vikṛtānanaśca ।
kirīṭakeyuravibhūṣitāṁgaḥ sadāstu me ketugaṇaḥ
praśāntaḥ ॥ 9 ॥

Having thus focussed your mind on the planets now recall the rest altogether with this mantra:

ओं अन्ये किरीटिनः कार्या वरदाभयपाणयः ।
om anye kirīṭinaḥ kāryā varadābhayapāṇayaḥ ।

Pūjā or worship should then follow such remembrance

and concentration, and obeisance should be paid with this mantra:

ओं भूर्भुवः स्वः आवाहिताभ्यो देवताभ्यो नमः । आसनं समर्पयामि । ओं भूर्भुवः स्वः आवाहिताभ्यो देवताभ्यो नमः । पाद्यं समर्पयामि । इत्यादिरीत्या, आचमनं समर्पयामि, स्नानं०, आचमनं०, वस्त्रं०, यज्ञोपवीतं०, गन्धं०, अक्षतं०, पुष्पं०, धूपं०, दीपं०, नैवेद्यं०, आचमनं०, फलं०, ताम्बूलं०, नीराजनं समर्पयामि ।

om bhūrbhuvaḥ svaḥ āvāhitābhyo devatābhyo namaḥ । āsanaṁ samarpayāmi । om bhūrbhuvaḥ svaḥ āvāhitābhyo devatābhyo namaḥ । pādyaṁ samarpayāmi । ityādirītya, ācamanaṁ samarpayāmi, snānaṁ . . . , ācamanaṁ . . . , vastraṁ . . . , yajñopavītaṁ . . . , gandhaṁ . . . , akṣataṁ. . . , puṣpaṁ . . . , dhūpaṁ . . . , dīpaṁ. . ., naivedyaṁ . . . , ācamanaṁ . . . , phalaṁ. . ., tāmbūlaṁ . . . , nīrājanaṁ samarpayāmi ।

The following mantra should be chanted while offering a banner to each planet in keeping with its colour:

ओं भूर्भुवः स्वः आदित्यादिनवग्रहेभ्यो नमः । तत्तद्वर्णपताकाः समर्पयामि ।।

om bhūrbhuvaḥ svaḥ ādityādinavagrahebhyo namaḥ । tattadvarṇapatākāḥ samarpayāmi ।

While worshipping the grahas, due obeisance should also be paid to their chosen and tutelary gods—to what is called *adhidaivata* and *pratyadhidaivata*. The order in which the planets, etc., have been invoked should be strictly followed while worshipping them. If the worshipper so desires, the pūjā rules do not forbid him to add the vyāhṛtis (bhūrbhuvaḥ svaḥ, भूर्भुवः स्वः) before each of the following invocatory mantras:

(नवग्रह)

(१) ओं आदित्याय नमः ।(२) ओं ईश्वराय नमः ।(३) ओं अग्नये नमः ।

(१) ओं सोमाय नमः । (२) ओं उमायै नमः । (३) ओं जलाय नमः ।
(१) ओं भौमाय नमः । (२) ओं स्कन्दाय नमः । (३) ओं भूम्यै नमः ।
(१) ओं बुधाय नमः । (२) ओं नारायणाय नमः । (३) ओं विष्णवे नमः ।
(१) ओं गुरवे नमः । (२) ओं ब्रह्मणे नमः । (३) ओं इन्द्राय नमः ।
(१) ओं शुक्राय नमः । (२) ओं इन्द्राय नमः । (३) ओं इन्द्राण्यै नमः ।
(१) ओं शनैश्चराय नमः । (२) ओं यमाय नमः । (३) ओं प्रजापतये नमः ।
(१) ओं राहवे नमः । (२) ओं कालाय नमः । (३) ओं सर्पेभ्यो नमः ।
(१) ओं केतवे नमः । (२) ओं चित्रगुप्ताय नमः (३) ओं ब्रह्मणे नमः ।।

(पंचलोकपाल)

(१) ओं विनायकाय नमः (२) ओं दुर्गायै नमः (३) ओं वायवे नमः (४) ओं आकाशाय नमः (५) ओं अश्विभ्यां नमः ।।
(१) ओं वास्तोष्पतये नमः (२) ओं क्षेत्राधिपतये (क्षेत्रपालाय) नमः ।।

(दशदिक्पाल)

(१) ओं इन्द्राय नमः (२) ओं अग्नये नमः (३) ओं यमाय नमः (४) ओं निर्ऋतये नमः (५) ओं वरुणाय नमः (६) ओं वायवे नमः (७) ओं कुबेराय (सोमाय) नमः (८) ओं ईशानाय नमः (९) ओं ब्रह्मणे नमः (१०) ओं अनन्ताय नमः ।

(For *Navagrahas*):

1. *om ādityāya namaḥ* । 2. *om īśvarāya namaḥ* । 3. *om agnaye namaḥ* । 1. *om somāya namaḥ* । 2. *om umāyai namaḥ* । 3. *om jalāya namaḥ* । 1. *om bhaumāya namaḥ* । 2. *om skandāya namaḥ* । 3. *om bhūmyai namaḥ* । 1. *om budhāya namaḥ*। 2. *om nārāyaṇāya namaḥ* । 3. *om viṣṇave namaḥ* । 1. *om gurave namaḥ* । 2. *om brahmaṇe namaḥ* । 3. *om indrāya namaḥ* । 1. *om śukrāya namaḥ* । 2. *om indrāya namaḥ* । 3. *om indrāṇyai namaḥ* । 1. *om śanaiścarāya namaḥ* । 2. *om yamāya namaḥ* । 3. *om prajāpataye namaḥ* । 1. *om rāhave namaḥ* । 2. *om kālāya namaḥ* । 3. *om sarpebhyo namaḥ* । 1. *om ketave namaḥ* । 2. *om citraguptāya namaḥ* । 3. *om brahmaṇe namaḥ* ॥

(For Pañcalokapālas):

1. *oṁ vināyakāya namaḥ* । 2. *oṁ durgāyai namaḥ* । 3. *oṁ vāyave namaḥ* । 4. *oṁ ākāśāya namaḥ* । 5. *oṁ aśvibhyāṁ namaḥ* ॥

1. *oṁ vāstoṣpataye namaḥ* । 2. *oṁ kṣetrādhipataye (kṣetrapālāya) namaḥ* ॥

(For Ten Dikpālas):

1. *oṁ indrāya namaḥ* । 2. *oṁ agnaye namaḥ* । 3. *oṁ yamāya namaḥ* । 4. *oṁ nirṛtaye namaḥ* । 5. *oṁ varuṇāya namaḥ* । 6. *oṁ vāyave namaḥ* । 7. *oṁ kuberāya (somāya) namaḥ* 8. *oṁ īśānāya namaḥ* । 9. *oṁ brahmaṇe namaḥ* । 10. *oṁ anantāya namaḥ* ॥

The same mantras can be used, if so desired, for Pañcopacāra or Ṣoḍaśopacāra. With flowers in folded palms offer the blossoms to all the planets, reciting the following mantras:

ओं ब्रह्मा मुरारिस्त्रिपुरान्तकारी भानुः शशी भूमिसुतो बुधश्च ।
गुरुश्च शुक्रः शनिराहुकेतवः सर्वे ग्रहाः शान्तिकरा भवन्तु ।।१।।
सूर्यः शौर्यमथेन्दुरुच्चपदवीं सन्मंगलं मंगलः ।
सद्बुद्धिं च बुधो गुरुश्च गुरुतां शुक्रःशुभं शं शनिः ।
राहुर्बाहुबलं करोतु सततं केतुःकुलस्योन्नतिं।
नित्यं प्रीतिकरा भवन्तु मम ते सर्वेऽनुकूला ग्रहाः ।।२।।

oṁ brahmā murārīstripurāntakārī bhānuḥ śaśī bhūmisuto budhaśca ।
guruśca śukraḥ śanirāhuketavaḥ sarve grahāḥ śāntikarā bhavantu ॥1॥
sūryaḥ śauryamathenduruccapadavīṁ sanmaṁgalaṁ maṁgalaḥ ।
sadbuddhiṁ ca budho guruśca gurutāṁ śukraḥśubhaṁ śaṁ śaniḥ ।
rāhurbāhubalaṁ karotu śatataṁ ketuḥ kulasyonnatiṁ ।
nityaṁ prītikarā bhavantu mama te sarve'nukūlā grahāḥ ॥2॥

Recitation of these mantras done, keep the blossoms on

each of the planets and other deities and bow to them with folded hands:

ओं आयुश्च वित्तं च तथा सुखं च धर्मार्थलाभौ बहुपुत्रतां च ।
शत्रुक्षयं राजसु पूज्यतां च तुष्टा ग्रहाः क्षेमकरा भवन्तु ।।
अनया पूजया आवाहिता देवाः प्रीयन्ताम् ।।

om āyuśca vittaṁ ca tathā sukhaṁ ca dharmārthalābhau bahuputratāṁ ca ||
śatrukṣayaṁ rājasu pūjyatāṁ ca tuṣṭā grahāḥ kṣemakarā bhavantu ||
anayā pūjayā āvāhitā devāḥ prīyantām ||

Last but not least is the saṁkalpa for the sacrificial fee to be paid to the officiating priest for conducting one of the most solemn of the pūjās. The saṁkalpa is as follows:

ओं अद्य पूर्वोक्तविशेषणविशिष्टायां शुभपुण्यतिथौ अमुकशर्म्माहम् अमुककर्मणि सवरुणादित्यादिग्रहाणामधिदैवतप्रत्यधिदैवतविनायकादिपंचलोकपालवास्तोष्पतिक्षेत्रपालेन्द्रादिदशदिक्पालसहितानां पूजायाः सांगतासिद्धये इमां दक्षिणाममुकपरिमितां यथानामगोत्राय ब्राह्मणाय दास्ये ओं तत्सन्न मम ।

om adya pūrvoktaviśeṣaṇaviśiṣṭāyāṁ śubhapuṇyatithau amukaśarmmāham amukakarmaṇi savaruṇādityādigrahāṇāmadhidaivatapratyadhidaivatavināyakādipaṁcalokapālavāstoṣpatikṣetrapālendrādidaśadikpālasahitānāṁ pūjāyāḥ sāṁgatāsiddhaye imāṁ dakṣiṇāmamukaparimitāṁ yathānāmagotrāya brāhmaṇāya dāsye aum tatsanna mama ।

Pay the fee as thus resolved. The purohita on his part should gratefully acknowledge it with ओं स्वस्ति (om svasti). The householder should then say ओं एतद्ग्रहाद्यर्चनं परिपूर्णमस्तु (om etadgrahādyarcanaṁ paripūrṇamastu). With his wonted courtesy and unaffected contentment, the brāhmaṇa would thus reply: ओं अस्तु परिपूर्णम् (om astu paripūrṇam).

Chapter III

The Tonsure

Such ceremonies as cūḍā and upanayana are performed in a pavilion especially erected for the purpose. The Maithils of Mithilā often ignore this custom. In Uttar Pradesh the practice of performing the saṁskāras in a pavilion is limited only to the marriages of daughters. What they do on such occasions is to implant the pole of a plough where they anoint the body of the boy with turmeric paste. This is done only when the upanayana is performed with the caula, although this should be done only in the latter case. In certain regions and states of the country they also tie a bracelet round the boy's hand. Generally speaking, this should be done before the day fixed for the performance of the caula and the upanayana. But remember that no ceremonial act should be performed on the third, sixth or ninth day prior to it. Some parents, who pride themselves on possessing an avant-garde taste, tie a sort of twisted hair round their son's head. The reason is that the natural hair is not allowed to grow. If there is no wig in place of the natural hair, on whom will the ceremony be performed?

It is necessary to bear in mind that what is called cūḍākaraṇa is 'keeping a lock of hair on the top of the head'. Dwelling at considerable length on what the caula or tonsure ceremony is, Swāmī Sahajānand Sarasvatī makes some important preliminary observations. He highlights, in the first place, the importance of the ceremony, its name and nature, and then adds that so long as a boy does not undergo the experience of tonsure the hairs on his head are of almost equal length.

With the tonsure ceremony duly performed, the most sacred part of which is the shaving and cutting these hairs, the boy begins to keep a single lock of hair appropriately called coṭī or śikhā in common parlance. A coṭī, śikhā or a cūḍā is only a tuft or lock of hair on the crown of the head. Suśruta, we are told, held the view that 'shaving and cutting the hair and nails remove impurities and give delight, lightness, prosperity, courage, and happiness'. To anthropologists however, the ceremony has a dedicatory purpose. The hairs of the boy were symbolically offered as a gift to propitiate a deity or to evoke his blessings. The anthropologists' stands in this respect are perhaps untenable. The Gṛhyasūtras and the smṛtis are silent on the question of the dedicatory motive underlying the cūḍākaraṇa, caula or tonsure ceremony.

The common Hindu in north India is not unaware of the importance of the ceremony and the variety of its name in the vernaculars. Some people also call it muṇḍana, the educated cūḍākaraṇa, yet others caula. One of the customs widely prevalent is that people perform the tonsure ceremony first at the time of the upanayana, which succeeds the former. No less regrettable is the fact that the saṁskāras of the Vedārambha and the samāvartana are now almost extinct. That is why householders prefer to perform the Vedārambha first, then the samāvartana immediately after the upanayana, thus tagging all these sacraments together. Lumping these ceremonies in this manner and performing them successively one after the other are not legitimatized by the śāstras.

The ninety-second mantra of chapter XIX of the *Śukla Yajurveda* brings out the symbolical meaning of the hairs and top-knot केशा न शीर्षन्यशसे श्रियै शिखा (keśā na śīrṣanyaśase śriyai śikhā). Here न (na) connotes 'च' (ca) yielding the meaning केशाश्च शीर्षन् यशसे श्रियै शिखा (keśāśca śīrṣan yaśase śriyai śikhā). 'Śīrṣan' signifies those on the head. Even science today gives credence to the belief that the top-knot is a kind of lightning conductor; and it is a human device, a preventive measure against external lightning and a stabilizer and controller of inner electric current. Thus what is superstitious absurdity to the moderns was a scientific necessity to the ancients. All arguments, their pros and cons, lead to the conclusion that when cutting the hair, a tuft or a lock must be left on the top of the head.

According to śāstras and the later law-givers, the cūḍākaraṇa is performed for envigorating the intellect, the centre that activates all other organs of the human body. A brain that suffers from torpidity needs to be whetted. That function is performed by this purificatory ceremony, the principal aim of its performance being cleansing the head. The boy whose head is shaved clean is thus licensed to keep his head hairless with only a tuft from time to time and not to let anything unclean accumulate there. An untidy head with dishevelled locks of hairs, all matted and lousy, affects the body and makes it unhealthy. The ceremony, which marks the cutting of boy's hairs with which he was born, has an explicit symbolical meaning as well. His animality born in the form of his hairs now comes to an end and he enters a new stage of life altogether—that of adolescence or of youth. Fully conscious that the ceremony of tonsure has a meaning more subtle than what meets the eye, the authorities had said:

कल्याणाय च लोकानां प्रयोगो बुद्धिज्ञानयोः ।
साफल्यं मानवीयस्य जीवनस्येह निश्चितम् ।।
kalyāṇāya ca lokānāṁ prayogo buddhijñānayoḥ ।
sāphalyaṁ mānavīyasya jīvanasyeha niścitam ॥

The meaning of the verse is simple: whatever is done for sharpening the mind and adding to knowledge is for the well-being of the world and, indeed, brings success to human endeavour. As for the age of the boy when the cūḍākaraṇa (also called keśānta) ceremony should take place, the Pāraskara Gṛhyasūtra maintains:

साम्वत्सरिकस्य चूडाकरणं, तृतीये वाऽप्रतिहते,
षोडशवर्षस्य केशांतो, यथा मंगलं वा ।

sāmvatsarikasya cūḍākaraṇaṁ, tṛtīye vā'pratihate, ṣoḍaśavarṣasya keśāṁto, yathā maṁgalaṁ vā ।

When the son is one year old, the cūḍākaraṇa (i.e. the tonsure of his head) should be performed. It may be performed before the lapse of the third year. When he is sixteen years old, the keśānta should be done. *Manusmṛti* confirms this view:

चूडाकर्म द्विजातीनां सर्वेषामेव जन्मतः ।
प्रथमेऽब्दे तृतीये वा कर्त्तव्यं श्रुतिचोदनात् ।।

cūḍākarma dvijātīnāṁ sarveṣāmeva janmataḥ ।
prathame'bde tṛtīye vā karttavyaṁ śruticodanāt ॥

According to the teaching of the revealed texts, the cūḍākarma (tonsure) must be performed, for the sake of spiritual merit, by all twice-born men in the first or third year.

Different castes and class perform the tonsure at different times. In certain families this ceremony is performed when the boy is five years old, while in certain others it takes place at the time of the initiation. In the event of the mother being pregnant in the third year of her son, the tonsure should be postponed to the fifth year. If providence so decrees that the mother be pregnant once again in her son's fifth year, then the age bar shall not apply nor will the mother's pregnancy be an hindrance. Performance of the tonsure at the time of the initiation is also permitted. The rules forbidding the performance of the tonsure, initiation and marriage ceremonies include the one concerning the mother's menstrual period when she is impure. All these ceremonies must be performed after or before the menstrual cycle, in a state of complete physical purity. In the event of the father's absence, any aged member of the family—grandfather, uncle, etc.—or even the mother can be invested with his role (i.e., play the part of the father). It may so happen that the boy falls ill on the eve of any of these functions. Care should be taken to initiate them only after the boy recovers and is physically sound once again.

In the opinion of the śāstras shaving of the head is forbidden for six months if the initiation, marriage, and other important ceremonies have taken place in the families of any of the relations up to three generations. The tonsure ceremony should not be performed until the obsequial rites, including the monthly obsequies have ended in the event of a death in the family of any of the relations up to four generations. No two brothers born of the same mother should have their keśānta ceremony performed in the same year (samvatsara). These are conditional injunctions. To these may be added one more: if a bereavement takes place after the ceremony has begun, the tonsure can be gone through after burnt oblations have been offered reciting the *Kuṣmāṇḍa*[1] and the gift of a cow has been made.

On an auspicious day and in an auspicious hour the parents should get ready for the ceremony, dressed up in all their finery after taking a bath. The boy should likewise be bathed and properly dressed; he should preferably be given the best garments his parents can afford. The mother, holding the boy in her lap, should take a pure seat, facing the sacrificial fire. The father likewise should occupy a comfortable seat, perform the ācamana and prāṇāyāma, and with the recitation of the following mantra and mentioning at the outset his native place and time, resolve that:

अमुककुमारस्य बीजगर्भसमुद्भवैनोनिबर्हणबलायुर्वर्चोमेधाऽभिवृद्धिद्वारा परमेश्वरप्रीत्यर्थं चौलकर्म करिष्ये ।
तत्र निर्विघ्नार्थं गणपतिपूजनं स्वस्तिपुण्याहवाचनं मातृकापूजनं च करिष्ये ।

amukakumārasya bījagarbhasamudbhavainonibarhaṇa-balāyurvarcomedhā'bhivṛddhidvārā parameśvara-prītyarthaṁ caulakarma kariṣye ।
tatra nirvighnārthaṁ gaṇapatipūjanaṁ svastipuṇyāha-vācanaṁ mātṛkāpūjanaṁ ca kariṣye ॥

---

1. Name of the verses VS. XX, 14-16 (spoken in a certain rīti for penance or expiation).

If the initiation is to follow the tonsure, then in place of 'caulakarma kariṣye' say 'cūḍopanayane kariṣye' and at the end of puṇyāhavācana say 'Prajāpatiḥ prīyatām'. For the full fruition of the tonsure ceremony let three brāhmaṇas be fed with resolve and offer an oblation with fire in accordance with the prescribed law. Then perform the first pañcabhūsaṁskāra[1] on the sacrificial altar. Having broomed the surface of the altar with three blades of kuśa grass, throw away the latter into the north-eastern quarter. It is then that the altar is coated with cowdung and with the root of the sruva three lines are drawn one after another from west to east. Throw away the earth from the grooves made by the sruva and sprinkle the altar with water. Having done so bring the sabhya[2] fire and, facing the west, position it. Thereafter the mother with her son in the lap, both elegantly dressed up, should sit to the west of the fire and on the left or north of the host. This follows the installation of the fire with pañcabhūsaṁskāra.

Then the latter should select the Brahmā, make him go round the fire and having seated him facing the north, keep the praṇītā vessel before him. Having kept the praṇītājar to the north of the fire spread four handfuls of kuśa grass around it (the fire) and seize the jar already kept (*prāksaṁstha pātrāsādana*) to the north of the fire. Then have five kuśa blades, three for pavitracchedana and two for purifying and sprinkling ghī, prokṣaṇī jar, vessel with clarified butter, sammārjana kuśa (kuśa for anointing, smearing), upayamana kuśa (a ladle used at sacrifices), three samidhās, sruva, clarified butter, jar filled with rice, etc. May these objects be arranged in the east of the pavitracchedana kuśas in order

1. 'Ground Preparation', a term for five methods of preparing and consecrating the khara (a quadrangular mound of earth for receiving the sacrificial vessel) at a ceremony.
2. One of the five sacred fires called pañcāgni.

stated. All other objects necessary for the caula should be arranged in the same order as all other objects; the brimful vessel brought at the end, the copper vessel containing some lukewarm water and then another containing cold water, ghī, curd, and butter, a small lump of any of these kept in a jar followed by a ten or twelve aṅgulas long pin which is white at three places in the middle obtained from *sāhī*,[1] twenty-seven kuśa blades with pointed tips all ten or twelve aṅgulas long (if possible divided into nine separate bunches of three blades each bound with hand-spun thread), an iron-knife with a copper handle or band, a barber, dung obtained from an uncastrated bull and kept in a bronze vessel, and the sacrificial fee for the ācārya. Keep all these in due order. Having done this perform the rest of the propitious rites, such as installation of the sacrificial fire[2] on the altar or in the pit especially dug for it, and all other functions related to it which sanctify an object or a ritual.

The next few steps in the ceremony include taking three chedana kuśas and cutting two of them, each of the span of the thumb and the forefinger. Then with the right hand which has a ring of kuśa grass on it pour the praṇītā water into the prokṣaṇī vessel three times. With the pavitras (two blades of kuśa grass) throw the prokṣaṇī water up into the air. This should be followed by pouring praṇītā water into that contained in the prokṣaṇī three times. The next act is sprinkling water on the butter bowl and keeping the prokṣaṇī right in the middle of the sacrificial fire and praṇītā. This done, pour clarified butter into the butter bowl with another container. Keep the butter on the fire, wave dry kuśas after having ignited them over it (clarified butter) and then throw them into the fire. These ceremonial acts are followed by

---

1. an animal with a small thorny body.
2. i.e. kuśakaṇḍikā which usually signifies this. It is placing the sacrificial fire into a special pit or on the altar.

heating the sruva (wooden ladle) three times and then having brushed them with the root of the kuśas, causing it to be wet with praṇītā water. Repeat a part of this process by heating the sruva three times once again and then keeping it on the ground towards the south of the sacrificial fire. The boiling ghṛta should then be brought down to cool and kept to the north. These sacrificial formalities do not come to an end with this. The householder is advised to keep patience, get up with the upayamana kuśas in his left hand, and with his mind fixed on Prajāpati offer an oblation of three firewoods, all drowned in ghī. This act of throwing the three pieces of firewood should be silently performed one after another without uttering any mantra. Then, taking his seat once again, the householder sprinkles water all around him while circulating the prokṣaṇī water from the north-east to the end of the north in a circumambulatory order. He should then keep the two kuśa blades (pavitras) into the praṇītā jar and abandon the prokṣaṇī. His next act is to touch the ground with the right knee and after being touched from behind by the Brahmā to offer butter oblations with the sruva to the sacrificial fire. After the oblation has been offered, let him drop with the same kuśa spoon the remaining drops of clarified butter into the prokṣaṇī. Now is the time when he should concentrate on Prajāpati and offer him an oblation by sprinkling clarified butter upon the sacrificial fire. This should be done silently. Offer two oblations of the āghāra, three of the mahāvyāhṛtis,[1] five of the sarvaprāyaścitta and two each

---

1. ॐ प्रजापतये स्वाहा । इदं प्रजापतये इति मनसा । ॐ इन्द्राय स्वाहा । इदमिन्द्राय इत्याघारौ । ॐ अग्नये स्वाहा । इदमग्नये । ॐ सोमाय स्वाहा । इदं सोमाय इत्याज्यभागौ । ॐ भूः स्वाहा । इदमग्नये । ॐ भुवः स्वाहा । इदं वायवे । ॐ स्वः स्वाहा । इदं सूर्य्याय । एता महाव्याहृतयः ।

om prajāpataye svāhā । idaṁ prajāpataye iti manasā । om indrāya svāhā । idamindrāya ityāghārau । om agnaye svāhā । idamagnaye । om somāya svāhā । idaṁ somāya ityājyabhāgau । om bhūḥ svāhā । idam-agnaye । om bhuvaḥ svāhā । idaṁ vāyave । om svaḥ svāhā । idaṁ sūryyāya । etā mahāvyāhṛtayaḥ ।

of the prājāpatya and sviṣṭakṛta. In this manner offer fourteen oblations altogether and then having drunk a little potion (saṁśravaprāśana), wash hands, sip a little water, offer the requisite sacrificial fee to the Brahmā and sprinkle a few drops of water on the head from the praṇītā. The householder should then drop the remaining water in the north-east quarter. His next act should be to mix up the ghṛta with the kuśas and then pick them up one by one and throw them into the fire.

Braiding

Now the customary rituals should be performed. While mixing hot water with cold, recite the following mantra and pour a little butter-milk into the water. A little butter or curd should also be dropped into it. The mantra to be spoken is as follows:

ॐ उष्णेन वाय उदकेनेह्यदिते केशान् वप ।
om uṣṇena vāya udakenehyadite keśān vapa ।

The boy, sitting with his face to the east, must have his hairs braided on the southern, western and northern sides. Moistening the first right side braid with the water mixed with butter, recite the following mantra:

ॐ सवित्रा प्रसूता दैव्या आप उन्दन्तु ते तनूम् ।
दीर्घायुत्वाय बलाय वर्चसे ।
om savitrā prasūtā daivyā āpa undantu te tanūm ।
dīrghāyutvāya balāya varcase ।

Now follow the following instructions:

Divide the hairs braided on the right side into three parts; separate the hairs from one another in each part with the pin (obtained from sāhī); now subdivide each part into three; recite the following mantra tucking the tips of three kuśas (picked up from the twenty-seven kuśa blades already kept there) in the roots of the first bunch of hairs out of the three:

ॐ ओषधे त्रायस्व–
om oṣadhe trāyasva

Having articulated the mantra, recite the following while picking up the razor:

ॐ शिवो नामासि स्वधितिस्ते पिता नमस्तेऽअस्तु मा मा हिꣳसीः ।
om śivo nāmāsi svadhitiste pitā namaste'astu mā mā hiṁsīḥ ।

While cutting the hairs with the three kuśas shoved into them, mutter the following:

ॐ निवर्तयाम्यायुषेऽन्नाद्याय प्रजननाय रायस्पोषाय सुप्रजास्त्वाय सुवीर्याय ।
om nivartayāmyāyuse'nnādyāya prajananāya rāyaspo-ṣāya suprajāstvāya suvīryāya ।

Other instructions to be followed thereafter may be stated as follows:

Of the three parts of the hairs on the right side, cut those on the western side along with the kuśas; keep the hair thus shaved on cowdung towards the north; do this in a sitting posture. The following mantra is to be chanted while cutting the boy's hair:

ॐ येनावपत् सविता क्षुरेण सोमस्य राज्ञो वरुणस्य विद्वान् ।
तेन ब्रह्माणो वपतेदमस्यायुष्यं जरदष्टिर्यथासत् ।
om yenāvapat savitā kṣureṇa somasya rājño varuṇasya vidvān ।
tena brahmāṇo vapatedamasyāyuṣyaṁ jaradaṣṭiryathā-sat ।

Now keep three kuśas in each of the two parts of the right-side braid already moistened. As before, cut them too and keep them on cowdung. But remember that no mantra is to be recited this time for the later rituals are performed with silent and unchanted mantra (tūṣṇīṁ mantrapāṭha).

Follow the same procedure with regard to the braid on the

western side of head, but do not recite any mantra while dividing the hairs into the three parts with sāhī's pin. The rest of the rituals are done with recitation of their relevant mantras. The first braid on the western side should be cut with the following:

ॐ त्र्यायुषं जमदग्नेः कश्यपस्य त्र्यायुषम् ।
यद्देवेषु त्र्यायुषं तन्नोऽअस्तु त्र्यायुषम् ।।
om tryāyuṣaṁ jamadagneḥ kaśyapasya tryāyuṣam ।
yaddeveṣu tryāyuṣaṁ tanno'astu tryāyuṣam ॥

The same process is repeated while cutting the braid on the northern side except that the following mantra is muttered when cutting the first of the three parts:

ॐ येन भूरिश्चरादिवं ज्योक्च पश्चाद्धि सूर्यम् ।
तेन ते वपामि ब्रह्मणा जीवातवे जीवनाय सुश्लोक्याय स्वस्तये ।
om yena bhūriścarādivaṁ jyokca paścāddhi sūryam ।
tena te vapāmi brahmaṇā jīvātave jīvanāya suślokyāya svastaye ॥

Once the hairs thus shaved are kept on the cowdung, the boy's head should be thoroughly moistened. Mutter the following formula while waving the razor three times all around the head in a circumambulatory order:

ॐ यत् क्षुरेण मज्जयता सुपेशसा वप्त्रा वा वपति केशाञ्छिन्धि शिरो मास्यायुः प्रमोषीः ।
om yat kṣureṇa majjayatā supeśasā vaptrā vā vapati keśāñcchindhi śiro māsyāyuḥ pramoṣīḥ ।

The first waving of the razor should accompany the recitation of this mantra, but not the remaining two. The shaving done, wet the whole head with what is a mixture of hot and cold water containing a little butter as well. Say 'ॐ अक्षिण्वन् परिवप' (om akṣiṇvan parivapa) while handing the razor to the barber. What it means is that the latter should now accomplish his task with great care.

Direction for Tonsure

The barber should perform his duties with considerable sense and circumspection. He should shave all except those which the family custom does not permit removal. Different families follow different traditions and customs of having their heads tonsured. The śāstras are therefore silent as to the amount of hair to be retained at the tonsure ceremony. One final act in the drama remains to be staged. This time the protagonist is none but the boy's mother who collects the hair cut by the barber, wraps it up in a new cloth and keeps it on a massed lump (piṇḍa) of cowdung, curd and milk. Her role contains two more functions: to offer the last oblation with the following mantra:

ॐ मूर्धानं दिवो अरतिं पृथिव्या वैश्वानरमृत आजातमग्निम् ।
कवि ꣡ सम्राजमतिथिं जनानामासन्ना पात्रं जनयन्त देवाः स्वाहा ।

om mūrdhānaṁ divo aratiṁ pṛthivyā vaiśvānaramṛta ājātamagnim ।
kaviṁ samrājamatithiṁ janānāmāsannā pātraṁ janayanta devāḥ svāhā ।

and collect some ashes from the fire altar with the root of the sruva and with the tip of her right ring finger to apply the same, with the muttering of the following sacred formula, to her own and the boy's forehead, throat, right arm and chest:

ॐ त्र्यायुषं जमदग्नेः, इति ललाटे ।
ॐ कश्यपस्य त्र्यायुषम्, इति ग्रीवायाम् ।
ॐ यद्देवेषु त्र्यायुषम्, इति दक्षिणबाहुमूले ।
ॐ तन्नो अस्तु त्र्यायुषम्, इति हृदि ।
om tryāyuṣaṁ jamadagneḥ, iti lalāṭe ।
om kaśyapasya tryāyuṣam, iti grīvāyām ।
om yaddeveṣu tryāyuṣam, iti dakṣiṇabāhumūle ।
om tanno astu tryāyuṣam, iti hṛdi ।

While applying the ashes to the boy substitute 'tatte' ('तत्ते') for 'tanno' ('तन्नो').

Having completed all these rites and rituals, carry the hairs wrapped in the piece of new cloth along with the cowdung to the cowshed, where these should be kept in a pit especially dug and designed for them. Alternatively, they can be buried on a river bank or on the bank of a pond. The last act with which the ceremony closes is that he offers the sacrificial fee or makes the gift of a cow to the officiating priest and, having pleased him, solicits his blessings and invites ten brāhmaṇas to luncheon.

CHAPTER IV

Upanayana

The importance of the upanayana[1] in the life of an orthodox Hindu is recognized by all institutors of the Hindu law. To them it is one of the sixteen saṁskāras or purificatory rites in which "the boy is invested with the sacred thread and thus endowed with second or spiritual birth and qualified to learn the Veda by heart." It is widely held that a brāhmaṇa is initiated in the eighth year, a kṣatriya in the eleventh and a vaiśya in the twelfth.[2] Manu, who must have been one of the earliest codifiers of the view if not its institutor, also proposes that the initiation of a brāhmaṇa who desires proficiency in sacred learning should take place in the fifth year after conception, that of a kṣatriya who wishes to become power-

1. The word 'upanayana' stands for that ceremony in which a boy goes to an ācārya well-versed in the Vedas with a view to be initiated into Vedic studies or a Guru draws a boy towards himself and initiates him into one of the three twice-born classes. The ceremony, as it is performed today, is only the shadowy outline of the original sacrament, its veneer devoid of its real spirit. Originally, when the student went to his ācārya, the first thing the latter did was to perform the boy's saṁskāra, which means purifying, rubbing, cleansing or removing impurities and blemishes before inculcating noble qualities. What is popularly designated as 'yajñopavīṭa' or 'janeū' today was in the past also called 'vratabandha', a name given to the ceremony in some parts of India even today. From the day the initiation ceremony took place, the young celibate committed himself to a life of austerity and abstinence; he chose to lead a life rigorously disciplined by vows and disciplinary rules. There was a time when such 'vratabandhas' marked the opening of a new chapter in the life of a true celibate who began after his initiation to sleep on the ground, maintain celibacy, etc.
2. See Appendix I.

ful in the sixth, and that of a vaiśya who longs for success in his business in the eighth.

ब्रह्मवर्चसकामस्य कार्यं विप्रस्य पञ्चमे ।
राज्ञो बलार्थिनः षष्ठे वैश्यस्येहार्थिनोऽष्टमे ।।
bramhavarcasakāmasya karyaṁ viprasya pañcame ।
rājño balārthinaḥ ṣaṣṭhe vaiśyasyehārthino'ṣṭame ॥

For others this code was modified, its alternative being contained in the verse that follows. In it Manu said that "In the eighth year after conception, one should perform the initiation of a brāhmaṇa, in the eleventh after conception that of a kṣatriya, but in the twelfth that of a vaiśya."

गर्भाष्टमेऽब्दे कुर्वीत ब्राह्मणस्योपनायनम् ।
गर्भादेकादशे राज्ञो गर्भात्तु द्वादशे विशः ।।
garbhāṣṭame'bde kurvīta brāhmaṇasyopanāyanam ।
garbhādekādaśe rājño garbhāttu dvādaśe viśaḥ ॥

Realizing the importance of the initiation ceremony Manu lays down elaborate instructions, including those with regard to the stuff of which the girdle should be made. The first and foremost among them is the following:

मौञ्जी त्रिवृत्समा श्लक्ष्णा कार्या विप्रस्य मेखला ।
क्षत्रियस्य तु मौर्वी ज्या वैश्यस्य शणतान्तवी ।।
mauñjī trivṛtsamā ślakṣṇā kāryā viprasya mekhalā ।
kṣatriyasya tu maurvī jyā vaiśyasya śaṇatāntavī ॥

The girdle of a brāhmaṇa shall consist of a triple cord of muñja grass, smooth and soft; that of a kṣatriya, of a bowstring, made of mūrvā fibres; that of a vaiśya of hempen threads. Aware that the sponsor of the ceremony may not find muñja grass easily available, he names its appropriate substitutes:

मुञ्जालाभे तु कर्तव्याः कुशाश्मन्तकबल्बजैः ।
त्रिवृता ग्रन्थिनैकेन त्रिभिः पञ्चभिरेव वा ।।

muñjālābhe tu kartavyāḥ kuśāśmantakabalbajaiḥ ।
trivṛtā granthinaikena tribhiḥ pañcabhireva vā ॥

If muñja grass be not procurable, the girdles may be made of kuśa, aśmantaka and balbaja fibres, with a single threefold knot, or with three or five knots according to the custom of the family. Having designated the inherent staff of the girdle, Manu then goes on to mention the stuff of which the sacred thread should be made:

कार्पासमुपवीतं स्याद्विप्रस्योर्ध्ववृतं त्रिवृत् ।
शणसूत्रमयं राज्ञो वैश्यस्याविकसौत्रिकम् ।।
kārpāsamupavītaṁ syādviprasyordhvavṛtaṁ trivṛt ।
śaṇasūtramayaṁ rājño vaiśyasyāvikasautrikam ॥

The sacrificial cord of a brāhmaṇa shall be made of cotton, it shall be twisted to the right, and consist of three threads; that of a kṣatriya of hempen threads, and that of a vaiśya of woollen threads. Lest one should think that the initiation ceremony in which the focal point is a mere cord or some twisted threads is a perfunctory ritual, it must be stressed that the so-called 'cord' is invested with considerable symbolical significance. It symbolizes submission to sensory discipline, to what is called 'vratabandha' or voluntary acceptance of a life which may ensure and lead to learning good conduct, robustness and sagacity. The word 'yajñopavīta' is a compound of 'yajña' and 'upavīta', the latter standing for that string, thread or cord which reaches the waist on its right side through the left shoulder, backbone and navel. The sacred thread in common use these days is unlike this. It falls lower than the waist which is not proper. The 'upavīta' is a mark and evidence of the fact that the bachelor wearing it can now perform sacrifices; he is now in full possession of this right which was denied to him earlier.

Performance of sacrifices presupposes a thorough knowledge of the Vedas and their auxiliaries. This is evident from Kṛṣṇa's postulate that it is in the Vedas that one finds the sacrifices elaborately dealt with and the modes of their performance:

एवं बहुविधा यज्ञा वितता ब्रह्मणो मुखे ।
evaṁ bahuvidhā yajñā vitatā brhmaṇo mukhe ।
(*The Gītā* 4.32)

By many people who have fully realized the sacredness of the thread they wear it is also called 'Brahmasūtra', the word 'Brahma' being a synonym for the Veda and 'sūtra' for the indicator or the interpreter. 'Brahmasūtra' therefore conveys that the bounden duty of a student is to study the Vedas and their auxiliaries, to acquire their true knowledge. It also distinguishes the bearer from others and shows that he is one of the three top varṇas, for, as Tulasī has said ''द्विज चिह्न जनेउ उघार तपी'' (dvija cihna janeu ughāra tapī).

The specialist's skill in making and weaving the sacred thread includes taking some hand-spun thread, making threefolds of it and then rolling them up ninety-six times round the four fingers of the right hand all touching one another. The length of the thread rolled up is sufficient enough to make a single piece of sacred thread. As a matter of fact, the word 'triguṇa' is often used to signify Ṛk, Yajuḥ and Sāma collectively called 'trayī', triple vidyā or threefold knowledge. The rolling up of the cotton thread round the four fingers signifies the four ways of muttering the three classes of the Vedic mantras, viz. padapāṭha, kramapāṭha, ghanapāṭha and jaṭāpāṭha.

The bachelor being initiated is required to carry a staff, an inviolable rule not to be infringed by the bachelor or his guardian. The staff is thus described:

ब्राह्मणो बैल्वपालाशौ क्षत्रियो वाटखादिरौ ।
पैलवौदुम्बरौ वैश्यो दण्डानर्हन्ति धर्मतः ।।
brāhmaṇo bailvapālāśau kṣatriyo vāṭakhādirau ।
pailavaudumbarau vaiśyo daṇḍānarhanti dharmataḥ ॥

A brāhmaṇa shall carry, according to the sacred law, a staff of bilva or palāśa; a kṣatriya of vaṭa or khadira; and a vaiśya, of pilu or udumbara. Manu was not unaware that staffs vary in size. An upholder of the rule of law as well as clarity and an arch-rejector of ambivalence, he specifies the size of the staff with the following verse:

केशान्तिको ब्राह्मणस्य दण्डः कार्यः प्रमाणतः ।
ललाटसंमितो राज्ञः स्यात्तु नासान्तिको विशः ।
keśāntiko brāhmaṇasya daṇḍaḥ kāryaḥ pramāṇataḥ ।
lalāṭasaṁmito rājñaḥ syāttu nāsāntiko viśaḥ ।

The staff of a brāhmaṇa shall be made of such length as to reach the end of his hair; that of kṣatriya, to reach his forehead; and that of a vaiśya, to reach the tip of his nose.

All this is indicative of the importance Manu attached to the ceremony of initiation. That the śūdras were debarred from performing this sacred rite and wearing yajñopavīta is no less evident from the writings of other law-givers. They are unanimous, however, in maintaining that 'without the upanayana none could call himself a twice-born'. For centuries the Hindus have excommunicated those who have not undergone this saṁskāra and obtained the dvija's passport to the literary treasures of the Hindus. "It was also a means of communion with the society," says Rājbalī Pandey, "because without it none could marry an Aryan girl. Thus the Hindu ideal made universal education the indispensable test and insignia of their community. The most striking fact in connection with the upanayana is that by virtue of its performance the initiated ranked as a dvija or twice-born. This transformation of man's personality by means of religious ceremonies compares well with the Christian rite of baptism, which is regarded as a sacrament and carries with it a spiritual effect to reform the life of man."

The saṁskāra has to be performed at an auspicious time. The sun should be in the northern hemisphere; in the case of vaiśya boys the sun could be in the southern hemisphere also. Here, again, distinctions between one caste and another were carried to extremes as in most other cases. The sacrament of initiation could be performed by different castes in different seasons. The brāhmaṇas could perform the ceremony in spring, the kṣatriya in summer, the vaiśya in autumn and a rathakāra in the rainy season. The allocation of different seasons to the different castes for the investiture ceremony has a symbolical overtone. The different seasons symbolized the different temperaments of the three varṇas. The spring, moderately cold and warm, is symbolical of the moderate temperament, the brāhmaṇic temperament; the summer heat symbolized the haughty kṣatriya, the hot-tempered knight; the autumn represented the season of brisk commercial activities suited to the trading class after the end of the rainy season. The rainy season, however irksome to many, was welcomed to the chariot-maker for the easy time it provided. In keeping with the tact and finesse for which the later Indian astrologers were noted, they attached different merits to different months from Māgha to Āṣāḍha:

माघे मासि महाधनो धनपतिः प्रज्ञायुतः फाल्गुने
मेधावी भवति व्रतोपनयने चैत्रे च वेदान्वितः ।
वैशाखे निखिलोपभोगसहितो ज्येष्ठे वरिष्ठो
बुधस्त्वाषाढे सुमहाविपक्षविजयी ख्यातो महापण्डितः ।।

māghe māsi mahādhano danapatiḥ prajñāyutaḥ phālgune
medhāvī bhavati vratopanayane caitre ca vedānvitaḥ ।
vaiśākhe nikhilopabhogasahito jyeṣthe variṣtho budha-
stvāṣāḍhe sumahāvipakṣavijayī khyāto mahāpaṇḍitaḥ ॥

A boy whose upanayana is performed in the month of Māgha becomes wealthy, in the month of Phālguna intelligent, in Caitra talented and well-versed in the Vedas, in Vaiśākha provided with all kinds of enjoyments, in Jyeṣṭha wise and great, and in Āṣāḍha a great conqueror of enemies and famous paṇḍita." Another restriction imposed by the astrologer and the family priest, who was generally adept in interpreting the almanac and astrological literature, was that the initiation ceremony should preferably be performed in the bright half of the month, the brightness being symbolical of learning and wisdom. Among inauspicious occasions unfit for the performance of initiation ceremony were counted all holidays, parvans, and the days of natural abnormality.

The Initiation Proper

On the day preceding that which is fixed for the initiation ceremony the boy should undertake an austerity vow; if he is a brāhmaṇa, he shall not be given any solid food. He should take only milk. If the boy comes of a kṣatriya family all he is permitted to take that day is boiled rice water or barley; the vaiśya boy will subsist on the drink called *śrīkhaṇḍa*. The parents, having washed their bodies with water perfumed, lavendered and sanctified with auspicious materials, should put on new garments, especially having borders. With sandal paste and saffron marks on their foreheads they should enter the pavilion erected a little further away from the pit of the sacrificial fire and facing the east take a seat made of a pure stuff. The father should see to it that his wife sits on his right and the boy on his wife's right. Having accomplished this part of the ceremony with due sincerity to the prescribed code, the householder is then required to utter the saṁkalpa, pronouncing his name, gotra, etc. for the success of the initiation rites. This, however, should follow the customary acts of ācamana and prāṇāyāma—sipping water and controlling the breath. From the very beginning of the ceremony should both the father and the son have their tufts (cūḍā) on the head properly tied, the father taking extra care to wear his sacred thread hanging from the left shoulder to his right side. The rules, however, forbid the householder to keep the crown tuft tied and the sacred thread in its usual position (from the left shoulder to the right side) while bathing and offering tarpaṇa to the pitṛs. All this presupposes that the householder has a crown tuft and wears a sacred thread, both of which distinguish a savarṇa Hindu.

The scriptures, mainly the sacerdotal law books and catechisms, enjoin the indispensability of the tuft and the thread to all those who profess orthodox Hinduism.

The prescribed saṁkalpa is as follows:

कृच्छ्रत्रयात्मकप्रायश्चित्तप्रत्याम्नायगोनिष्क्रयी भूतयथाशक्तिरजतद्रव्य-दानपूर्वकं द्वादशसहस्त्रं द्वादशाधिकसहस्त्रं वा गायत्रीजपमहं ब्राह्मणद्वारा कारयिष्ये ।

kṛcchratrayātmakaprāyaścittapratyāmnāyagoniṣkrayī bhūtayathāśaktirajatadravyadānapūrvakaṁ dvādaśa sahasraṁ dvādaśādhikasahasraṁ vā gāyatrījapamahaṁ brāhmaṇadvārā kārayiṣye ।

The meaning of all this is that the householder will have twelve thousand or one thousand and twelve Gāyatrī mantras chanted by a brāhmaṇa. It should be borne in mind that if the householder's desire is to have twelve thousand Gāyatrīs muttered, he must not say 'द्वादशाधिकसहस्त्रं' (dvādaśādhikasahasraṁ); if, however, he wants a thousand and twelve Gāyatrīs to be repeated, he should drop 'द्वादशसहस्त्रं' (dvādaśasahasraṁ) from the saṁkalpa. If the householder decides to mutter the Gāyatrī formulas himself, and not get it recited by a brāhmaṇa, he should just say 'करिष्ये' (kariṣye) instead of 'ब्राह्मणद्वारा कारयिष्ये' (brāhmaṇadvārā kārayiṣye). The householder's preoccupation with other duties and responsibilities often prevents him from doing the *japa* himself. It is for this reason that brāhmaṇas are appointed to do the job immediately after the saṁkalpa is uttered. Let a brāhmaṇa be entrusted with the responsibility of repeating the Gāyatrī mantras.

The meaning and significance of the saṁkalpa made by the boy should be explained to him; he should be apprised that by uttering his saṁkalpa he has resolved that he would atone for his transgressions by making gifts of silver equivalent to the price of a cow and having twelve thousand or a thousand and twelve Gāyatrī mantras repeated by a brāhmaṇa. With the brāhmaṇa condescending to repeat the Gāyatrī mantras and taking his seat for the purpose the father should express his resolve to perform the upanayana saṁkalpa in the following words:

> **अस्य कुमारस्य द्विजत्वसिद्धिद्वारा वेदत्रय्यधिकारसिद्ध्यर्थं श्रीपरमेश्वर प्रीत्यर्थं चोपनयनमद्य श्वो वा करिष्ये ।**
> *asya kumārasya dvijatvasiddhidvārā vedatrayyadhikārasiddhyarthaṁ śrīparameśvara prītyarthaṁ copanayanamadya śvo vā kariṣye* ।

In other words, "With a view to pleasing the Almighty so that the boy may by becoming a dvija or twice-born, possess the right of learning the Vedas, I shall have his initiation performed today or tomorrow." If the initiation is to be performed along with the tonsure, the householder should say 'चूडाकर्मोपनयनाख्ये कर्मणी अहं करिष्ये' (cūḍākarmopanayanākhye karmaṇī ahaṁ kariṣye).

What adds to the solemnity of the ceremonies is the performance of a number of 'pūjās', such as Gaṇapatipūjana, svastipuṇyāhavācana, mātṛkāpūjana, nāndīśrāddha, grahapūjā, etc. Each of these ceremonial obeisances should be made with due saṁkalpas and as prescribed by the law books. All this is done on the day preceding that on which the actual initiation rites are performed. The ceremonies mentioned so far are all auxiliaries, complementary and integral, but not the actual initiation. What follows relates directly to and is the ceremony of investiture. The day begins with the tonsure of the boy whose initiation is being performed. Follow the instructions mentioned earlier in the chapter 'The Tonsure'. If the boy has already been tonsured, the ceremonies related and integral to the tonsure need not be performed again. The śāstras forbid the repetition of even as solemn a saṁkalpa as the one called 'pañcabhū' if it was performed on the earlier occasion of the tonsure.

The day, historic according to the Hindu dharmaśāstras in the life of the boy, opens with the priest summoning the boy clad in new clothes and decked with whatever ornaments his parents can afford to the pavilion and making him stand or sit to his right and to the west of the sacrificial fire. The other brāhmaṇas assembled there should then bless him, uttering अब्रह्मन्नित्यम् (abrahmannityam). The ācārya acting as the family priest should ask the boy to repeat the following:

ब्रह्मचर्यमागाम् । (brahmacaryamāgām)
ब्रह्मचार्यसानि । (brahmacāryasāni)

This done, the ācārya should repeat the following mantra while the boy wears the cotton waistband (kaṭisūtra) and the piece of cloth (kaupīna), etc. used by ascetics to cover their privities:

ॐ येनेन्द्राय बृहस्पतिर्वासः पर्यदधादमृतम् ।
तेन त्वा परिदधाम्यायुषे दीर्घायुत्वाय बलाय वर्चसे ।
om yenendrāya bṛhaspatirvāsaḥ paryadadhādamṛtam ।
tena tvā paridadhāmyāyuṣe dīrghāyutvāya balāya varcase ।

The same mantra should be muttered while the boy puts on whatever clothing is necessary for him at this time. This should be followed by the ācamana (the ceremonial sipping of water) by the boy. It is at this stage that the brahmacārī is made to wear a girdle with as many knots in it as there are his seniors (pravaras). A brāhmaṇa's girdle is made of the muñja grass with triple cords, a kṣatriya's of mūrvā fibres and a vaiśya's of hempen threads. Note that these girdles are made strictly in accordance with the varṇa of the boy. It is the ācārya's duty to repeat the following mantra while tying the girdle into a knot after its triple cords have been wound around the waist of the boy one after another.

ॐ इयं दुरुक्तं परिबाधमाना वर्णं पवित्रं पुनती म आगात् ।
प्राणापानाभ्यां बलमादधाना स्वसा देवी सुभगा मेखलेयम् ।
om iyaṁ duruktaṁ paribādhamānā varṇaṁ pavitraṁ

punatī ma āgāt ।
prāṇāpānābhyāṁ balamādadhānā svasā devī subhagā mekhaleyam ।

In keeping with the practice, offer a pair of sacred thread to each brāhmaṇa present. Other offerings to be made to the brāhmaṇas consist of twenty-four small earthen pots filled with grains and sacrificial gifts. While doing so the following mantra should be recited:

ॐ तत्सदद्य (अमुक) गोत्रो (अमुक) शर्मा, वर्मा, गुप्तः अहं स्वकीयोपनयनकर्मविषयकसत्संस्कारप्राप्त्यर्थमिदं भाण्डाष्टात्रयं सयज्ञोपवीतं सदक्षिणं नानानामगोत्रेभ्यो ब्राह्मणेभ्यः संप्रददे ।
om tatsadadya (amuka) gotro (amuka) śarmā, varmā, guptaḥ ahaṁ svakīyopanayanakarmaviṣayakasat-saṁskāraprāptyarthamidaṁ bhāṇḍāṣṭātrayaṁ sayajño-pavītaṁ sadakṣiṇaṁ nānānāmagotrebhyo brāhmaṇe-bhyaḥ saṁpradade ।

After the gifts have been distributed among the brāhmaṇas, the ācārya or the family priest gets ready for performing the initiation. His first act now is to sprinkle a little water on the sacred thread with the recitation of the following three mantras:

ॐ आपो हि ष्ठा मयोभुवस्ता न ऊर्जे दधातन ।
महे रणाय चक्षसे ।। १ ।।
ॐ यो वः शिवतमो रसस्तस्य भाजयतेह नः ।
उशतीरिव मातरः ।। २ ।।
ॐ तस्मा अरं गमाम वो यस्य क्षयाय जिन्वथ ।
आपो जनयथा च नः ।। ३ ।।
om āpo hi ṣṭhā mayobhuvastā na ūrje dadhātana ।
mahe raṇāya cakṣase ॥ 1 ॥
om yo vaḥ śivatamo rasastasya bhājayateha naḥ ।
uśatīriva mātaraḥ ॥ 2 ॥
om tasmā araṁ gamāma vo yasya kṣayāya jinvatha ।

āpo janayathā ca naḥ ॥ 3 ॥

अंगुष्ठभ्रामणक्रिया (*aṁguṣṭhabhrāmaṇakriyā*)

Let the ācārya wave his thumb upon and round the sacred thread with the following three mantras:

ॐ ब्रह्म जज्ञानं प्रथमं पुरस्ताद्विसीमतः सुरुचो वेन आवः ।
स बुध्न्या उपमा अस्य विष्ठाः सतश्चयोनिमसतश्च विवः ।।१।।
ॐ इदं विष्णुर्विचक्रमे त्रेधा निदधे पदम् ।
समूढमस्य पा छं सुरे ।।२।।
ॐ नमस्ते रुद्र मन्यव उतोत इषवे नमः बाहुभ्यामुत ते नमः ।।३।।

om brahma jajñānaṁ prathamaṁ purastādvisīmataḥ suruco vena āvaḥ ।
sa budhnyā upamā asya viṣṭhāḥ sataścayonimasataśca vivaḥ ॥ 1 ॥
om idaṁ viṣṇurvicakrame tredhā nidadhe padam samūḍhamasya pāṁsure ॥ 2 ॥
om namaste rudra manyava utota iṣave namaḥ bāhubhyāmuta te namaḥ ॥ 3 ॥

As soon as the third mantra has been recited the ācārya sanctifies the nine cords or strings of the sacred thread by embedding nine of the gods like Oṁkāra, Agni, Nāga, Soma, Indra, Prajāpati, Vāyu, Sūrya, and Viśvedevas in them. While placing the gods on the nine cords mutter the following nine formulas one after another.

(१) ओंकारं प्रथमे तन्तौ विन्यस्यामि ।
(२) अग्निं द्वितीये तन्तौ विन्यस्यामि ।
(३) नागान् तृतीये तन्तौ विन्यस्यामि ।
(४) सोमं चतुर्थे तन्तौ विन्यस्यामि ।
(५) इन्द्रं पंचमे तन्तौ विन्यस्यामि ।
(६) प्रजापतिं षष्ठे तन्तौ विन्यस्यामि ।
(७) वायुं सप्तमे तन्तौ विन्यस्यामि ।
(८) सूर्यं अष्टमे तन्तौ विन्यस्यामि ।

(९) विश्वेदेवान् नवमे तन्तौ विन्यस्यामि ।

1. *oṁkāraṁ prathame tantau vinyasyāmi* ।
2. *agniṁ dvitīye tantau vinyasyāmi* ।
3. *nāgān tṛtīye tantau vinyasyāmi* ।
4. *somaṁ caturthe tantau vinyasyāmi* ।
5. *indraṁ paṁcame tantau vinyasyāmi* ।
6. *prajāpatiṁ ṣaṣṭhe tantau vinyasyāmi* ।
7. *vāyuṁ saptame tantau vinyasyāmi* ।
8. *sūryaṁ aṣṭame tantau vinyasyāmi* ।
9. *viśvedevān navame tantau vinyasyāmi* ।

The next mandatory injunction is to repeat the Gāyatrī—

ॐ भूर्भुवः स्वः तत्सवितुर्वरेण्यं भर्गो देवस्य धीमहि धियो यो नः प्रचोदयात्
om bhūrbhuvaḥ svaḥ tatsaviturvareṇyaṁ bhargo devasya dhīmahi dhiyo yo naḥ pracodayāt

—ten times with the eyes riveted to the sacred thread. Then displaying the latter to the Sun, let the ācārya repeat the following:

ॐ उपयाम गृहीतोऽसि सावित्रोऽसि च नोधाश्च नोधा असि च नो मयि धेहि ।
जिन्व यज्ञं जिन्व यज्ञपतिं भगाय देवाय त्वा सवित्रे ।
om upayāma gṛhīto'si sāvitro'si ca nodhāśca nodhā asi ca no mayi dhehi ।
jinva yajñaṁ jinva yajñapatiṁ bhagāya devāya tvā savitre ।

Having done so, the ācārya himself should offer the 'yajñopavīta' to the boy who acknowledges the gift with the following mantra:

ॐ यज्ञोपवीतं परमं पवित्रं प्रजापतेर्यत्सहजं पुरस्तात् ।
आयुष्यमग्र्यं प्रतिमुञ्च शुभ्रं यज्ञोपवीतं बलमस्तु तेजः ।
यज्ञोपवीतमसि यज्ञस्य त्वा यज्ञोपवीतेनोपनह्यामि ।।
om yajñopavītaṁ paramaṁ pavitraṁ prajāpateryat-sahajaṁ purastāt ।
āyuṣyamagryaṁ pratimuñca śubhraṁ yajñopavītaṁ balamastu tejaḥ ।

yajñopavītamasi yajñasya tvā yajñopavītenopanahyāmi ||

The boy should raise his right arm and wear the sacred thread on his left shoulder and a new cotton cloth, as directed by the ācārya, who chants the following mantra while the boy is engaged in doing so.

ॐ युवा सुवासाः परिवीत आगात्स उ श्रेयान् भवति जायमानः ।
तं धीरासः कवय उन्नयन्ति स्वाध्यो मनसा देवयन्तः ।।
om yuvā suvāsāḥ parivīta āgātsa u śreyān bhavati jāyamānaḥ ||
taṁ dhīrāsaḥ kavaya unnayanti svādhyo manasā devayantaḥ ||

He also offers him a scarf of deerskin. The young bachelor should accept the muffler with the following:

ॐ मित्रस्य चक्षुर्धरुणं बलीयस्तेजो यशस्वि स्थविर ं समिद्धम् ।
अनाहनस्यं वसनं जरिष्णुः परीदं वाज्यजिनं दधेऽहम् ।
om mitrasya cakṣurdharuṇaṁ balīyastejo yaśasvi sthaviraṁ samiddham |
anāhanasyaṁ vasanaṁ jariṣṇuḥ parīdaṁ vājyajinaṁ dadhe'ham |

The next step in the ceremony is the offer of a staff to the boy by the ācārya and the muttering of the following mantra by the former:

ॐ यो मे दण्डः परापतद्वैहायसोऽधिभूम्याम् ।
तमहं पुनरादद आयुषे ब्रह्मणे ब्रह्मवर्चसाय ।।
om yo me daṇḍaḥ parāpatadvaihāyaso'dhibhūmyām |
tamahaṁ punarādada āyuṣe brahmaṇe brahmavarcasāya ||

Another school of the priestly class adds that after handing the staff to the bachelor, the ācārya fills his open palms with water and pours it three times into the boy's with the repetition of the following mantras:

ॐ आपो हि ष्ठा मयो भुवस्ता न ऊर्जे दधातन ।

महे रणाय चक्षसे ।। १ ।।
ॐ यो वः शिवतमो रसस्तस्य भाजयतेह नः
उशतीरि व मातरः ।। २ ।।
ॐ तस्मा अरं गमाम वो यस्य क्षयाय जिन्वथ ।
आपो जनयथा च नः ।। ३ ।।

om āpo hi ṣṭhā mayo bhuvastā na ūrje dadhātana ।
mahe raṇāya cakṣase ॥ 1 ॥
om yo vaḥ śivatamo rasastasya bhājayateha naḥ
uśatīri va mātaraḥ ॥ 2 ॥
om tasmā araṁ gamāma vo yasya kṣayāya jinvatha ।
āpo janayathā ca naḥ ॥ 3 ॥

While the officiating priest is muttering these sacred formulas the boy should offer water oblation to the sun with his cupped palms at the end of each mantra. The ācārya would say 'सूर्यमुदीक्षस्व' (sūryamudīkṣasva) and the boy would recite thus looking at the sun:

ॐ तच्चक्षुर्देवहितं पुरस्ताच्छुक्रमुच्चरत् । पश्येम शरदः शत ँ जीवेम शरदः शत ँ शृणुयाम शरदः शतं प्रब्रवाम शरदः शतमदीनाः स्याम शरदः शतं भूयश्च शरदः शतात् ।।

om taccakṣurdevahitaṁ purastācchukramuccarat ।
paśyema śaradaḥ śataṁ jīvema śaradaḥ śataṁ śṛṇuyāma śaradaḥ śataṁ prabravāma śaradaḥ śatamadīnāḥ śyāma śaradaḥ śataṁ bhūyaśca śaradaḥ śatāt ॥

The ācārya should now carry his hand from the boy's right shoulder to his heart, touching his bosom with the following mantra:

ॐ मम व्रते ते हृदयं दधामि मम चित्तमनुचित्तं ते अस्तु ।
मम वाचमेकमना जुषस्व बृहस्पतिष्ट्वा नियुनक्तु मह्यम् ।।

om mama vrate te hṛdayaṁ dadhāmi mama cittamanu-cittaṁ te astu ।
mama vācamekamanā juṣasva bṛhaspatiṣṭvā niyunaktu mahyam ॥

He should ask the boy's name, saying 'को नामासि?' (ko nāmāsi). This should accompany his catching hold with his right hand the boy's right hand, including its thumb, at this propitious moment. In reply the boy should mention his name thus: अमुक (so and so) 'शर्माऽहं भोः' (śarmā'haṁ bhoḥ) three times; if he is a kṣatriya he would mention his name and his title 'वर्माऽहं' (varmā'haṁ); in case he is a vaiśya he would do the same but his title would be 'गुप्तोऽहं' (gupto'haṁ). The priest would repeat his question three times, evoking the same reply from the boy each time the question is put to him. This interesting dialogue should continue, the ācārya asking 'कस्य ब्रह्मचार्यसि?' (kasya brahmacāryasi?) and the bachelor replying 'भवतः' (bhavataḥ). The ācārya should cite a mantra which is as follows:

ॐ इन्द्रस्य ब्रह्मचार्यस्यग्निराचार्यस्तवाहमाचार्यस्तव (अमुक) ।
om indrasya brahmacāryasyagnirācāryastavāhamā-cāryastava (amuka) ।

In this what is important is that the priest should mention the boy's name in place of अमुक (amuka) and end with śarmā, varmā and gupta. Thereafter the boy should turn towards the various quarters with folded hands. He faces the east first while the ācārya mutters the following mantra:

ॐ प्रजापतये त्वा परिददामि ।
om prajāpataye tvā paridadāmi ।

The next mantra muttered by the priest when the boy faces the southern quarter is:

ॐ देवाय त्वा सवित्रे परिददामि ।
om devāya tvā savitre paridadāmi ।

The mantra for the western quarter is as follows:

ॐ अद्भ्यस्त्वौषधीभ्यः परिददामि ।

om adbhyastvauṣadhībhyaḥ paridadāmi ।

The one repeated by the priest on the boy facing north is:

ॐ द्यावापृथिवीभ्यां त्वा परिददामि ।
om dyāvāpṛthivībhyāṁ tvā paridadāmi ।

Now the boy should look downward as the priest chants:

ॐ विश्वेभ्यस्त्वा भूतेभ्यः परिददामि ।
om viśvebhyastvā bhūtebhyaḥ paridadāmi ।

and

ॐ सर्वेभ्यस्त्वा भूतेभ्यः परिददामि ।
om sarvebhyastvā bhūtebhyaḥ paridadāmi ।

as the boy looks up towards the sky. This part of the solemn drill ends after the boy goes round the sacrificial fire, sprinkling water all around it without uttering any mantra. He takes his seat on the left (north) of the ācārya and taking flower, sandal, betel leaves and garments, select the brahmā with the recitation of the following:

ॐ अद्य कर्त्तव्योपनयनहोमकर्मणि कृताकृतावेक्षणरूपब्रह्मकर्म कर्त्तुम् (अमुक) गोत्र (अमुक) शर्माहं ब्राह्मणमेभिः पुष्पचन्दनताम्बूलवासोभिर्ब्रह्मत्वेन त्वामहं वृणे ।
om adya karttavyopanayanahomakarmaṇi kṛtākṛtāvekṣanarūpabrahmakarma karttum (amuka) gotra (amuka) śarmāhaṁ brāhmaṇamebhiḥ puṣpacandanatāmbūlavāsobhirbrahmatvena tvāmahaṁ vṛṇe ।

The brahmā on his part should accept the offering of flowers, etc. and utter 'ॐ वृतोऽस्मि' (om vṛto'smi). He is seated to the south of the sacrificial fire on a wooden bed properly covered with kuśa blades whose tips are towards the east. Before taking his seat the brahmā should go round the festal fire. The householder then steps in with the following mantra:

अस्मिन् कर्मणि त्वं मे ब्रह्मा भव ।
asmin karmaṇi tvaṁ me brahmā bhava ।

Replying, the brahmā should say 'भवानि' (bhavāni). After the brahmā has taken his seat with his face to the north, the host should place the praṇītā before him, fill it with water, and cover it with kuśa blades. He should then look at the brahmā's face and keep the praṇītā vessel to the north of the sacrificial fire and ahead of everything else. Having done this, he should take four handfuls of kuśa grass, spread it all around the sacrificial fire and seize the jar (prāksaṁstha pātrāsādana) already kept to the north of the fire. Then follow the instructions given for the performance of the pañcabhū saṁskāra. The performer is advised to have five kuśa blades, three for pavitrachedana and two for purifying and sprinkling ghī, a prokṣaṇī jar, a vessel with clarified butter, sammārjana kuśa blades, upayamana kuśa blades, three samidhās, a sruva, clarified butter, a jar filled with 256 handfuls of rice, etc. These objects should be arranged in the east of the pavitrachedana kuśa in order stated.

ततः पवित्रच्छेदनकुशैः स्वप्रादेशमात्रे पवित्रे छित्त्वा सपवित्रकरेण त्रिवारं प्रणीतोदकं त्रिः प्रोक्षणीपात्रे निधाय अनामिकाङ्गुष्ठाभ्याम् उत्तराग्रे पवित्रे गृहीत्वा त्रिरुत्पवनम् । ततः प्रोक्षणीपात्रं वामहस्ते कृत्वा अनामिकांगुष्ठाभ्यां गृहीतपवित्राभ्यां प्रोक्षणीजलं किंचिदुत्क्षिप्य प्रणीतोदकेनाभ्युक्ष्य ततः प्रोक्षणीजलेन यथासादितवस्तुसेचनं ततोऽग्निप्रणीतयोर्मध्ये प्रोक्षणीपात्रं निदध्यात् ।
tataḥ pavitracchedanakuśaiḥ svaprādeśamātre pavitre chittvā sapavitrakareṇa trivāraṁ praṇītodakaṁ triḥ prokṣaṇīpātre nidhāya anāmikāṅguṣṭhābhyām uttarāgre pavitre gṛhītvā trirutpavanam । *tataḥ prokṣaṇīpātraṁ vāmahaste kṛtvā anāmikāṁguṣṭhābhyāṁ gṛhītapavitrā-bhyāṁ prokṣaṇījalaṁ kiṁcidutkṣipya praṇītodakenā-bhyukṣya tataḥ prokṣaṇījalena yathāsāditavastusecanaṁ tato'gnipraṇītayormadhye prokṣaṇīpātraṁ nidadhyāt* ।

Then the following rites are recommended:

First, cut the kuśas into small pieces, each as long as a handspan. Holding two kuśa blades or pavitra (used for holding offerings or for sprinkling ghī), drop the water of the praṇītāpātra into the prokṣaṇīpātra three times. Again, holding the two kuśa strainers with their points to the north, seizing them between the ring finger and the thumb, sprinkle water overhead three times. Then holding the prokṣaṇīpātra in the left hand and the two kuśa blades between the ring finger and the thumb, toss up the water of the prokṣaṇī a little bit. And then sprinkle the water of the praṇītāpātra over everything before these are sprinkled with the water of the prokṣaṇī. Having done so, keep the prokṣaṇī vessel between the fire and the praṇītā vessel.

आज्यस्थाल्यामाज्यं निरुप्य वह्नावधिश्रित्य ततो ज्वलत्तृणादिना हविर्वेष्ट-यित्वा प्रदक्षिणक्रमेण वह्नौ तत्प्रक्षेपः । ततः स्त्रुवप्रतपनम् । संमार्जन-कुशानामग्रैरग्रं मूलैर्मूलं मध्यैर्मध्यं स्त्रुवं प्रणीतोदकेनाभ्युक्ष्य पुनः प्रतप्य स्त्रुवं दक्षिणतो निदध्यात् ।

ājyasthālyāmājyaṁ nirupya vahnāvadhiśritya tato jvalattṛṇādinā havirveṣṭayitvā pradakṣiṇakrameṇa vahnau tatprakṣepaḥ । *tataḥ sruvapratapanam* । *sammārjana-kuśānāmagrairagraṁ mūlairmūlaṁ madhyairmadhyaṁ sruvaṁ praṇītodakenābhyukṣya punaḥ pratapya sruvaṁ dakṣiṇato nidadhyāt* ।

Pour a little clarified butter (ājya) in a small platter which should then be heated to cause the ghī to melt. After this, let the clarified butter be stirred round the platter with a burning straw (tṛṇa) which should then be thrown into the fire after waving it around (the fire). The next few instructions include heating the sruva spoon (the wooden ladle) and cleaning its front part with the point (agrabhāga) of the kuśa grass meant for this purpose. The middle portion of the sruva be cleaned with the middle of the kuśa, while the bottom should be wiped with the roots of it. Then shall the saṁskāras be performed followed by keeping the heated sruva towards the south close to the brahmā after sprinkling it with the water kept in the holy vessel praṇītā.

ततः आज्यस्थालीमग्नेरवतार्य्य अग्रे धृत्वा प्रोक्षणीवदुत्पूय अवेक्ष्य सत्यपद्रव्ये तन्निरसनं पुनः प्रोक्षण्युत्पवनं ततः उपयमनकुशान् वामहस्ते कृत्वा उत्तिष्ठन् प्रजापतिं मनसा ध्यात्वा तूष्णीमेवाग्नौ घृताक्ताः समिध[1]स्तिस्रः क्षिपेत् । तत उप विश्य सपवित्रप्रोक्षण्युदकेन प्रदक्षिणक्रमेणाग्निपर्युक्षणं कृत्वा प्रणीतापात्रे पवित्रे निधाय पातितदक्षिणजानुः कुशेन ब्रह्मणान्वारब्धः समिद्धतमेऽग्नौ स्रुवेणाज्याहुतीर्जुहुयात् ।

tataḥ ājyasthālīmagneravatāryya agre dhṛtvā prokṣaṇī-vadutpūya avekṣya satyapadravye tannirasanaṁ punaḥ prokṣaṇyutpavanaṁ tataḥ upayamanakuśān vāmahaste kṛtvā uttiṣṭhan prajāpatiṁ manasā dhyātvā tūṣṇīmevāgnau ghṛtāktāḥ samidhastisraḥ kṣipet । tata upaviśya sapavitraprokṣaṇyudakena pradakṣiṇa-krameṇāgniparyukṣaṇaṁ kṛtvā praṇītāpātre pavitre nidhāya pātitadakṣiṇajānuḥ kuśena brahmaṇānvāra-bdhaḥ samiddhatame'gnau sruveṇājyāhutīrjuhuyāt ।

---

1. यादृश्यो समिधो निरूपितास्ता: प्रोक्ता
व्यासकात्यायनवसिष्ठगौतमभरद्वाजै: ।।
पलाशखदिराश्वत्थशम्युदुम्बरजा समित् ।
अपामार्गार्कदूर्वाश्च कुशाश्चेत्यपरे विदु: ।।
सत्वच: समिध: स्थाप्या: ऋजुश्लक्ष्णा: समास्तथा ।
शस्ता दशाङ्गुलास्तास्तु द्वादशाङ्गुलिकास्तु ता: ।।
आर्द्रा: पक्वा: समच्छेदास्तर्जन्यङ्गुलिवर्तुला: ।
अपाटिताश्च विशिखा: कृमिदोषविवर्जिता: ।
ईदृशीर्होमयेत् प्राज्ञ: प्राप्नोति विपुलां श्रियम् ।।
yādṛśyo samidho nirūpitāstāḥ proktā ।
vyāsakātyāyanavasiṣṭhagautamabharadvājaiḥ ॥
palāśakhadirāśvatthaśamyudumbarajā samit ।
apāmārgārkadūrvāśca kuśāścetyapare viduḥ ॥
satvacaḥ samidhaḥ sthāpyāḥ ṛjuślakṣṇāḥ samāstathā ।
śastā daśāṅgulāstāstu dvādaśāṅgulikāstu tāḥ ॥
ārdrāḥ pakvāḥ samacchedāstarjanyaṅgulivartulāḥ ।
apāṭitāśca viśikhāḥ kṛmidoṣavivarjitāḥ ॥
īdṛśīrhomayet prājnaḥ prāpnoti vipulāṁ śriyam ।

These instructions, not yet complete, should be followed by removing the ghī jar from the fire, keeping it in front, and purifying the ghī with the pavitras (two kuśa leaves for holding offerings or for sprinkling ghī) as one sanctifies the water contained in the prokṣaṇī. Do not miss to have a close look at the ghī jar; if anything impure (such as an insect or a fly) has defiled it, it must be removed forthwith and the ghī be purified as one purifies the prokṣaṇī. Then, taking the kuśa grass serving as an *upayamana* (sprinkling ladle) in the left hand and fixing the mind on Prajāpati, wet the three samidhās (firewood, fuel) with ghī and throw them quietly into the fire. Then take your seat, with the pavitras throw a little of the water kept in the prokṣaṇī first into the fire; keep the pavitras in the praṇītā jar; bend your right knee and having touched Brahmā with kuśa, offer oblation of ghī with the sruva to the flaming fire, thus performing the homa (i.e. the act of making an oblation to the devas or gods by casting clarified butter into the fire).

तत्राघारादारभ्य द्वादशाहुतिषु तत्तदाहुत्यनन्तरं स्रुवावस्थितहुतशेषघृतस्य प्रोक्षणीपात्रे प्रक्षेपः ।

tatrāghārādārabhya dvādaśāhutiṣu tattadāhutyanan-taraṁ sruvāvasthitahutaśeṣaghṛtasya prokṣaṇīpātre prakṣepaḥ ।

The oblation to be performed next is called āghāra, meaning, according to Monier Monier Williams, "sprinkling clarified butter upon the fire at certain sacrifices." From this āghāra homa to the twelfth oblation drop the residual ghī into the prokṣaṇī jar with the sruva.

ततः ॐ एषो ह देवः प्रदिशोऽनु सर्वाः पूर्वो ह जातः स उ गर्भे अन्तः । स एव जातः स जनिष्यमाणः प्रत्यङ् जनस्तिष्ठति सर्वतोमुखः ।। इति मंत्रेणाग्नेः सम्मुखीकरणम् । अथ स्रुवपूजनम् । मंगलं भगवान् विष्णुर्मंगलं गरुडध्वजः । मंगलं पुण्डरीकाक्षः मंगलायतनो हरिः ।।

tataḥ om eṣo ha devaḥ pradiśo'nu sarvāḥ pūrvo ha jātaḥ sa u garbhe antaḥ । *sa eva jātaḥ sa janiṣyamāṇaḥ pratyaṅ janastiṣṭhati sarvatomukhaḥ* ॥ *iti maṁtreṇāgneḥ sammukhīkaraṇam* । *atha sruvapūjanam* । *maṁgalaṁ bhagavān viṣṇurmaṁgalaṁ garuḍadhvajaḥ* । *maṁgalaṁ puṇḍarīkākṣaḥ maṁgalāyatano hariḥ* ।

This pre-eminent Agnideva or the supreme Puruṣa is immanent in all the quarters (sarvaḥ pradiśaḥ). O men, this celebrated Deva appears as the very first being, establishes himself in the middle of the womb (garbhe antaḥ), and then reveals himself. It is he who enters every object and is omnifaced, inscrutable and omnipotent.

Pronouncing this mantra and facing the fire, do obeisance to the sruva with the śloka 'maṁgalaṁ bhagavān viṣṇuḥ maṁgalaṁ garuḍadhvajaḥ maṁgalaṁ puṇḍarīkākṣaḥ maṁgalāyatano hariḥ'.

ॐ प्रजापतये स्वाहा । इदं प्रजापतये इति मनसा । ॐ इन्द्राय स्वाहा । इदमिन्द्राय इत्याघारौ । ॐ अग्नये स्वाहा । इदमग्नये । ॐ सोमाय स्वाहा । इदं सोमाय इत्याज्यभागौ । ॐ भूः स्वाहा । इदमग्नये । ॐ भुवः स्वाहा । इदं वायवे । ॐ स्वः स्वाहा । इदं सूर्य्याय । एता महाव्याहृतयः ।

om prajāpataye svāhā । *idaṁ prajāpataye iti manasā* । *om indrāya svāhā idamindrāya ityāghārau* । *om agnaye svāhā* । *idamagnaye* । *om somāya svāhā* । *idaṁ somāya ityājyabhāgau* । *om bhūḥ svāhā* । *idamagnaye* । *om bhuvaḥ svāhā* । *idam vāyave* । *om svaḥ svāhā* । *idaṁ sūryyāya* । *etā mahāvyāhṛtayaḥ* ।

With your mind fully focused on 'om prajāpataye svāhā' and muttering it, make the oblation. This and 'om indrāya svāhā' are the two oblations which are called āghāra, while 'om agnaye svāhā' and 'om somāya svāhā' are called ājyabhāga (the two portions of clarified butter belonging to Agni and Soma). 'om bhūḥ svāhā', 'om bhuvaḥ svāhā', and 'om svaḥ svāhā'—these are three other oblations called mahāvyāhṛtis (because they constitute the mystical formula 'om bhūḥ bhuvaḥ svaḥ').

ॐ त्वं नोऽअग्ने वरुणस्य विद्वान् देवस्य हेडो अवयासिसीष्ठाः । यजिष्ठो वह्नितमः शोशुचानो विश्वा द्वेषाꣳसि प्रमुमुग्ध्यस्मत् स्वाहा—इदमग्नी-वरुणाभ्याम् ।। १ ।।

om tvaṁ no'agne varuṇasya vidvān devasya heḍo avayā-sisīṣṭhāḥ । yajiṣṭho vahnitamaḥ śośucāno viśvā dveṣāṁ̐si pramumugdhyasmat svāhā—idamagnīvaruṇābhyām ॥ 1 ॥

O Fire! If there is any flaw or imperfection (if there is anything lacking) in the performance of this ceremony, let not Varuṇa fly into rage (vaiguṇyādeva varuṇasya devasya heḍaḥ krodhaṁ avayāsisīṣṭhāḥ apanayetyarthaḥ). Considering me dull-witted (yadvā no'smān pramattān mandamatīniti jānan), let not only Varuṇa's fury (kiñca na kevalaṁ varuṇakrodhamapanaya) be quelled but also let all the sacrilege committed by me be forgiven and obtain for me all the great luxuries and objects of supreme enjoyment (kintu asmat iti asmabhyaṁ viśvā dveṣāṁsi sarvāṇi bhāgyāni pramumugdhi). You are surpassingly the greatest of all the gods of sacrifice and the most effulgent of them all (punaḥ kīdṛśastvaṁ vahnitamaḥ sakalayajñāṁśabhāgibhyaḥ svasvāṁśaprāpaṇena sātiśayaḥ).

ॐ स त्वं नो अग्नेऽवमो भवोती नेदिष्ठो अस्या उषसो व्युष्टौ । अवयक्ष्व नो वरुणं रराणो वीहि मृडीकं सुहवो न एधि स्वाहा—इदमग्नीवरुणाभ्याम् ।। २ ।।

om sa tvaṁ no agne'vamo bhavotī nediṣṭho asyā uṣaso vyuṣṭau ।
avayakṣva no varuṇaṁ rarāṇo vīhi mṛḍīkaṁ suhavo na edhi svāhā—idamagnīvaruṇābhyām ॥ 2 ॥

O Fire! Whatever you are, be my nourisher and sustainer. Explaining when precisely he should offer his protection and patronage, he says, he should do so from the early hours of the morning (asya uṣaso vyuṣṭau) and not just protect (na kevalametadeva) him but also, in response to his glad invitation (kintu āgatya mṛḍīkaṁ sukhakaraṁ), willingly and happily appear and reward him with plenty of foodgrains, such as paddy, etc. (no vīhi asmatsaṁbandhi vrīhyādikaṁ rarānaḥ dadānaḥ san) and let him obtain whatever food he has wished to offer to the gods and for which he has worshipped Varuṇa, the presiding Lord of Sacrifice (varuṇaṁ yajñādhiṣṭhātāraṁ avayakṣva pūjayetyarthaḥ).

ॐ अयाश्चाग्नेऽस्यनभिशस्तिश्च सत्यमित्त्वमया असि ।
अया नो यज्ञं वहास्यया नो धेहि भेषजं स्वाहा—इदमग्नये ॥ ३ ॥
om ayāścāgne'syanabhiśastiśca satyamittvamayā asi ।
ayā no yajñaṁ vahāsyayā no dhehi bheṣajaṁ svāhā—
idamagnaye ॥ 3 ॥

O Agni! You dwell everywhere, both inside and outside. (You are familiar with all the urgings and instincts of men, their intrinsic as well as extrinsic motivations.) As a purifying agent, you destroy all defilements and by purging men of their impurities, you make them pure like yourself and then protect them. (One is purged of one's sins if one sincerely repents of his transgressions and leads a life dedicated to altruistic activities, holy deeds or *karmas*, and to the performance of sacrifices, penance, etc. To be sincerely penitent is to burn in the fire of redeeming self-reproach. When one experiences the stings of conscience and burns in the fire of remorse and self-reproof, one is slowly purged of sins.) You are, O Agni, undeniably the way leading to auspicious action. Pray be so kind to me that I may perform this sacrifice with a sincere heart and may thus propitiate the celestial deities. Making me in your own image, bless me with the faculty of recognizing the real source of happiness and of destroying that which leads to suffering (*duḥkha*).

ॐ ये ते शतं वरुण ये सहस्त्रं यज्ञियाः पाशा वितता महान्तः ।
तेभिर्नो ऽअद्य सवितोत विष्णुर्विश्वे मुञ्चन्तु मरुतः स्वर्क्काः स्वाहा ॥ इदं
वरुणाय सवित्रे विष्णवे विश्वेभ्यो मरुद्भयः स्वर्क्केभ्यः ॥ ४ ॥
om ye te śataṁ varuṇa ye sahasraṁ yajñiyāḥ pāśā vitatā mahāntaḥ ।
tebhirno 'adya savitota viṣṇurviśve muñcantu marutaḥ svarkkāḥ svāhā ॥

idaṁ varuṇāya savitre viṣṇave viśvebhyo marudbhyaḥ svarkkebhyaḥ ॥4॥

O Varuṇa! The myriads of fetters which result from the irregularities in and obstructions to the performance of sacrifices and which cannot be destroyed, howsoever one may try, have kept me manacled. May Savitā, Viṣṇu, Indra, Viśvedeva, Maruta, and Āditya Devatā, famed for his beautiful heart, free me and by accepting the oblation made to them in the sacrifice, be pleased with me and purify me everywhere.

ॐ उदुत्तमं वरुण पाशमस्मदवाधमं वि मध्यमꣳश्रथाय ।
अथा वयमादित्य व्रते तवानागसोऽदितये स्याम स्वाहा ।।इदं वरुणाय ।।५।।
उदकोपस्पर्शनम् । एताः प्रायश्चित्तसंज्ञिकाः[1] ।

om uduttamaṁ varuṇa pāśamasmadavādhamaṁ vi madhyamaṁśrathāya । *athā vayamāditya vrate tavānāgaso'ditaye syāma svāhā* ॥ *idaṁ varuṇāya* ॥ 5 ॥
udakopasparśanam । *etāḥ prāyaścittasaṁjñikāḥ* ।

1. होमकर्मणि पराशरः । आघारावाज्यभागौ च महाव्याहृतयस्तथा । सर्वप्राय. . . स्तथा ।। प्राजापत्यं स्विष्टकृतोऽग्नेर्होमश्च सर्वतः । होमकर्म्मण्याहुतीनां चतुर्द्दशकमीरितम् ।। सर्वप्रायश्चित्तं त्वं नोऽग्ने इत्यारभ्य उदुत्तममित्यन्तमाहुतिपञ्चकम् । प्राजापत्यं प्राजापत्याहुतिः ।। अथ विवाहहोममप्याह सांख्यायनः—विवाहे होमयेन्नित्यं राष्ट्रभृद्द्वादशाहुतीः । जयाहुतीर्दश त्रींश्च होमयेत् तत्र चेच्छया ।। अष्टादशापि जुहुयादभ्याता आहुतीस्तथा ।। आहुतित्रितयं दद्यादविवाहे साक्षिकाग्नये। साक्षीदानादिपूज्योतोग्निं साक्षिणमोह्वयेद् इति ।। धर्म्म आत्मा सदा साक्षी धर्मो धारयते प्रजाः । अतो वैवस्वतं धर्म्ममाहुतिभ्यां प्रपूजयेत् ।। इति वचनात् । वैवस्वतायाप्याहुतिद्वयम् ।।

homakarmaṇi parāśaraḥ / āghārāvājyabhāgau ca mahāvyāhṛtayastathā / sarvaprāya. . .stathā // prājāpatyaṁ sviṣṭakṛto'gnerhomaśca sarvataḥ / homakarmmaṇyāhutīnāṁ caturddaśakamīritam // sarvaprāyaścittaṁ tvaṁ no'gne ityārabhya uduttamamityantamāhutipañcakam /prājāpatyaṁ prājāpatyāhutiḥ // atha vivāhahomamapyāha sāṁkhyāyanaḥ—vivāhe homayennityaṁ rāṣṭrabhṛddvādaśāhutīḥ / jayāhutīrdaśa trīṁśca homayet tatra cecchayā // aṣṭādaśāpi juhuyādabhyātā āhutīstathā // āhutitritayaṁ dadyādavivāhe sākṣikāgnaye / sākṣidānādipūjyo'togniṁ sākṣiṇamohvayed iti // dharmma ātmā sadā sākṣī dharmo dhārayate prajāḥ / ato vaivasvataṁ dharmmamāhutibhyāṁ prapūjayet // iti vacanāt / vaivasvatāyāpyāhutidvayam //

O Varuṇa! May you protect me from your noose, which is of three kinds: the most excellent, the middling, and the vilest or the worst. Loosen the hangman's noose and save me. Having done so, O Varuṇa, son of Aditi, rid me of my sense of helplessness just as you forgave me the sins I committed in not observing the vow of celibacy.

Join all the five fingers of the right hand and touch water. These five oblations are penitential and are, therefore, called 'prāyaścitta'.

Now, offer two oblations of Prājāpatya and Sviṣṭakṛt with the following mantra:

ॐ प्रजापतये स्वाहा, इदं प्रजापतये न मम ।
इति मनसा प्राजापत्यम् ।
ॐ अग्नये स्विष्टकृते स्वाहा ।
इदमग्नये स्विष्टकृते न मम ।

om prajāpataye svāhā, idaṁ prajāpataye na mama ।
iti manasā prājāpatyam ।
om agnaye sviṣṭakṛte svāhā ।
idamagnaye sviṣṭakṛte na mama ।

After thus offering fourteen oblations wash your hands and give the sacrificial fee to the brahmā with the recitation of the following saṁkalpa:

ॐ अद्यैतस्मिन्नुपनयनहोमकर्मणि कृताकृतावेक्षणरूपब्रह्मकर्मप्रतिष्ठार्थमिदं पूर्णपात्रं प्रजापतिदैवतं अमुकगोत्रायामुकशर्मणे ब्रह्मणे ब्राह्मणाय दक्षिणां तुभ्यमहं संप्रददे ।

om adyaitasminnupanayanahomakarmaṇi kṛtā-kṛtāvekṣaṇarūpabrahmakarmapratiṣṭhārthamidaṁ pūrṇapātraṁ prajāpatidaivataṁ amukagotrāyāmu-kaśarmaṇe brahmaṇe brāhmaṇāya dakṣiṇāṁ tubhyamahaṁ saṁpradade ।

The brahmā should accept the fee saying 'ॐ स्वस्ति' (om svasti) and should sprinkle the praṇītā water with the pavitras on his head:

ॐ सुमित्रिया न आप ओषधयः सन्तु ।
om sumitriyā na āpa oṣadhyaḥ santu ।

Now drop the praṇītā water in the north-east quarter and recite the following:

ॐ दुर्मित्रियास्तस्मै सन्तु योऽस्मान् द्वेष्टि यं च वयं द्विष्मः ।
om durmitriyāstasmai santu yo'smān dveṣṭi yaṁ ca vayaṁ dviṣmaḥ ।

Then mix the pavitras with the kuśas spread on the ground and pick them up in the order in which they were spread on the ground. After picking them smear them with clarified butter and throw them in the fire with the following mantra:

ॐ देवा गातुविदो गातुं वित्त्वा गातुमित ।
मनस्पत इमं देवयज्ञ ँ स्वाहा वातेधाः स्वाहा ।
इदम् वाताय न मम ।।
om devā gātuvido gātuṁ vittvā gātumita ।
manaspata imaṁ devayajñaṁ svāhā vātedhāḥ svāhā ।
idam vātāya na mama ॥

The Ācārya's Instructions

Having done all this, the priest should thus instruct the initiate, who should gratefully acknowledge it.

Ācārya— 'ब्रह्मचार्यसि' (brahmacāryasi). You are a celibate now entitled to perform all that is enjoined by the Vedas.

Student— 'भवानि' (bhavāni). So be it.

Ācārya— 'अपोऽशान' (apo'śāna). Perform the ācamana.

Student— 'अशानि' (aśāni). I shall act accordingly.

Ācārya— 'कर्म कुरु' (karma kuru). Perform your evening ablutions, study the Vedas and go about begging alms.

Student— 'करवाणि' (karavāṇi). I shall do all these.

Ācārya— 'मा दिवा सुषुप्था: (mā divā suṣupthā). Avoid all mid-day siesta.

Student— 'न स्वपानि' (na svapāni). I shall not sleep in the early afternoon.

Ācārya— 'वाचं यच्छ' (vācaṁ yaccha). Maintain silence while eating and defecating.

Student— 'यच्छानि' (yacchāni). I shall not utter a word on either occasion.

Ācārya— 'अध्ययनं सम्पादय' (adhyayanaṁ sampādaya). You should study the Vedas regularly in accordance with the prescribed rule.

Student— 'सम्पादयानि' (sampādayāni). I shall study the Vedas regularly.

Ācārya— 'समिधमाधेहि' (samidhamādhehi). You should offer oblation of firewood or fuel to agni every day.

Student— 'आदधानि' (ādadhāni). I shall offer such an oblation with unceasing regularity.

Ācārya— 'अपोऽशान' (apo'śāna). Perform ācamana after every meal.

Student— 'अशानि' (aśāni). I shall not fail to do so.

Having listened to the ācārya's instructions with rapt seriousness and acquiescence, the boy being initiated should touch his feet and take his seat facing the west to the north of the fire. The student and the ācārya should sit facing each other. In that case the ācārya would face the east and, while thus facing the young bachelor, discourse on the Gāyatrī mantra. This, however, should follow the act of strewing some rice grains over a bronze platter and writing the Gāyatrī with the praṇava and the vyāhṛtis with a gold or silver or copper stick. The following saṁkalpa should be uttered after this:

ओमद्य मम ब्रह्मवर्चसवेदाध्ययनाधिकारसिद्ध्यर्थं गायत्र्युपदेशांगविहितं

गायत्रीसावित्रीसरस्वतीपूजनपूर्वकमाचार्यपूजनं करिष्ये ।
omadya mama brahmavarcasavedādhyayanādhikārasiddhyarthaṁ gāyatryupadesāṁgavihitaṁ gāyatrīsāvitrīsarasvatīpūjanapūrvakamācāryapūjanaṁ kariṣye ।

This is expressive of the celibate's resolve that for the attainment of divine glory, superhuman powers and rights to study the Vedas, he would reverence his ācārya along with Gāyatrī and Sarasvatī, both described as an integral part of the Gāyatrī mantra. The next few rituals are performed in the following order: the saṁkalpa should be followed by the installation of Gāyatrī with such mantras as ॐ मनोजूतिर्जुषतां (om manojūtirjuṣatāṁ) etc., and worship of Gāyatrī and other goddesses with 'श्रीश्च ते...' (śrīśca te...), etc. on the rice grains strewn over the platter; the ritual of paying homage to the ācārya is performed next. First of all, this should be followed by the ācārya's explication of each and every foot of the Gāyatrī mantra with the praṇava and the vyāhṛtis in the following manner:

ॐ भूर्भुवः स्वः–तत्सवितुर्वरेण्यम् ।
ॐ भूर्भुवः स्वः–भर्गो देवस्य धीमहि ।
ॐ भूर्भुवः स्वः–धियो यो नः प्रचोदयात् ।
om bhūrbhuvaḥ svaḥ—tatsaviturvareṇyam ।
om bhūrbhuvaḥ svaḥ—bhargo devasya dhīmahi ।
om bhūrbhuvaḥ svaḥ—dhiyo yo naḥ pracodayāt ।

This completes the first cycle. In the second let the praṇava and the vyāhṛtis be added to the first half ṛcā in the same manner. For example:

ॐ भूर्भुवः स्वः–तत्सवितुर्वरेण्यम्–भर्गो देवस्य धीमहि ।
ॐ भूर्भुवः स्वः–धियो यो नः प्रचोदयात् ।
om bhūrbhuvaḥ svaḥ—tatsaviturvareṇyam—bhargo devasya dhīmahi ।
om bhūrbhuvaḥ svaḥ—dhiyo yo naḥ pracodayāt ।

This is another repetition. In the third complete the mantra *in toto* with the praṇava and the vyāhṛtis:

ॐ भूर्भुवः स्वः–तत्सवितुर्वरेण्यं भर्गो देवस्य धीमहि । धियो यो नः प्रचोदयात् ।

om bhūrbhuvaḥ svaḥ—tatsaviturvareṇyaṁ bhargo devasya dhīmahi । *dhiyo yo naḥ pracodayāt* ।

Thus shall the ācārya repeat the mantra which the boy should simultaneously parrot. The teacher and the pupil, the young celibate and the preceptor should both then say 'ॐ स्वस्ति' (om svasti). The śāstras enjoin that the ācārya should discourse on the Sāvitrī mantra at least once in the course of a year, in six months, in twenty-four days, in twelve days, in six days, in the course of three days. And they are reliable authorities. If the student is mature enough to grasp the spirit, not only the letters of the mantras, he should not be denied the opportunity of receiving them without delay. To a learned brāhmaṇa celibate the instructions can be delivered at any opportune moment. What we have said about the mode of imparting instructions on the Savitā Gāyatrī applies to the brāhmaṇa student. The kṣatriya student should, however, receive his instructions on the Gāyatrī written in the *triṣṭup* metre. The seer (ṛṣi) who composed it is Bṛhaspati and the deity to whom it is addressed is Savitā, its presiding god:

ॐ देव सवितः प्रसुव यज्ञं प्रसुव यज्ञपतिं भगाय ।
दिव्यो गन्धर्वः केतपूः केतं नः पुनातु वाचस्पतिर्वाचं नः स्वदतु ।।

om deva savitaḥ prasuva yajñaṁ prasuva yajñapatiṁ bhagāya ।
divyo gandharvaḥ ketapūḥ ketaṃ naḥ punātu vācaspatir-vācaṃ naḥ svadatu ॥

For vaiśya student use the Gāyatrī written in Jagatī metre presided over by Savitā and composed by Prajāpati, the seer (ṛṣi). This mantra is as follows:

ॐ विश्वा रूपाणि प्रति मुञ्चते कविः प्रासावीद् भद्रं द्विपदे चतुष्पदे ।
विनाकमख्यत् सविता वरेण्योऽनुप्रयाणमुषसो विराजति ।।

om viśvā rūpāṇi prati muñcate kaviḥ prāsāvīd bhadraṁ dvipade catuṣpade ।
vinākamakhyat savitā vareṇyo'nuprayāṇamuṣaso virājati ॥

This again derives its authenticity from the scriptures. It is also stated that a student belonging to any of the three varṇas—brāhmaṇa, kṣatriya and vaiśya—if he is desirous of attaining divine glory and is possessed of super human brilliance, is authorised to receive the same instructions on the Gāyatrī which has been described above as the first of the three modes of repeating it.

Samidādhāna

The offering of firewood to agni follows the instructions imparted on the Gāyatrī. For performing the ritual, the bachelor, seated facing the east to the south of the ācārya and to the west of the fire, should throw with his right hand dry cowdung cakes soaked in clarified butter into the fire with the recitation of the following five mantras:

ॐ अग्ने सुश्रवः सुश्रवसं मा कुरु स्वाहा ।। १ ।।
ॐ यथा त्वमग्ने सुश्रवः सुश्रवा असि स्वाहा ।। २ ।।
ॐ एवं मा ꣳ सुश्रवः सौश्रवसं कुरु स्वाहा ।। ३ ।।
ॐ यथा त्वमग्ने देवानां यज्ञस्य निधिपोऽसि स्वाहा ।। ४ ।।
ॐ एवमहं मनुष्याणां वेदस्य निधिपो भूयासम् स्वाहा ।। ५ ।।

om agne suśravaḥ suśravasaṁ mā kuru svāhā ॥ 1 ॥
om yathā tvamagne suśravaḥ suśravā asi svāhā ॥ 2 ॥
om evaṁ māṁ suśravaḥ sauśravasaṁ kuru svāhā ॥ 3 ॥
om yathā tvamagne devānāṁ yajñasya nidhipo'si svāhā ॥ 4 ॥
om evamahaṁ manuṣyāṇāṁ vedasya nidhipo bhūyāsam svāhā ॥ 5 ॥

This should be followed by pouring water around the fire

with the right hand or in a wee pot from the north-east quarter to the north in a circumambulatory fashion. Having performed this part of the ceremony, the bachelor should pick up three pieces of firewood, soak them in clarified butter as far in length as measures the distance between the thumb and the little finger (when you stretch your hand as widely as possible). He should throw the pieces of firewood one after another into the fire and offer the oblation with the following two mantras or with either of them:

ॐ अग्नये समिधमाहार्षं बृहते जातवेदसे यथा त्वमग्ने समिधा समिध्यसि एवमहमायुषा मेधया वचसा प्रजया पशुभिर्ब्रह्मवर्चसेन समिन्धे जीवपुत्रो ममाचार्यो मेधाव्यहमसान्यनिराकरिष्णुर्यशस्वी तेजस्वी ब्रह्मवर्चस्यन्नादो भूयासम् ।।१।।
ॐ एषा ते अग्ने समित्तया वर्धस्व चा च प्यायस्व वर्धिषीमहि च वयमाच प्यासिषीमहि स्वाहा ।।२।।

om agnaye samidhamāhārṣaṁ bṛhate jātavedase yathā tvamagne samidhā samidhyasi evamahamāyuṣā medhayā vacasā prajayā paśubhirbrahmavarcasena samindhe jīvaputro mamācāryo medhāvyahamasānyanirākariṣṇuryaśasvī tejasvī brahmavarcasyannādo bhūyāsam ॥ 1 ॥
om eṣā te agne samittayā vardhasva cā ca pyāyasva vardhiṣīmahi ca vayamāca pyāsiṣīmahi svāhā ॥ 2 ॥

This should be repeated everytime the firewood is offered. As a matter of fact either of the mantras or both should be uttered as long as the pupil intends to remain an unmarried religious student.

Taking his seat he should then offer the oblation of the cowdung cakes soaked in clarified butter into the sacrificial fire with the repetition of 'ॐ अग्ने सुश्रव:' (om agne suśravaḥ), etc. Once again he should pour a little water around the fire. And warming his hands without uttering any mantra touch his face. The last act, i.e. while touching the face, should, however, be done with the recitation of the following seven mantras:

ॐ तनूपा अग्नेऽसि तन्वं मे पाहि ।। १ ।।
ॐ आयुर्दा अग्नेऽस्यायुर्मेदेहि ।। २ ।।
ॐ वर्चोदा अग्नेऽसि वर्चो मे देहि ।। ३ ।।
ॐ अग्ने यन्मे तन्वा ऊनं तन्म आपृण ।। ४ ।।
ॐ मेधां मे देवः सविता आदधातु ।। ५ ।।
ॐ मेधां मे देवी सरस्वती आदधातु ।। ६ ।।
ॐ मेधां मेऽश्विनौ देवावाधत्तां पुष्करस्त्रजौ ।। ७ ।।
om tanūpā agne'si tanvaṁ me pāhi ॥ 1 ॥
om āyurdā agne'syāyurme dehi ॥ 2 ॥
om varcodā agne'si varco me dehi ॥ 3 ॥
om agne yanme tanvā ūnaṁ tanma āpṛṇa ॥ 4 ॥
om medhāṁ me devaḥ savitā ādadhātu ॥ 5 ॥
om medhāṁ me devi sarasvatī ādadhātu ॥ 6 ॥
om medhāṁ me'śvinau devāvādhattāṁ puṣkarasrajau ॥ 7 ॥

Having done this, he should touch his body from head to foot with his right hand with the recitation of the following five sacred formulas:

ॐ अंगानि च म आप्यायन्ताम् ।। १ ।।
ॐ वाक् च आप्यायताम् । इति मुखम् ।। २ ।।
ॐ प्राणश्च म आप्यायताम् । इति नासाम् ।। ३ ।।
ॐ चक्षुश्च म आप्यायताम् । इति चक्षुषी युगपत् ।। ४ ।।
ॐ श्रोत्रं च म आप्यायताम् ।। ५ ।।
om aṁgāni ca ma āpyāyantām ॥ 1 ॥
om vāk ca āpyāyatām । *iti mukham* ॥ 2 ॥
om prāṇaśca ma āpyāyatām । *iti nāsām* ॥ 3 ॥
om cakṣuśca ma āpyāyatām । *iti cakṣuṣī yugapat* ॥ 4 ॥
om śrotraṁ ca ma āpyāyatām ॥ 5 ॥

In other words, the first mantra 'ॐ अंगानि०' (om aṁgāni. . .) should be muttered while touching all the organs of the body, the second while touching the face, the third while touching the nose, the fourth while applying the hands to the eyes, and the fifth while applying them to the ears. The sixth mantra ॐ यशोबलं च म आप्यायताम् (om yaśobalaṁ ca ma āpyāyatām) should be muttered while touching the two arms. The following four mantras are then chanted when applying the ashes of the firewood to the forehead, throat, right shoulder and bosom in this very order:

ॐ त्र्यायुषं जमदग्नेः ।। १ ।। इति ललाटे ।
ॐ कश्यपस्य त्र्यायुषम् ।। २ ।। इति ग्रीवायाम् ।
ॐ यद्देवेषु त्र्यायुषम् ।। ३ ।। इति दक्षिणांसे ।
ॐ तन्नो अस्तु त्र्यायुषम् ।। ४ ।। इति हृदि ।
om tryāyuṣaṁ jamadagneḥ ॥ 1 ॥ *iti lalāṭe* ।
om kaśyapasya tryāyuṣam ॥ 2 ॥ *iti grīvāyām* ।
om yaddeveṣu tryāyuṣam ॥ 3 ॥ *iti dakṣiṇāṁse* ।
om tanno astu tryāyuṣam ॥ 4 ॥ *iti hṛdi* ।

Salutation and Greeting

Now the ceremony enters a phase when all the gods collectively or Agni and the Sun are saluted with due devotion and concentration. The mantras spoken while greeting them as well as the ācārya, who is saluted immediately after the gods, are as follows:

(१) 'अमुकगोत्रः अमुकप्रवरः अमुक (शर्मा, वर्मा, गुप्तः) अहं वैश्वानर त्वामभिवादये' ।
(२) 'अमुकगोत्रः अमुकप्रवरः अमुक. . . अहं सूर्यदेव त्वामभिवादये' ।
(३) 'अमुकगोत्रः अमुकप्रवरः अमुकनामाहं भो'

1. *'amukagotraḥ amukapravaraḥ amuka (śarmā, varmā, guptaḥ) ahaṁ vaiśvānara tvāmabhivādaye'* ।
2. *'amukagotraḥ amukapravaraḥ amuka. . .ahaṁ sūryadeva tvāmabhivādaye'* ।
3. *'amukagotraḥ amukapravaraḥ amukanāmāhaṁ bho'*

Replying, the ācārya and other brāhmaṇas should bless the boy with āyuṣmān bhava ('आयुष्मान् भव'). It is then that the student should salute his parents and other elders and teachers and receive their good wishes.

Mendicancy

Then a symbolic act of begging is performed. The student is required to hold a begging bowl in his hand and go about begging. Each of these varṇas has its own style of begging:

(Brāhmaṇa): 'भवति भिक्षां देहि' (bhavati bhikṣāṁ dehi)।
(Kṣatriya): 'भिक्षां भवति देहि' (bhikṣāṁ bhavati dehi)।
(Vaiśya): 'भिक्षां देहि भवति' (bhikṣāṁ dehi bhavati)।

It is obvious that the *varṇa* of the student determines the kind of sentence he has to articulate in begging. He should accept whatever alms he receives from women belonging to his own *varṇa*. They can be three, six, twelve or indeterminate in number. According to some reliable authorities, the first woman to be approached by the mendicant is his own mother. A motherless student can, however, approach his own elder sister for alms. Where a mendicant is bereaved of both mother and sister, his mother's sister should be thought of as the first woman to be approached. It is mandatory that no raw food grains should be offered to the ceremonial beggar. The ritual of begging demands that only cooked grains be offered to the student. Whosoever responds to his begging should be gratefully thanked with 'ॐ स्वस्ति' (om svasti) and the alms received should be kept before the ācārya. On receiving the ācārya's permission with 'भैक्षं भुङ्क्ष्व' (bhaikṣaṁ bhuṅkṣva) he should partake of the food offered. The student is then put to a hard disciplinary test when he is required to keep standing without uttering a word till sun-down. It is relaxable only in the case of a student physically handicapped and too weak to stand the test. Such a student can sit with the permission of the preceptor. The śāstras require him to perform his evening ablutions, which include hymning 'ॐ अग्ने सुश्रवः सुश्रवसं' (om agne suśravaḥ suśravasaṁ), etc., and to end his silence after performing all the actions from offering cowdung cakes into the festal fire to the salutation of the elders and the ācārya.

The sacrificial fire kindled for the sacrament of the sacred thread should be kept burning for three days. The saṁskāra should come to an end with the ācārya and all the other brāhmaṇas blessing the boy with such mantras as 'आ ब्रह्मन्' (ā brahman. . .) 'ब्रह्मवर्चसी भव' (brahmavarcasī bhava). Finally must the ācārya be saluted, fed, paid the sacrificial fee and duly reverenced. The latter on his part should bless the boy who then bids farewell to the divine mothers. One of the last acts is to feed at least fifty brāhmaṇas as enjoined by the smṛtis with due saṁkalpa. According to other sources, however, the number of brāhmaṇas to be invited on the valedictory occasion depends on the financial resources of the host, for in that lie the vindication and maintenance of his honour.

The wearer of the sacred thread is expected to observe certain codes of conduct and discipline his life accordingly. Transgressions of the rules laid down for students who have been invested with the sacred thread are deemed culpable and incur upon the transgressor some punishments and rigorous disciplinary actions. The student who has undergone the initiation ceremony and wears the sacred thread should, say the seers, lead a life of abstemiousness and asceticism, subjecting his senses to the rigours of inexorable discipline. All sensual pleasures are to him anathema; he must sleep on the ground and eat plain food, avoiding all stimulants and spicy dishes. The laws of Manu, deemed inviolable by all brāhmaṇas, are often quoted *in extenso* in this regard:

अग्नीन्धनं भैक्षचर्यामधःशय्यां गुरोर्हितम् ।
आसमावर्तनात् कुर्यात् कृतोपनयनो द्विजः ।।
agnīndhanaṁ bhaikṣacaryāmadhaḥśayyāṁ gurorhitam ।
āsamāvartanāt kuryāt kṛtopanayano dvijaḥ ॥

Manu distinguishes the natural father from the teacher-father. What he says about the two categories of fathers can be summed up as follows. According to the injunctions of the revealed texts, the first birth of an Aryan is from his natural mother, the second happens on the tying of the girdle of muñja grass and the third on the initiation to the performance of a śrauta sacrifice. Among those three the birth which is symbolised by the investiture with the girdle of muñja grass, is his birth for the sake of the Veda; they declare that in that birth the Sāvitrī verse is his mother and the teacher his father. Not less important are Manu's verses on the respective rules to be followed by all those who have been initiated:

कृतोपनयनस्यास्य व्रतादेशनमिष्यते ।
ब्रह्मणो ग्रहणं चैव क्रमेण विधिपूर्वकम् ।।
यद्यस्य विहितं चर्म यत्सूत्रं या च मेखला ।
यो दण्डो यच्च वसनं तत्तदस्य व्रतेष्वपि ।।
सेवेतेमांस्तु नियमान्ब्रह्मचारी गुरौ वसन् ।
सन्नियम्येन्द्रियग्रामं तपोवृद्ध्यर्थमात्मनः ।।

kṛtopanayanasyāsya vratādeśanamiṣyate ।
brahmaṇo grahaṇaṁ caiva krameṇa vidhipūrvakam ॥
yadyasya vihitaṁ carma yat sūtraṁ yā ca mekhalā ।
yo daṇḍo yacca vasanaṁ tattadasya vrateṣvapi ॥
sevetemāṁstu niyamānbrahmacārī gurau vasan ।
sanniyamyendriyagrāmaṁ tapovṛddhyarthamātmanaḥ ॥

The student who has been initiated must be instructed in the performance of the vows, and gradually learn the Veda, observing the prescribed rules. Whatever dress of skin, sacred thread, girdle, staff, and lower garment are prescribed for a student at the initiation, the like must again be used at the performance of the vows. But a student who resides with his teacher must observe the following restrictive rules, duly controlling all his organs, in order to increase his spiritual merit.

The punctuality and seriousness with which the brahmacārī

has to observe the rules of studentship after initiation[1] can be realized from the following:

नित्यं स्नात्वा शुचिः कुर्याद्देवर्षिपितृतर्पणम् ।
देवताऽभ्यर्चनं चैव समिदाधानमेव च ।।
वर्जयेन् मधु मांसं च गन्धं माल्यं रसानि स्त्रयः ।
शुक्तानि यानि सर्वाणि प्राणिनां चैव हिंसनम् ।।
अभ्यङ्गमञ्जनं चाक्ष्णोरुपानच्छत्रधारणम् ।
कामं क्रोधं च लोभं च नर्तनं गीतवादनम् ।।
द्यूतं च जनवादं च परिवादं तथानृतम् ।
स्त्रीणां च प्रेक्षणालम्भमुपघातं परस्य च ।।
एकः शयीत सर्वत्र न रेतः स्कन्दयेत् क्वचित् ।
कामाद्धि स्कन्दयन् रेतो हिनस्ति व्रतमात्मनः ।।

nityaṁ snātvā śuciḥ kuryāddevarṣipitṛtarpaṇam ।
devatā'bhyarcanaṁ caiva samidādhānameva ca ॥
varjayen madhu māṁsaṁ ca gandhaṁ mālyaṁ rasāni srayaḥ ।
śuktāni yāni sarvāṇi prāṇināṁ caiva hiṁsanam ॥
abhyaṅgamañjanaṁ cākṣṇorupānacchatradhāraṇaṃ ।
kāmaṁ krodhaṁ ca lobhaṁ ca nartanaṁ gītavādanam ॥
dyūtaṁ ca janavādaṁ ca parivādaṁ tathānṛtam ।
strīṇāṁ ca prekṣaṇālambhamupaghātaṁ parasya ca ॥
ekaḥ śayīta sarvatra na retaḥ skandayet kvacit ।
kāmāddhi skandayan reto hinasti vratamātmanaḥ ॥

Everyday, having bathed, and being purified, he must offer libations of water to the gods, sages and manes, worship the images of the gods, and place fuel on the sacred fire. Let him abstain from honey, meat, perfumes, garlands, substances used for flavouring food, woman, all substances turned acid, and from doing injury to living creatures, from anointing his body, applying collyrium to his eyes, from the use of shoes and of an umbrella or parasol, from sensual

1. See Appendix II.

desire, anger, covetousness, dancing, singing, and playing musical instruments, from gambling, idle disputes, backbiting and lying, from looking at and touching women, and from hurting others. Let him always sleep alone, let him never waste his manhood; for he who voluntarily wastes his manhood, breaks his vow.

Those were the days when all this was possible and the student could sleep on the ground. The abstemious life recommended by Manu could be led and the vows performed with due seriousness and regularity. But climate as well as the capability of the student often eludes the performance of such vows and sacrifices which the law-givers have enjoined. Where the climate is much too cold, it would be difficult to sleep on the ground or abstain from subsisting on what is essentially a non-vegetarian diet. The laws may, if necessary, be modified in unfavourable circumstances and emergency. Would it be possible for a Hindu immigrant to bathe in the Thames? The laws enjoined that one should not bathe in the river, but use a metal pot while bathing and washing one's body. Some of the Hindu sages forbid bathing in the river on the ground that it stimulates the sensual organs. As a matter of fact, they forbid the student to do anything likely to prevent him from performing his vows and leading a life appropriate to his career and calling. Nothing should hamper him by any obstructive and unbecoming action, by anything which would prevent him from performing his duties or discharging his responsibilities. The sages strongly felt that a midday sleep, anointing the body with deodorants, keeping a sleepless vigil at night, looking at one's own reflection every now and again in the mirror, heavy and frequent toiletries, eating what is stale and left over, frequenting the theatre, reading erotic literature, etc. are harmful and calculated to ruin one's sense of discipline and decorum. So long as one is a student, one should desirably subsist on charity and be dressed plainly like a mendicant. If and where possible he should also carry a suitable staff in his hand. Neither his clothes nor his staff should be tattered, broken or ramshackle. The sacred thread, if broken, must be replaced at once by a new one. The appropriate mantra should be muttered in the process of this replacement. The state of impeccable moral purity and celibacy should be maintained as long as the Vedas are not fully mastered. Alternatively, one can remain in this state for nine, eighteen, thirty-six, or forty-eight years.

Reinitiation

Reinitiation becomes inevitable under certain unavoidable circumstances. Scholars are, however, not unanimous on this issue. According to Śātātapa:

लशुनं गृंजनं जग्ध्वा पलाण्डुं च तथा शुनम् ।
उष्ट्रमानुषकेभाश्वरासभीक्षीरभोजनम् ।
उपनयनं पुनः कुर्यात्तप्तकृच्छ्रं चरेन्मुहुः ।।
laśunaṁ gṛṁjanaṁ jagdhvā palāṇḍuṁ ca tathā śunam ।
uṣṭramānuṣakebhāśva rāsabhīkṣīrabhojanam ।
upanayanaṁ punaḥ kuryāttaptakṛcchraṁ carenmuhuḥ ॥

In other words, reinitiation of him who has partaken of garlic, onion or canine carrion or drunk the milk of a she-camel, a woman, a she-elephant, a mare, or a she-ass, must be performed. This is also confirmed by Manu:

लशुनं गृञ्जनं चैव पलाण्डुं कवकानि च ।
अभक्ष्याणि द्विजातीनाममेध्यप्रभवाणि च ।।५ ।।
laśunaṁ gṛñjanaṁ caiva palāṇḍuṁ kavakāni ca ।
abhakṣyāṇi dvijātīnāmamedhyaprabhavāṇi ca ॥

Garlic, leeks and onions, mushrooms and all plants, springing from impure substances, are unfit to be eaten by twice-born men. He who survives after suicide, an attempt on his life, accident, etc. must be reinitiated. Such is the opinion of elder Manu:

जीवन् यदि समागच्छेद् घृतकुम्भे निमज्ज्य च ।

उद्धृत्य स्थापयित्वाऽस्य जातकर्मादि कारयेत् ।।
jīvan yadi samāgacched ghṛtakumbhe nimajjya ca ।
uddhṛtya sthāpayitvā'sya jātakarmādi kārayet ॥

In other words, if a person drowned in a reservoir comes out alive, he should perform all the sacraments such as the jātakarma (Birth ceremonies), etc., again. Reinitiation is recommended in the case of one who wittingly or unconsciously gobbles an impure object. Manu's view in this regard is expressed in his institutes in the chapter entitled 'Penances for Minor Offences' (XI, 151):

अज्ञानात् प्राश्य विण्मूत्रं सुरासंसृष्टमेव च ।
पुनः संस्कारमर्हन्ति त्रयो वर्णा द्विजातयः ।।
ajñānāt prāśya viṇmūtraṁ surāsaṁsṛṣṭameva ca ।
punaḥ saṁskāramarhanti trayo varṇā dvijātayaḥ ॥

He who becomes a householder once again after reinitiation must perform all the saṁskāras. What Parāśara says in his Smṛti confirms this:

यः प्रत्यवसितो विप्रः प्रव्रज्यातो विनिर्गतः ।
अनाशकनिवृत्तश्च गार्हस्थ्यं चेच्कीर्षति ।।
सचरेत् त्रीणि कृच्छ्राणि त्रीणि चान्द्रायणानि च ।
जातकर्मादिभिः सर्वैः संस्कृतः शुद्धिमाप्नुयात् ।।
yaḥ pratyavasito vipraḥ pravrajyāto vinirgataḥ ।
anāśakanivṛttaśca gārhasthyaṁ ceckīrṣati ॥
sacaret trīṇi kṛcchrāṇi trīṇi cāndrāyaṇāni ca ।
jātakarmādibhiḥ sarvaiḥ saṁskṛtaḥ śuddhimāpnuyāt ॥

If a recluse returns home and becomes a householder and if he has not taken any impure food, he must, if he desires to lead a worldly life, observe three Prājāpatya vows and perform all the saṁskāras, including jātakarma, etc., to purify himself. Those who accept the gift of bed in the last rites of a dead person are also advised to perform all the saṁskāras. This has been aptly expressed by Hemādri:

'प्रेतशय्याप्रतिग्राही पुनः संस्कारमर्हति'
(pretaśayyāpratigrāhī punaḥ saṁskāramarhati)
though all the rites of reinitiation are not to be necessarily observed. For example:

अजिनमेखलादण्डो भैक्षचर्या व्रतानि च ।
निवर्त्तन्ते द्विजातीनां पुनः संस्कारकर्मणि ।।
ajinamekhalādaṇḍo bhaikṣacaryā vratāni ca ।
nivarttante dvijātīnāṁ punaḥ saṁskārakarmaṇi ॥

In other words, in the second initiation deerskin, girdle, staff, begging and other essentials may be left out. The śāstras enjoin that if the sacred thread becomes impure or snaps, it should be replaced by a new one duly sanctified. The following verse is expressive of this view:

यज्ञोपवीतमजिनं मौञ्जी दण्डं च धारयेत् ।।
नष्टे भ्रष्टे नवं मन्त्राद् धृत्वा भ्रष्टं जले क्षिपेत् ।।
yajñopavītamajinaṁ mauñjī daṇḍaṁ ca dhārayet ।
naṣṭe bhraṣṭe navaṁ mantrād dhṛtvā bhraṣṭaṁ jale kṣipet ॥

It also enjoins that the old, broken thread should be thrown away into a river.

Penances for the Vrātyas

He who has not been initiated till his twenty-third year is deprived of grace and is called a 'vrātya'. It is, therefore, necessary that a brāhmaṇa bachelor must be initiated by the time he reaches his fifteenth year. If he is not initiated by the time he is fifteen years old he becomes a 'vrātya'. A kṣatriya bachelor has to be initiated by the time he is twenty years old and vaiśya by the time he reaches his twenty-third year.

Penury often prevents parents to perform their children's initiation ceremony. The great Hindu preceptors are of the view that if a brāhmaṇa bachelor does not have his initiation performed till the sixteenth year, a kṣatriya till his twenty-second and a vaiśya till his twenty-fourth, the penance to be done by them is the observance of a cāndrāyaṇa vow, or, alternatively, a vow for three continuous days to which should be added the gift of a bull and ten cows. Yet another alternative is that they should do the sort of penance one does when one slaughters a cow. If even this is not feasible a handful of ground gram (*sattu*) should be quaffed with water everyday for twenty days and at the end five brāhmaṇas be fed. Where this is not possible for such a length of time, the transgressor is permitted to take pound barley for two months, only milk for a month, curd for fifteen days, clarified butter of cow's milk for eight days and abstain from taking food or water for a day. Having done this penance they should go in for the initiation ceremony.

The Penance for Transgressing Studentship

Penances are recommended for those who break the vow of studentship and celibacy. Let us first know what the transgression of a vow is:

> **अत्र शौचाचमनसन्ध्यावन्दनदर्भभिक्षाग्निकार्यराहित्यशूद्रादिस्पर्शकौपीनकटिसूत्रयज्ञोपवीतमेखलादण्डाजिनत्यागदिवास्वापछत्रधारणपादुकाध्यारोहणमालाधारणोद्वर्तनानुलेपनाञ्जनजलक्रीडाद्यूतनृत्यगीतवाद्याभिरतिपाखण्ड्यादिभाषणअष्टविधमैथुनवीर्यस्खलनपर्युषितभोजनादिव्रतलोपसकलदोषपरिहारार्थं मध्ये समाप्तौ वा कृच्छ्रत्रयं चरेन्महाव्याहृत्याद्यनादिष्टहोमं च कुर्यात् ।**
>
> *atra śaucācamanasandhyāvandanadarbhabhikṣāgnikāryarāhityaśūdrādisparśakaupinakaṭisūtrayajño-pavītamekhalādaṇḍājinatyāgadivāsvāpachatradhāraṇa-pādukādhyārohaṇamālādhāraṇodvartanānulepanāñjana-jalakrīḍādyūtanṛtyagītavādyabhiratipākhaṇḍyādi-bhāṣaṇāaṣṭavidhamaithunavīryaskhalanaparyuṣita-bhojanādivratalopasakaladoṣaparihārārthaṁ madhye samāptau vā kṛcchratrayaṁ carenmahāvyāhṛtyādyanādiṣṭahomaṁ ca kuryāt* ।

Baudhāyana's list of offences which make men impure is fairly comprehensive: gambling, performing incantations, subsisting by gleaning corn though one does not perform an agnihotra, subsisting by alms after one has finished one's studentship, living, after that has been finished, longer than four months in the house of one's teacher, and teaching such a person who has finished his studentship, gaining one's livelihood by astrology, and so forth. "But the expiation of these offences," according to Baudhāyana, "is to perform penances during twelve months, during twelve fortnights, during twelve times ten days, during twelve times ten nights, during twelve times three days, during twelve days, during six days, during three days, during a day and a night, during one day, in proportion to the offence committed."

Conclusion

The initiation rituals and the materials used for their performance are all instinct with profound symbolism. The *mekhalā* or girdle which the pupil is required to wear is no exception. The following hymns of the *Atharva Veda*, for example, reveal its subtle symbolical meaning, awakening and coming of age:

य इमां देवो मेखलामाबबन्ध यः संननाह य उ नो युयोज ।
यस्य देवस्य प्रशिषा चरामः स पारमिच्छात् स उ नो विमुञ्चात् ।। १ ।।
आहुतास्यभिहुता ऋषीणामस्यायुधम् ।
पूर्वा व्रतस्य प्राश्नती वीरघ्नी भव मेखले ।। २ ।।

ya imāṁ devo mekhalāmābabandha yaḥ saṃnanāha ya u no yuyoja ।
yasya devasya praśiṣā carāmaḥ sa pāramicchāt sa u no vimuñcāt ॥ 1 ॥
āhutāsyabhihutā ṛṣīṇāmasyāyudham ।
pūrvā vratasya prāśnatī vīraghnī bhava mekhale ॥ 2 ॥

In *The Vedic Experience* the author, Raimundo Panikkar, renders these mantras into English prose as follows:

> The divine Power who has bound this girdle round us,
> who tied us together and yoked us in one,
> the divine Power under whose direction we progress,
> may he lead us to the other shore and free us!
> Daughter of Faith, born out of Fervour,
> sister of the sages who mould[1] the world,
> grant to us, Girdle, powers of thought and wisdom,
> grant to us ardour and vigour.

The girdle extolled here, says Panikkar, is "a powerful

1. Spellings anglicized by me—author.

symbol of human maturity, power, and restraint, that is to say, of a disciplined freedom (for one is bound by one's own freedom); it possesses a material concreteness, but represents also a spiritual reality. The girdle is what the three highest *varṇas* of tradition are accustomed to wear as a sign of their second birth, that is, of having undergone the initiation that makes them *dvija*, 'born again'. At the time of initiation the girdle is a symbol of chastity and obedience and thus it represents the condition of the *brahmacārin*, the student, who is bent on gaining wisdom and progressing on the spiritual path".[1]

The presentation of the girdle, we are further told, is the handing of an object which symbolizes the goddess of the spirit of austerity (*tapas*) and both physical and mental vigour. The new garment presented by the *ācārya* (teacher) to the boy symbolizes the new period of his life. The ceremony of presentation includes a prayer offered to the goddess who wove the piece of cloth. The sacred thread or sacrificial cord which is presented gives the initiate the right, or the power, to take part in the offering of the ritual sacrifice. The presentation of the deerskin, followed by prayers, symbolizes the beseeching of the gods to aid the student in his knowledge of the wisdom embodied in the Vedas. The presentation of the staff is accompanied by a prayer in which the student is entrusted to the divine hierarchy.

The rest of the ceremony may be divided into the following stages:

> Having entrusted the student to the vigilant protection of the gods, the *ācārya* accepts him as a disciple. The unity that has to exist between master and pupil is expressed in prayer and in the touching of the heart.
>
> The Sāvitrī mantra, by which the *dvitīya janma* or second birth is achieved, is now taught to the student.
>
> Next follows the ceremony of the Fire, which sets a seal

1. See Raimundo Panikkar, *The Vedic Experience: Mantramañjari*, pp. 238-39.

> upon the unity of life which is to exist within a student.
>
> The second section, the ceremony of the *departure*, consists of a *ritual bath* taken by the student at the end of his stay (which is generally of several years) with his master.
>
> Before the bath the young man lights the ritual fire. The prayers during the bath, unlike those of the initiation ceremony which contain a note of austerity and renunciation, are full of joy and rejoicing in the good things of life.
>
> Then, putting to one side his ascetic garb, the young man arrays himself in fine new clothing, bedecks himself with flowers, puts on a turban, earrings and new shoewear. He takes an umbrella in his hand and a bamboo staff.
>
> He is now ready to live to the full his adult life, a life that will take its inspiration from the wisdom of the Scriptures.[1]

With the completion of the ceremony, the student awakens and comes of age. He evaluates things around man from now on and contains a reflection on man himself. Having performed the initiatory pūjās, he begins to discover himself and his own projection in the outside world. He finds the road to humanness now open. The Hindus of today, like their forefathers, are convinced that no man, and much less the Hindus, can dispense with rites, that is why from olden times *rites de passage* developed and became an integral part of the orthodox Hindu life. "Initiation, however", says Panikkar, "would have no meaning or would have to be interpreted in an almost magical way, if man had not already awakened to the mystery of human life, that is, to the personal discovery of love, though still without an object."[2] The initiation of the student symbolizes "a coming-of-age so as to take one's life into one's own hands—except that the

1 Raimundo Panikkar, *op. cit.*, p. 247. Also see Appendix III.

2. *Ibid.*, p. 242.

'one' is not necessarily always the individual. There is a period in human life, however, in which living implies more than sheer passivity. Both biologically and also intellectually and spiritually, creative force appears at a certain age. Man enters into life by living, that is, by overcoming death, setting limits for himself, and following his own path. Initiation is the relatively modern technical word for the *rite de passage* implied in reaching human maturity."[1]

The pre-eminence of the initiation ceremony among the Hindu sacraments has always been recognized and extolled by the sacred law of the Hindus. In his aphorisms Āpastamba, for example, remarks that for all the castes, excepting śūdras and those who have committed bad actions, are ordained the initiation, the study of the Vedas, and the kindling of the sacred fire. Defining what initiation is, he uses the word in the sense of 'consecration in accordance with the text of the Veda, of a male who is desirous of and can make use of sacred knowledge'. Āpastamba rejects the right of all unlearned brāhmaṇas to perform the initiation ceremonies when he says:

> Coming out of darkness, he indeed enters darkness, whom a man unlearned in the Vedas, initiates, and so does he who, without being learned in the Vedas, performs the rite of initiation. That has been declared in a Brāhmaṇa.
>
> As performer of this rite of initiation he shall seek to obtain a man in whose family sacred learning is hereditary, who himself possesses it, and who is devout in following the law.

The *ācārya* (teacher or guru) is the man from whom the pupil gathers the knowledge of his religious duties (or *dharma*). This is supported by Gautama who in his *Institutes of the Sacred Law* maintains that the 'person from whom the pupil receives initiation is called the *ācārya*'. The law-givers, who

1. Raimundo Panikkar, *op. cit.*, p. 246.

were all aware of the pre-eminent position the pūjās associated with the upanayana occupied, do not leave out any detail relevant to the ceremony. Their details include the stuff of which the girdle, the upper and the lower garments are made. One instance of the care the law-givers bestow upon the sacrificial details is provided by Gautama, who says:

> The girdles worn by students shall be strings of muñja grass, a bow string, or a wool thread, according to the order of the castes. Their upper garments shall be skins of black-bucks, spotted deer, or he-goats. Hempen or linen cloth, the inner bark of trees, and woollen blankets may be worn as lower garments by students of all castes, and undyed cotton cloth. Some declare that it even may be dyed red. In that case the garment of a brāhmaṇa shall be dyed with a red dye produced from a tree, and those of students of the other two castes shall be dyed with madder or turmeric. The staff carried by a student of the brāhmaṇa caste shall be made of bilva or palāśa wood. Staves made of aśvattha or pīlu wood are fit for students of the remaining two castes. Or a staff cut from a tree that is fit to be used at a sacrifice may be carried by students of all castes. The staves must be unblemished, bent at the lop like a sacrificial post, and covered by their bark. They shall reach the crown of the head, the forehead, or the tip of the nose according to the caste of the wearer.

Details with regard to the materials used for the performance of the initiation rites in accordance with the sacred law are not wanting. Quite a good number of rituals centre round a *kalaśa*, a *kumbha*, a jar, or a vessel that is above time, the *Atharva Veda* tells us. The placing of the pitcher in the sacrificial pavilion has a symbolical meaning, for the jar is so full that 'it is the origin of time inexhaustible'. The Upaniṣadic seers, we are told, "attempt to peep into and take possession of the jar in its entirety. The Vedas themselves had suggested the method: breaking the jar by means of sacrifice. The Upaniṣads now assert that this sacrifice must be an internal and spiritual one."[1] In order that the rituals may not be marred by the teacher's negligence or the pupil's ignorance the law-givers are punctilious about every little detail and ask the performer not to rush through the rituals in a haphazard way. If water has to be sprinkled around the sacrificial fire, it must be done with kuśa blades; if the brahman has to be placed somewhere, it must be placed in a particular direction with the words *bhūr bhuvaḥ svaḥ*; if grass has to be strewn around the fire, the purohita must see to it that the pupil strews eastward-pointed kuśa grass around it in three or in five layers, beginning on the east side, then to the west, then again to the west; the praṇītā waters are carried forward on a particular side with the words 'who carries ye forward?'; the ājya pot must be taken up with the words, 'Milk of the cows art thou', etc., etc.

Baudhāyana's aphorisms do not ignore these details. His purohita uses girdles consisting of a rope made of muñja grass, a bow-string, or a rope made of hemp, the skins those of a black antelope, of a spotted deer, or of a he-goat. The staff, he says, shall reach the crown of the head, the forehead, or the tip of the nose, and be made of a tree fit for a sacrifice. As regards begging, he insists that the student should beg, employing a formula consisting of seven syllables, with the word 'bhavati' in the beginning, with the word 'bhikṣāṁ' in the middle, and with the verb expressing the request at the end; and let him not produce loudly the syllables 'kṣā' and 'hi.'

The initiation ceremony, the mantras of which have been given above, is one of the most important Hindu sacraments and is performed in the Hindu homes with painstaking care, often with unbounded zeal and fanfare. The occasion is as much religious as festive and is celebrated as a real awakening of the boy, not as a mere symbolical entry into dvijahood.

---

1. Raimundo Panikkar, *op. cit.*, p. 220.

APPENDICES

Appendix I

According to the *Śāṅkhāyana Gṛhyasūtra*, a brāhmaṇa has to be initiated with an antelopeskin in the eighth or tenth year after the conception. We learn from the same authority that in the eleventh year after the conception a kṣatriya and in the twelfth year after the conception a vaiśya should be initiated. Of these two varṇas, the kṣatriya student is initiated with the skin of a spotted deer and the vaiśya with a cow-hide. Śāṅkhāyana modifies these sūtras by adding that until the sixteenth year the time has not passed for a brāhmaṇa, until the twenty-second for a kṣatriya, and until the twenty-fourth for a vaiśya. After that time has passed, they become *patitasāvitrika* or men who have lost their right of learning the Sāvitrī.

What this Gṛhyasūtra lays down as the proper age for the initiation of an unmarried student is essentially a representative view common to the institutes of Āśvalāyana, Pāraskara, Gobhila, and Baudhāyana. A typical description of the initiation ceremony is found also in Hiraṇyakeśin's Gṛhyasūtra which, though compendious to many, is ample enough and gives the reader a fairly elaborate idea of how the institutors of the Hindu domestic ceremonies looked upon them. It is a typical example of a work on which the family priest has been drawing on ceremonial occasions from the day it was compiled. The following instructions are taken from this compilation; they provide, precis-fashion, as the ācāryas think, a significant account of the rituals associated with or performed at the initiation ceremony.

Let him initiate a brāhmaṇa, says Hiraṇyakeśin, at the age of seven years, a rājanya of eleven, a vaiśya of twelve; a brāhmaṇa in the spring, a rājanya in the summer, a vaiśya in the autumn. In the time of the increasing moon, under an auspicious constellation, preferably under a constellation the name of which is masculine, he should serve food to an even number of brāhmaṇas and should cause them to say, 'An auspicious day! Hail! Good luck!' Then he should have the boy seated, should have his hair shaven, and after the boy has bathed and has been decked with ornaments, he should dress him in a new garment which has not yet been washed.

From these simple details Hiraṇyakeśin now turns to what are rather elaborate, though regarded by some as reasonably extended. In a place, he observes, inclined towards the east or towards the north or north-east or in an even place, he raises the surface on which he intends to sacrifice, sprinkles it with water, kindles fire by attrition, or fetches common fire, puts the fire down, and puts wood on the fire. He strews eastward-pointed *darbha* grass (a tuft or bunch of grass, especially of kuśa, used for sacrificial purposes) round the fire; or the grass which is strewn to the west and to the east of the fire may be northward-pointed.

How should the darbha blades be arranged? Answering this, the Gṛhyasūtra observes that he arranges these blades so as to lay the southern blades uppermost, the northern ones below, if their points are turned partly towards the east and partly towards the north. Having strewn darbha grass, to the south of the fire, in the place destined for the brāhmaṇa, having with the two verses, 'I take the fire to myself,' and, 'The fire which has entered'—taken possession of the fire, and having, to the north of the fire, spread out darbha grass, he prepares the following objects, according as they are required for the ceremony which he is going to perform: a stone, a new garment which has not yet been washed, a skin of an antelope, or a spotted deer, etc., a threefold-twisted girdle of *muñja* grass if he is a brāhmaṇa who shall be initiated, a bow string for a rājanya, a woollen thread for a vaiśya, a staff of *bilva* or of *palāśa* wood for a brāhmaṇa, of *nyagrodha* wood for a rājanya, of *udumbara* wood for a vaiśya.

With remarkable exactitude Hiraṇyakeśin follows the Gṛhyasūtras and goes on to describe the minutiae of the ceremony. One of the duties of the person performing the ceremony, he says, is to bind together the fuel, twenty-one pieces of wood, or as many as there are oblations to be made. Together with that fuel he ties up the three sticks of wood which are to be laid round the fire, which should have the shape of pegs. He gets ready, besides, the spoon called *darvī*, a bunch of grass, the *ājya* pot, the pot for the praṇītā water, and whatever else is required; all those objects together, or one after the other as it happens. At that time the brāhmaṇa suspends the sacrificial cord over his left shoulder, sips water, passes by the fire, on its west side, to the south side, throws away a grass blade from the brāhmaṇa's seat, touches water, and sits down with his face turned towards the fire. He takes as 'purifiers' two straight darbha blades with unbroken points of one span's length, cuts them off with something else than his nail, wipes them with water, pours water into a vessel over which he has laid the purifiers, fills that vessel up to near the brim, purifies the water three times with the two darbha strainers, holding their points to the north, places the water on darbha grass on the north side of the fire, and covers it with darbha grass. Having consecrated the prokṣaṇī water by means of the purifiers as before, having placed the vessels upright, and having untied the fuel, he sprinkles the sacrificial vessels three times with the whole prokṣaṇī water. Having warmed the *darvī* spoon over the fire, having wiped it, and warmed it again, he puts it down. Having besprinkled with water the darbha grass with which the fuel was tied together, he throws it into the fire. He melts the *ājya*, pours the *ājya* into the *ājya* pot over which he has laid the purifiers, takes some coals from the fire towards the north, puts the *ājya* on these coals, throws light on the *ājya* by means of burning darbha blades, throws two young darbha shoots into it, moves a fire-brand round it three times, takes it from the coals towards the north, pushes the coals back into the fire, purifies the *ājya* three times with the two purifiers, holding their points towards the north, drawing them through the *ājya* from west to east and taking them back to the west each time, throws the two purifiers into the fire, and lays the three pegs round the fire. On the west side of the fire he places the middle peg, with its broad end to the north, on the south side of the fire the second peg, so that it touches the middle one, with its broad end to the east, on the north side of the fire the third peg, so that it touches the middle one, with its broad end to the east, to the west of the fire the teacher, who is going to initiate the student, sits down with his face turned towards the east.

The amplitude and capaciousness of the details do not end here. In fact, what follows is no less elaborate, midway though the ceremony is by the time we reach this point. Hiraṇyakeśin takes pains not to leave out any significant detail relevant to the initiation ceremony, including such seemingly unimportant matters as how the teacher and the pupil should sit. To the south of the teacher, the law-giver points at, the boy, wearing the sacrificial cord over his left shoulder, having sipped water, sits down and touches the teacher. Then the teacher sprinkles water round the fire in the following way: on the south side of the fire he sprinkles water from west to east with the words, 'Aditi! Give thy consent!' On the west side, from south to north, with the words, 'Anumati! Give thy consent!' On the north side, from west to east, with the words, 'Sarasvatī! Give thy consent!' On all sides, so as to keep his right side turned towards the fire, with the mantra, 'God Savitṛ! Give thy impulse!'

Having thus sprinkled water round the fire, and having anointed the fuel with ājya, he puts it on the fire with the mantra, 'This fuel is thyself, Jātavedas! Thereby thou shalt be inflamed and shalt grow. Inflame us and make us grow; through offspring, cattle, holy lustre, and through the enjoyment of food make us increase. Svāhā!'

He then sacrifices with the spoon called darvī the following oblations:

Approaching the darvī to the fire by the northerly junction of the pegs laid round the fire, and fixing his mind on the formula, 'To Prajāpati, to Manu, svāhā !' Without pronouncing that mantra, he sacrifices a straight, long, uninterrupted stream of ājya, directed towards the south-east. Approaching the darvī to the fire by the southern junction of the pegs laid round the fire, he sacrifices a straight stream of ājya, directed towards the north-east, with the mantra which he pronounces, 'To Indra, svāhā!'

Having thus poured out the two āghāra oblations, he sacrifices the two ājyabhāgas, with the words, 'To Agni, svāhā!' over the easterly part of the northerly part of the fire; with the words, 'To Soma, svāhā!' over the easterly part of the southerly part of the fire. Between them he sacrifices the other oblations. He makes four oblations with the following mantras: 'Thou whom we have set to work, Jātavedas! carry forward our offerings. Agni! Perceive this work (i.e. the sacrifice), as it is performed by us. Thou art a healer, a creater of medicine. Through thee may we obtain cows, horses, and men. Svāhā! Thou who liest down athwart, thinking, "It is I who keep all things asunder:" to thee who art propitious to me, I sacrifice this stream of ghī in the fire. Svāhā! To the propitious goddess svāhā! To the accomplishing goddess svāhā!'

This is the rite for all darvī-sacrifices. At the end of the mantras constantly the word svāhā is pronounced. Oblations for which no mantras are prescribed are made merely with the words, 'To such and such a deity svāhā!'—according to the deity to whom the oblation is made. He sacrifices with the vyāhṛtis, 'bhūḥ! bhuvaḥ! svaḥ!'—with the single three vyāhṛtis and with the three together. The mantras for the two chief oblations are, the verse, 'Life-giving, Agni!' and, 'Life-giving, O god, choosing long life, thou whose face is full of ghī, whose back is full of ghī, Agni, drinking ghī, the noble ambrosia that comes from the cow, lead this boy to old age, as a father leads his son. Svāhā!' Then follow oblations with the verses, 'This, O Varuṇa', 'For this I entreat thee', 'Thou, Agni', 'Thus thou, Agni', 'Thou Agni, art quick. Being quick, appointed by us in our mind as our messenger, thou who art quick, carriest the offering to the gods. O quick one, bestow medicine on us! Svāhā!' and finally the verse, 'Prajāpati!' With the verse, 'What I have done too much in this sacrifice, or what I have done here deficiently, all that may Agni sviṣṭakṛt, he who knows it make well sacrificed and well offered for me. To Agni sviṣṭakṛt, the offerer of well-offered sacrifices, the offerer of everything, to him who makes us succeed in our offerings and in our wishes, svāhā!'—he offers the sviṣṭakṛt oblation over the easterly part of the northerly part of the fire, separated from the other oblations. Here some add as subordinate oblations, before the sviṣṭakṛt, the jaya, abhyātana, and rāṣṭrabhṛt oblations. The jayā oblations he sacrifices with the thirteen mantras, 'Thought, svāhā! Thinking, svāhā!'—or, 'To thought svāhā! To thinking svāhā!'

The amplitude of the description of the upanayana rituals given by Hiraṇyakeśin shows the importance his Gṛhyasūtra attached to it. He goes on to expand the details, to mention every little rite, and to point to the mantras appropriate to it. Needless to say, those interested in these details will find Hiraṇyakeśin extremely useful.[1]

1. See *Sacred Books of the East*, Vol. 30, pp. 137-58.

Appendix II

Just as the teacher and the householder have certain duties assigned to them by the law-givers, so is the student's life circumscribed by his responsibilities and rules of conduct. He is not free to behave like a householder or in whatever manner he chooses to behave. Decorum should be his watch-word, pursuit of propriety his *summum bonum*. Devoted to his studies with full concentration and a certain élan, he must not offend his guru or circumvent the gurukula rules. What the law-givers lay down as the duties of a snātaka may be found in most of the extant codes of conduct and rules of behaviour. The following extracts have been selected from *Vaśiṣṭha's Dharmaśāstras* for its representative value:

Now, therefore, the duties of a snātaka will be explained.

Let him not beg from anybody except from a king and a pupil.

But let him ask, if pressed by hunger, for some small gift only, a cultivated or uncultivated field, a cow, a goat or a sheep, or at the last extremity, for gold, grain or food.

But the injunction given by those who know the law is, 'A snātaka shall not be faint with hunger.'

Let him not dwell together with a person whose clothes are foul; let him not cohabit with a woman during her courses, not with an unfit one.

Let him not be a stay-at-home.

Let him not step over a stretched rope to which a calf or cow is tied.

Let him not look at the sun when he rises or sets.

Let him not void excrements or urine in water, nor spit into it.

Let him ease himself, after wrapping up his head and covering the ground with grass that is not fit to be used at a sacrifice, and turning towards the north in the daytime, turning towards the south at night, sitting with his face towards the north in the twilight.

Now they quote also the following verses: 'But snātakas shall always wear a lower garment and an upper one, two sacrificial threads, shall carry a staff and a vessel filled with water.'

'It is declared, that a vessel becomes pure if cleaned with water, or with the hand, or with a stick, or with fire. Therefore he shall clean his vessel with water and with his right hand.'

'For Manu, the lord of created beings, calls this mode of cleaning encircling it with fire.'

'He who is perfectly acquainted with the rules of purification shall sip water out of this vessel, after he has relieved the necessities of nature.'

Let him eat his food facing the east.

Silently let him swallow the entire mouthful, introducing it into the mouth with the four fingers and with the thumb; and let him not make a noise while eating.

Let him approach his wife in the proper season, except on the parva days.

Let him not commit a crime against nature with her.

Now they quote also the following verse: The ancestors of a man who commits an unnatural crime with a wedded wife, feed during that month on his semen. All unnatural intercourse is against the sacred law.

It is also declared in the Kāṭhaka, when the women asked Indra, "May even those among us, who are soon to be mothers be allowed to cohabit with their husbands," he granted that wish.

Let him not ascend a tree.

Let him not descend into a well.

Let him not blow the fire with his mouth.

Let him not pass between a fire and a brāhmaṇa, nor

between two fires; nor between two brāhmaṇas; or he may do it after having asked for permission.

Let him not dine together with his wife. For it is declared in the Vājasaneyaka, 'His children will be destitute of manly vigour.'

Let him not point out a rainbow calling it by its proper name, 'Indra's bow.'

Let him call it 'the jewelled bow' (maṇidhanuḥ).

Let him avoid seats, clogs, sticks for cleaning the teeth, and other implements made of palāśa wood.

Let him not eat food placed in his lap.

Let him not eat food placed on a chair.

Let him carry a staff of bamboo, and wear two golden earrings.

Let him not wear any visible wreath excepting a golden one; and let him disdain assemblies and crowds.

Now they quote also the following verse: 'To deny the authority of the Vedas, to carp at the teaching of the ṛṣis, to waver with respect to any matter of duty, that is to destroy one's soul.'

Let him not go to a sacrifice except if he is chosen to be an officiating priest. But if he goes, he must, on returning home, turn his right hand towards the place.

Let him not set out on a journey when the sun stands over the trees.

Let him not ascend an unsafe boat or any unsafe conveyance.

Let him not cross a river, swimming.

When he has risen in the last watch of the night and has recited the Veda he shall not lie down again.

In the muhūrta sacred to Prajāpati a brāhmaṇa shall fulfil some sacred duties.

Appendix III

We give here a brief note on the manner of using the ceremonial objects and the mantras used when doing so. This note forms part of Panikkar's *The Vedic Experience* (Part II; Germination and Growth):

New Garment

HGS I, 1, 4, 2

(i) After the boy has removed his old attire the teacher clothes him in a new garment that has not yet been washed, saying:

"May the Goddess who spun, who wove, who measured and fashioned this garment, clothe you with long life! Put on this garment, endowed with life and strength.

"Clothe him! By this garment may he attain a life span of a hundred years. Lengthen his days. Bṛhaspati gave this garment to King Soma to put on.

"May you live to old age! Put on this garment. Be a protector of mankind against menacing speeches. Live a hundred years, full of vigor. Clothe yourself in ever increasing wealth."

PGS II, 2, 7

(ii) "As Bṛhaspati clothed Indra in the garment of immortality, even so I clothe you, with prayer for long life, a good old age, strength, and splendor."

HGS I, 1, 4, 3

(iii) Thus clothed [the boy], the following prayers [are said by the teacher]:

"For your own well-being you have put on this

garment. You have become a protector of your friends against the curses of men. Live a hundred long years. May you be noble, blessed with fullness of life, sharing generously your wealth."

The Girdle

SGS II, 1, 28-29

(iv) 28. After the teacher has offered sacrifice, they both stand behind the fire, the teacher facing East, the other facing West.

29. He should initiate him standing.

II, 2, 1

He ties the girdle from left to right [around the waist of the boy] three times, saying:

"Here has come to us this blessed girdle, friendly Goddess for our defense against evil words and for the purification of our family, investing us with strength by inhalation and exhalation."

The Sacred Thread

SGS II, 2, 3-12

(v) 3. He fixes the sacred thread (saying):

"You are the sacred thread. With the sacred thread of sacrifice I initiate you."

4. He takes water in the hollow of his joined hands, the student also joining his hands, and says:

"What is your name?"

5. "I am so-and-so, Sir," replies the student.
6. "Descending from the same patriarchal sages?" asks the teacher.
7. "Descending from the same patriarchal sages," says the student.
8. "Declare yourself as a student."
9. "I am a student, Sir."

10. Then he sprinkles water three times with his joined hands on the joined hands of the student, saying: *"bhūr, bhuvaḥ svaḥ!"*
11. Then, grasping the student's hands, with right hand uppermost, he says:
12. "By the vivifying power of God Savitṛ, with the strength of the two Aśvins and with Pūṣan's aid, I initiate you, so-and-so."

The Deerskin

HGS I, 1, 4, 6

(vi) He then puts on him a deerskin as an outer covering and says:

"Put on this skin, noble so-and-so; may the firm strong eye of Mitra, his glorious splendor, powerful and shining, be a token of swiftness and self-control. Let Aditi gird your loins that you may know the Vedas, that you may acquire insight and faith, and, keeping what you have learned, that you may be endowed with goodness and shining purity."

The Staff

PGS II, 2, 11-12

(vii) 11. The teacher hands him the staff.
12. The student accepts it saying:

"This staff which is falling from the sky upon the earth I now take up again, with prayer for life, fullness of spirit, and the splendor of Brahman."

The Dedication

SGS II, 3, 1-5

(viii) 1. The teacher then says:

"Bhaga has grasped your hand,

Savitṛ has grasped your hand,
Pūṣan has grasped your hand,
Aryaman has grasped your hand,
Mitra are you now by law,
Agni has become now your master,
along with myself, so-and-so.
Agni, I entrust this student to you,
Indra, I entrust this student to you,
Āditya, I entrust this student to you,
All Gods, I entrust this student to you,
that he may have long life, a blessed posterity,
strength, frequent increase of riches, authority
in all the Vedas, high renown, and happiness."

3. The teacher touches the student's heart saying: "May your pure heart ever hold me dear."
4. He then turns, silently, from right to left.
5. And then, putting his hand with the palm up on the student's heart, he prays in a low voice.

SGS II, 4, 1; 5

(ix) 1. "Under my direction I place your heart.
Your mind will follow my mind.
In my word you will rejoice with all your spirit.
May Bṛhaspati unite you with me.

5. "You are a student. Tend the fire. Drink only water.
Perform your service. Do not sleep in the daytime.
Keep silence till the lighting of the fire."

The Sāvitrī Mantra

SGS II, 5, 1-3; 8-12

(x) 1. After a year the teacher recites the Sāvitrī mantra (to the student).
2. Or, after three nights,
3. or, immediately.
8. They sit to the north side of the fire.
9. The teacher turning towards the East, the student toward the West.

10. Then the student says: "Recite, Sir!"
11. The teacher, after uttering the syllable OM, invites the student to say the mantra: "Recite the Sāvitrī, Sir."
12. Then he recites for him the Sāvitrī, that verse, "That glorious Sāvitrī," at first verse by verse then line by line, and finally the whole at one stretch.

The Sacred Fire

PGS II, 4, 2-3; 8

(xi) 2. The student heaps up the fire with his hand, speaking these words:

"O Lord, the glorious one, make me glorious,
as you, glorious Lord, yourself are glorious.
As you, Lord, are custodian of sacrifice for the Gods
even so may I be custodian of Sacred Knowledge for men."

3. Having sprinkled water around the fire from left to right, he places some wood on the fire and says, standing:

"To the Lord, the great Seers have brought some wood.
As you, O Lord, are set ablaze by wood,
so may I be set ablaze by life, intelligence, and vigor,
by means of offspring, cattle, and divine glory.
May my teacher be one whose sons are living.
May I be capable of insight, not obstructive.
May I increase in honor and divine glory.
May I integrate everything into the cosmic dynamism of the sacrifice. Svāhā!"

8. He warms his hands at the fire and puts them to his mouth and says:

"You, Lord, are the protector of bodies. Protect my body.
You, Lord, are the giver of life. Grant life to me.

You, Lord, are the giver of vigor. Impart vigor to me. What is imperfect, Lord, in my body, that restore to fullness.
May the God Savitṛ give me wisdom,
may the Goddess Sarasvatī give me wisdom,
may the two divine Aśvins, wreathed with lotus, give me wisdom."

The End of Student Life

PGS II, 6, 25-26; 29-31

(xii) 25. He puts a turban on his head, reciting:
"A young man, well-dressed."

26. He puts on the two earrings, saying:
"An ornament are you. May I have more!"

29. He takes an umbrella in his hand and says:
"You are the protection of Bṛhaspati;
protect me, then, from evil,
but do not protect me from splendor and renown!"

30. Next he puts on the pair of sandals:
"You are my defense. Defend me from every side."

31. He takes, finally, a bamboo staff, reciting:
"From all destructive powers preserve me on all sides."

Sanskrit Glossary*

Aṁguṣṭha (aṁgūṭhā) :	the thumb.
Aṁjali :	the open hands placed side by side and slightly hollowed; a libation to the manes; when raised to the forehead, a mark of supplication; reverence, salutation.
Aditi :	personified as mother of the Gods called Ādityas; Aditi is the symbol of unbound, divine freedom and generosity, of inexhaustible fullness.
Agni :	the fire of sacrifice and the divine Fire, one of the most important Gods or divine manifestations, the mediator or priest to Men and Gods.
Agnihotra :	daily fire-sacrifice which was performed morning and evening in every household of the higher castes, consisting in an oblation of milk sprinkled on the fire.
Agnikuṁḍa :	fire-pit.
Agnikārya :	kindling or feeding the sacrificial fire with clarified butter.
Agnisthāpana :	installation of fire.
Agniṣṭoma :	Soma sacrifice, lasting for several

* Only those words are listed here which, besides being technical, have been frequently used in the text or in the rendition.

		(usually five) days; one of the most important Vedic sacrifices.
Anvārambha	:	touching from behind.
Apasavya	:	wearing of the sacred thread from the right shoulder to the left side.
Aham	:	'I', the first person.
Ahiṁsā	:	'non-violence'; respect for life; non-killing.
Akṣata	:	raw rice grains; unhusked barley-corns.
Akṣara	:	syllable; smallest part of speech; imperishable.
Amṛta	:	immortal, imperishable; the sacred drink (ambrosia), the nectar of immortality.
Aṁtarikṣa	:	the 'in-between', the airy space between heaven and earth, atmosphere, midspace.
Antaryāmi	:	the 'inner Controller' (antar-yam).
Anāmikā	:	the ring finger.
Aśmārohaṇa	:	the ceremony of placing the foot on a stone.
Ācamana	:	sipping water from the palm of the hand (before religious ceremonies, before meals) for purification.
Ācārya	:	teacher, guru.
Āditya	:	son of Aditi.
Ājya	:	clarified butter (ghī) used for oblations, or for pouring into the holy fire at the sacrifice, or for anointing anything sacrificed or offered.

Ājyasthālī	:	a vessel for clarified butter.
Āhuti	:	calling, invoking; an oblation or offering, especially to a deity; a sacrifice.
Āsādana	:	putting or lying down, reaching, getting possession of.
Īśānakoṇa	:	north-eastern quarter.
Upavīta	:	the sacred thread
Kanyā rāśi	:	Virgo.
Kamalāsana	:	Lotus posture.
Karka rāśi	:	Cancer.
Kalaśa	:	sacrificial (festal) vessel.
Kula	:	clan, lineage.
Kuśa	:	the sacred grass used at certain religious ceremonies.
Kuśakaṇḍikā	:	installation of the sacrificial fire into a kuṇḍa or an altar especially prepared for it.
Kumbha rāśi	:	Aquarius.
Kautukāgāra	:	a room for festivity, a pleasure-house.
Khīla	:	parched rice.
Gotra	:	a family, race, lineage; a name, appellation.
Candana	:	sandal.
Chāyāpātra	:	a small bowl, plate, platter, etc. filled with clarified butter in which one sees his face reflected.
Tulā rāśi	:	Libra.
Tṛṇa	:	blade of grass; straw.

Dūrvā	: bent grass.
Dhanu rāśi	: Sagittarius.
Pañcabhūsaṁskāra	: 'ground preparation', a term for five methods of preparing and consecrating the khara (a quadrangular mound of earth for receiving the sacrificial vessels) at a ceremony.
Pañcāgni	: the five sacred fires (viz. Anvāhāryapacana or Dakṣiṇa, Gārhapatya, Āhavanīya, Sabhya and Āvasathya.)
Pañcopacāra	: the five modes of worship.
Parikramā	: circumambulation; walking round or about.
Pavitra	: a small sieve or strainer; two kuśa leaves for holding offerings or for sprinkling and purifying ghī.
Prājāpatya	: relating or sacred to Prajāpati.
Prāyaścitta	: expiation, atonement.
Putreṣṭi	: a sacrifice performed to obtain male children or one performed at the time of adoption.
Purohita	: family priest.
Praṇītā pātra	: the vessel for the holy water.
Prokṣaṇī pātra	: a vessel for sprinkling water.
Maṇḍapa	: a temporary shed erected on festive occasions; pavilion; tent.
Makara rāśi	: Capricorn.
Mithuna rāśi	: Gemini.
Mīna rāśi	: Pisces.
Meṣa rāśi	: Aries.

Yajña	:	act of worship or devotion; offering; oblation; sacrifice.
Yajñopavīta	:	sacred thread.
Yajamāna	:	the person paying the cost of a sacrifice; the institutor of a sacrifice (who to perform it employs a priest or priests, who are often hereditary functionaries in a family); host.
Lājā	:	fried or parched rice.
Vedī	:	an elevated piece of ground serving for a sacrificial altar (generally strewn with Kuśa grass, and having receptacles for the sacrificial fire.
Vyāhṛti	:	the mystical utterance of the names of the seven worlds (viz. bhūr, bhuvar or bhuvaḥ, svar, mahar, janas, tapas, satya), the first three of which, called 'the great Vyāhṛtis', are pronounced after *OM* by every Brāhmaṇa in commencing his daily prayers and are personified as the daughters of Sāvitrī and Pṛaśni.
Vṛścika rāśi	:	Scorpio.
Vṛṣa rāśi	:	Taurus.
Śikhā	:	the tuft on the crown of the head.
Ṣoḍaśopacāra	:	the sixteen modes of worship.
Ṣoḍaśamātṛkā	:	the sixteen divine mothers.
Saṁkalpa	:	a solemn vow or determination to perform any ritual observance; definite intention.
Sāṁkalpika	:	based on or produced by the will or imagination.

Saṁskāra	:	sacraments.
Saṁantraka	:	possessing charms or spills.
Savya	:	wearing the sacred thread from the left shoulder to the right side.
Siṁha rāśi	:	Leo.
Sruva	:	a wooden ladle shaped like a spoon.
Svadhā	:	the sacrificial offering due to each god, especially the food or libation or refreshing drink offered to the pitṛs or spirits of deceased ancestors. The exclamation or benediction used on presenting (or as a substitute for) the above oblation or libation to the gods or departed ancestors.
Sviṣṭakṛta	:	oblation for the fulfilment of desire.
Havis	:	an oblation or burnt offering; anything offered as an oblation with fire (as clarified butter, milk, Soma, grain, etc.)
Havya	:	anything to be offered as an oblation; sacrificial gift or food.
Havana	:	a hole made in the ground for the sacrificial fire which is to receive a burnt oblation; the act of offering an oblation with fire.
Homa	:	the act of making an oblation to the Devas or gods by casting clarified butter into the fire; oblation with fire, burnt-offering, any oblation or sacrifice.

Index

Abhāva, 36
Ābhyudayịka, 63
Ācārya, 3, 9, 24, 105, 122-29, 139, 140, 142, 143, 146-47, 158, 160
Ācamana, 113, 14, 32, 59, 64, 103, 119, 122
Ācamanī, 13
Adhidaivata, 85, 95
Aditi, 138
Āghāra, 24, 106, 133, 134
Agni, 6, 7, 25, 26, 38, 81, 89, 124, 134, 136, 146
Agnicayana, 28
Agnihotra, 7, 34, 156
Agniṣṭoma, 7
Agnyādheya, 7
Āgrahāyaṇeṣṭi, 7
Ājya, 26, 131, 134, 162, 164, 168
Āka, 34
Ākāśa, 86, 87
Akṣata, 29
Akṣamālā, 26
Ananta, 91
Aṅgulas, 24, 25, 26, 105
Antyeṣṭi, 35, 61
Annaprāśana, 38
Aupāsana, 35
Apāna, 13
Apāmārga, 27
Apasavya, 63
Āpastamba, 160
Āratī, 33
Arghya, 29, 32, 33, 59, 62
Arka, 27
Aryan, 4, 5, 117, 149
Āsana, 32, 59
Asthikaṇṭaka, 24
Aṣṭakā, 7
Aśvinīkumāra, 86, 88
Āśvāyujī, 7
Atha, 23
Atharva Veda, 157
Atirātra, 7
Ātmadevatā, 28
Atyagniṣṭoma, 7
Aupāsana, 35, 38
Āvasathya, 35
Āvāhana, 32, 59, 62
Aveṣṭi, 8
Āyuṣya, 60, 62

Bali, 27
Baudhāyana, 4, 5, 155, 156, 162
Bhikṣāṁ, 162
Brahma, 57
Brahmā, 6, 24, 25, 78, 83, 86, 91, 104, 106, 107, 116, 129, 130, 132, 133
Brāhmaṇa, 1,2, 3, 4, 8, 9, 26, 29, 39, 45, 46, 48, 50, 51, 52, 53, 54, 56, 67, 68, 69, 70, 104, 111-115, 118, 119, 120, 121, 122, 123, 142, 143, 146, 147, 148, 154, 155, 160, 161
Brahmasūtra, 116
Bṛhaspati, 142

Caitrī, 7
Candana, 32
Cāndrāyaṇa, 154
Caru, 24, 27
Cāturmāsya, 7
Caula, 99, 100, 105
Citragupta, 85
Coṭī, 100
Cuḍā, 38, 99, 100, 101, 102, 119

Cūrṇa, 28

Dakṣiṇā, 28, 29
Dānavas, 24
Darbha, 25, 26
Darśapaurṇamāsa, 7
Devas, 24, 133, 134
Devasenā, 28, 57
Ḍhāka, 64
Dharma, 6
Dhṛti, 28, 57
Dhyāna, 33
Dhūpa, 33, 36, 59
Dikpāla, 89, 91
Dīpa, 33, 59
Dravya, 36
Dṛṣṭi, 28
Duḥkha, 136
Dūrvā, 28, 33, 40, 74
Durgā, 86
Dvija, 117, 121, 158

Gaṅgā, 33, 42
Gaṇa, 27
Gandha, 59
Gaṇeśa, 17, 20, 27, 29, 39, 57, 58, 59
Gaṇeśapūjā, 17, 121
Garbhādhāna, 38
Gauṇa Āśvina, 35
Gautama, 4, 160, 161
Gaurī, 28, 57
Gāyatrī, 31, 120, 121, 125, 140-43
Graha, 95
Grahamaṇḍala, 86, 89
Grahapūjā, 12, 70, 71, 79, 121
Gṛhya, 35
Gṛhyasūtras, 1, 3, 100, 101
Guggula, 27
Guru, 3

Hasta, 27
Havana, 36
Havis, 27, 28
Haviryajñas, 7
Hemādri, 62, 153
Hindu, 1, 79, 100, 113, 117, 119, 121, 151, 159, 160, 162
Homa, 26, 27, 133
Hotṛ, 25

Indra, 38, 83, 84, 124, 137
Indrāṇī, 84
Īśa, 91
Īśvara, 81

Jagatī, 142
Jātakarma, 35, 153
Jayā, 28, 57

Kāla, 85
Kalaśa, 15, 16, 17, 36, 41, 42, 71, 161
Kāma, 35
Kāmanā, 35
Kāmya, 34, 35
Karmakāṇḍas, 8, 9, 31, 78
Kaṭisūtra, 122
Kātyāyana, 62
Keśānta, 38, 101, 102, 103
Ketaka, 34
Ketu, 27, 85, 86, 88
Khadira, 26, 27, 117
Kṛṣṇa, 115
Kratudakṣa, 38
Kṣatriya, 8, 9, 113, 114, 115, 117, 118, 119, 122, 128, 143, 154
Kṣetrādhipati, 86, 88
Kṣetrapāla, 86
Kubera, 91
Kumbhaka, 14

Madhuparka, 36
Mahābhārata, 8
Mahādeva, 91
Maṇḍala, 81, 86
Maṁgala, 82
Maṇḍapa, 36

Manu, 1-3, 36, 113-115, 117, 148, 151, 152, 153
Manusmṛti, 102
Maruta, 5, 137
Mātṛkā, 28, 39, 57, 59, 70, 121
Mātṛyāga, 28
Medhā, 28, 57
Mekhalā, 157
Mithilā, 99
Monier-Williams, Monier, 133
Mudrā, 27
Muṇḍana, 100
Muñja, 114, 122, 149, 161, 166

Nāga, 63, 124
Naimittika, 34, 35
Nairṛti, 90
Naivedya, 16, 20, 28, 29, 33, 59
Nāmakaraṇa, 38
Nāndīśrāddha, 38, 39, 61-63, 70, 121
Namaskāra, 33
Nārada, 23
Nārāyaṇa, 82
Navagraha, 92
Niruddhapaśubandhaka, 7
Nīrājana, 29
Niṣāda, 8, 11
Nitya, 34, 35
Niyamas, 6
Nyāsa, 13, 14

Oṁkāra, 23, 38, 124

Padmā, 28, 57
Pādya, 29, 32, 33, 59, 64
Pala, 25, 28
Palāśa, 10, 26, 27, 28, 64, 117, 161
Pañcabhū, 104, 121, 130
Pañcadhārā, 57
Pañcagavya, 36
Pañcāmṛta, 36
Pañcalokapāla, 86
Pañcaratna, 36, 37, 41
Pañcapallava, 16, 36, 37, 41
Pañcavaruṇa, 26
Pañcavāyu, 14
Pañcopacāra, 31-33, 97
Parāśara, 153
Pāraskara, 101
Parisamūhana, 23
Pāvaka, 38
Pavitra, 24, 105, 106, 130, 131, 133, 138, 139
Piṇḍa, 62, 110
Pitṛ, 24, 35, 61, 62, 64, 103, 119
Prāṇa, 14
Prāṇāyāma, 13, 14, 64, 103, 119
Prajāpati, 26, 38, 84, 106, 124, 133, 142
Pārvaṇaśrāddha, 7
Pradakṣiṇā, 33, 59
Pradhānakalaśasthāpana, 70
Prāksaṁstha pātrāsādana, 104, 130
Praśna 62
Pratyadhidaivata, 86, 95
Praṇāma, 33
Praṇītā, 25, 104, 105, 106, 107, 130, 131, 132, 133, 138, 139, 162
Pravara, 122
Proddharana, 24
Prokṣaṇī, 24, 25, 104, 105, 106, 107, 130, 131, 132, 133
Pūjā, 31, 34, 80, 86, 95, 98, 121, 159
Pūraka, 14
Pūrṇāhuti, 26
Purāṇa, 5-8, 23, 57
Purohita, 2, 9, 10, 16, 17, 23, 162
Puṣpa, 33, 59
Puṣṭi, 28, 59
Putreṣṭi, 35
Pūrvamīmāṁsā, 8

Rāhu, 27, 85, 86, 87
Raimundo Panikkar, 157
Rajbali, Pandey, 117

Rathakāra, 8, 118
Recaka, 14
Ṛk, 116
Rolī, 16, 71
Ṛṣi, 142
Ṛtviks, 24

Sabhya, 104
Śacī, 28, 57
Sāhī, 105, 107, 109
Sahjānanda Sarasvatī, 9, 99
Śākhā, 24
Śakti, 26
Śālāgni, 35
Samāna, 14
Samāvartana, 63, 64, 100
Śamī, 26
Samidhā, 27, 104, 133
Sāma, 116
Saṁkalpa, 38, 39, 57, 58, 62, 64, 72, 80, 98, 120, 121, 138, 140, 141, 148
Saṁsāra, 12
Saṁvatsara, 103
Saṁskāra, 1, 8, 10, 11, 12, 15, 16, 17, 23, 31, 36, 38, 56, 63, 64, 99, 100, 113, 117, 130, 131, 148, 153
Sammārjana, 25, 104, 130
Sandhyopāsana, 34
Śāntipāṭha, 11
Saptadhānya, 36, 37, 73
Saptadhātu, 36, 37
Saptamṛttikā, 36, 37, 41
Sarpa, 85
Sarasvatī, 141
Sarvagandha, 36, 37
Sarvauṣadhi, 36, 37, 40
Śāstra, 57, 63, 91, 100, 103, 110, 121, 142, 147
Ṣaṣṭikā, 28
Śātātapa, 151
Satyavasu, 38, 64
Saubhāgya, 24
Sautrāmaṇī, 7
Savarṇa, 119
Savitā, 38, 142
Sāvitrī, 28, 57, 142, 149
Savya, 63
Śikhābandhana, 13, 14
Śiva, 9, 34
Smṛtis, 3, 25, 36, 100, 148, 153
Smārtta, 34-36
Snāna, 32, 59
Snātaka, 3, 4
Ṣoḍaśī, 7
Ṣoḍaśamātṛkāpūjana, 56
Ṣoḍaśopacāra, 17, 31, 39, 97
Soma, 63, 91, 124, 134
Somasaṁsthās, 7
Śrāddha, 6, 35, 38, 61-65
Śrauta, 34, 35, 149
Śrāvaṇī, 7
Śrīkhaṇḍa, 119
Śrīparṇī, 26
Sruk, 25, 26
Sruva, 24-26, 104, 131, 133, 134
Sthālī, 25
Sthālīpāka, 38
Śūdras,8, 26, 117
Sūrya, 38, 124
Suśruta, 100
Svadhāvācana, 62
Svadhā, 28, 57
Svāhā, 28, 57
Svastika, 16, 40
Svastivācana, 12, 38, 39, 41, 57, 121
Sviṣṭakṛta, 26, 106

Tāmbūla, 59
Tarpaṇa, 35, 119
Thames, the, 151
Tīrtha, 5, 16, 42
Tuṣṭi, 28, 57

Udāna, 14
Udumbara, 27, 117
Uktha, 7
Umā, 81

Upacāra, 32
Upanayana, 31, 38, 99, 100, 106, 113, 117, 118, 121
Upaniṣad, 162
Upavāyu, 14
Upavīta, 32, 115
Upayamana, 25, 104, 130, 133

Vaidhṛti, 28
Vaiśya, 8, 9, 113-15, 117, 118, 119, 122, 128, 142, 143, 154
Vaitānika, 35
Vaivāhika, 35
Vājapeyaka, 7
Varṇa, 9, 118, 122, 143, 147, 158
Varuṇa, 42, 76, 90, 135-38
Vasordhārā, 28, 57
Vastra, 32, 59
Vasu, 28
Vāstoṣpati, 86, 88
Vāyu, 5, 86, 87, 90, 124
Veda, 1-4, 8, 9, 11, 36, 54, 113, 115, 116, 118, 121, 141, 149, 158, 160, 161
Vedārambha, 38, 100
Vedikā, 25
Vijayā, 28, 57
Vikaṇṭaka, 26
Vikira, 62
Vināyaka, 27, 86
Viriñci, 25
Visarjana, 33
Viṣṇu, 34, 39, 82, 137
Viśvedeva, 38, 64, 67, 69, 124, 137
Vṛddhiśrāddha, 62
Vyāhṛtis, 26, 95, 106, 134, 140-42
Vyāna, 14

Yajamāna, 24
Yajña, 6, 24, 26, 115
Yajñopavīta, 59, 115, 117, 125
Yajurveda, 100, 116
Yama, 6, 25, 84, 85, 90
Yamunā, 33
Yoga, 6
Yogin, 6